HOW TO MEDITATE

An Anthology of Talks on Meditation and
"Meditation: The Bridge Is Flowing
But The River Is Not"

Additional books, recorded talks and music related to Rama - Dr. Frederick P. Lenz's teachings of American Buddhism, are available through the online storefront of the Frederick P. Lenz Foundation for American Buddhism: *www.fredericklenzfoundation.org*.

Editors' note: These talks have been lightly edited to maintain the extemporaneous quality of speech.

How to Meditate

An Anthology of Talks on Meditation and
"Meditation: The Bridge Is Flowing But the River Is Not"

Rama - Dr. Frederick P. Lenz

HOW TO MEDITATE
An Anthology of Talks on Meditation
And "Meditation: The Bridge Is Flowing But The River Is Not."

Published By
The Frederick P. Lenz Foundation for American Buddhism
9899 Santa Monica Blvd., PMB 180
Beverly Hills, CA 90212
www.fredericklenzfoundation.org

ISBN 1-932206-10-8

Book cover design by Janis Wilkins
Back cover photo of Dr. Lenz by Greg Gorman

This book is dedicated to Rama - Dr. Frederick P. Lenz and to the principles of American Buddhism he cherished, embodied, and tirelessly taught.

I come into the world to be of service to beings who seek knowledge, empowerment, enlightenment; who seek to grow, evolve, develop; who want to have more fun with their lives and experience the profundity of being; who want to become more conscious in their short time in an incarnate form. I'm a teacher.

— Rama - Dr. Frederick P. Lenz

TABLE OF CONTENTS

How to Meditate
An Anthology of Talks on Meditation

Meditation: The Bridge Is Flowing But The River Is Not

Introduction

Meditate and realize that when you meditate, no matter how high you go, no matter how deeply you perceive, that you're only touching the bare surface of infinity. Just hold in mind the fact that beyond your perception is ecstasy. Not far beyond. Just with the stoppage of thought there's ecstasy—power, understanding, in limitless amounts.
— Rama - Dr. Frederick P. Lenz

In the thousands of talks he gave on Buddhism and self-discovery from 1980 to 1998, Rama-Dr. Frederick P. Lenz spoke with ease and eloquence on a vast range of topics. Yet every talk he gave had one theme in common—the importance of daily meditation. Whether he was speaking of career success, sports, dressing well, reincarnation or liberation and self-realization, all topics were founded on one nexus: the ability to meditate well.

For Dr. Lenz, "meditation" was not a passive word implying relaxation or mental contemplation. Rather, meditation as he taught and expressed it, was transformational, essential, revolutionary. Without meditating well, he emphasized, no Buddhist realization is possible. He did not feel meditation—the practice of stopping all thought in the mind—was easy to do; he said it was hard to do and that was one of the things he loved about it.

In *How to Meditate*, Dr. Lenz's recorded talks that specifically focus on meditation have been assembled into a single volume. Serving as both a primer and refresher, this series of talks is as valuable for the experienced meditator as for the beginner.

The talks are presented in order, most recent first. This is an important point because over his years of teaching, as tens of thousands of people attended his public seminars, Dr. Lenz evolved his perception of what meditation techniques work best in Western society.

The meditation practice that he ultimately determined was most helpful and powerful is described in the first two chapters of this book, "Meditation" and "Intermediate Meditation." Recorded in 1992, these lectures present in-depth descriptions of Dr. Lenz's preferred meditation technique. In addition, they discuss how to maintain the momentum of meditation practice going forward.

These chapters also refer to the electronic music that Dr. Lenz produced with his band, Zazen. These CDs, specifically "Enlightenment," "Canyons of Light" and "Samadhi," do more than provide a simple musical background for meditation. Dr. Lenz infused these works with the meditative energy of his own enlightenment. Through the music he gives teaching empowerments that aid tremendously in learning to meditate. The CDs are available through the online storefront of the Frederick P. Lenz Foundation for American Buddhism (www.fredericklenzfoundation.org).

The first two chapters in this book, then, may be considered the touchstone knowledge in the series. Nonetheless, as one goes back in time with Dr. Lenz, one's view of meditation expands and many details of the practice become increasingly clear.

For example, in four talks on meditation from the "Tantric Buddhism" series, he begins with an overview, goes on to explain in detail how to start meditating, then addresses what to do when you have begun to meditate regularly. Finally he discusses advanced meditation, assuming that all his listeners/readers will need this knowledge as they progress:

Meditation is about ecstasy. It's about the understanding of truth. It's about us changing ourselves and making ourselves God-like. Our mind melds with the mind of infinity and we become infinity.

Dr. Lenz approaches meditation from the Zen point of view in his 1986 talk, "Zen: Concentration and Meditation"

Think of meditation as a summer night. The crickets are chirping, life is going on, with or without us, within or without us. Life is going on, on the stage of life in front of our eyes and senses. In the house next door that we may not be aware of, life is going on—in countries other than our own, in worlds other than ours, distant galaxies. Life exists in the sub-atomic regions, in the quasars. Life is all there is. That's meditation.

In Dr. Lenz's talks recorded between 1982 through 1986, the reader learns additional ways of meditating – occasionally using a mantra (a sound such as Aum), a yantra (a visual meditation tool) or other ways of visually focusing one's attention on an object such as a candle flame or flower. While Dr. Lenz did not emphasize these ways of meditating in his later teaching cycle, he often said that whatever meditation technique works to stop thought is the best way to meditate. That way will undoubtedly change from time to time, thus it's helpful to know more than one way to meditate. Several of the talks from this time period were given before live audiences of between 600 to 800 people. Dr. Lenz often used humor in his talks, switching voices and poking fun at himself and at solemn concepts. The comment (Audience laughs) that appears throughout these talks is frequently an understatement. Often, the audience was howling with laughter.

At the conclusion of the twelve talks on meditation is a book by Dr. Lenz that is dedicated to the art of silencing the mind. Published in 1983, *Meditation: The Bridge Is Flowing But The River Is Not* beautifully captures Dr. Lenz's love of meditation and distills his how-to wisdom. Written in lyrical verse and poetry, the book contains three sections. The first section is "The Way of Meditation."

Meditation should always be practiced with love.

Meditate on Light and you will become Light. Meditate on Peace and you will become Peace. Meditate on Eternity and you will become Eternity. Meditate without trying and you will go beyond all suffering and enter into Nirvana.

The second section is "The Art of Meditation."

The possibilities of Immortality are endless!
Here you sit reading these words – a butterfly resting on a flower.
Never before have you had so many reasons to celebrate yourself! You are immortal. You are infinite. You are mortal. You are finite. By celebrating yourself, you commence your education in the eternal schools of consciousness and becoming.

The third section is "How to Meditate."

Enjoy the experience.
Don't expect anything.
Whenever you expect something
From a meditation, you set yourself up for
Immediate frustration.

Don't program your meditation.
Sit and enjoy it.

For the new or continuing student of meditation, *How to Meditate* and *Meditation: The Bridge Is Flowing But The River Is Not* provide a full range of tools, knowledge and wisdom to deepen meditation practice and understand meditation's essential role in daily life. Open the book at any time to any page, and you will receive your daily quota of inspiration.

There is nothing but hope. How could anyone dare to even think anything else? Hope is the bridge that binds all of the worlds together. Hope is the dream that lies just beyond sight. When you meditate with hope, there is no end to your meditation. You will be bliss – light – and perfection. This is hope.

Meditation is the short path to happiness. It is the way to become completely happy. It streamlines the process. It takes you beyond the desire-aversion operating system that offers very limited happiness and a great deal of frustration. As you practice meditation—it's no good just to talk about it but you need to do it—if you can bring an earnestness to your meditation, if you can really try, in other words, you will find that happiness is something that will run through your life constantly.

— *Enlightenment Cycle:* Personal Happiness

Enlightenment Cycle: MEDITATION *1992*

Meditation is a process of expanding your awareness. When you meditate, you get in touch with the deepest part of yourself. You know from your own point of view what's right, what's wrong, what you should do and shouldn't in any situation. Meditation makes you tough, makes you strong, conscious, happy, and eventually, enlightened. Meditation is a process of silencing your thoughts.

Beyond the world of thought and sensorial impressions, there are planes and dimensions of perfect light, knowledge and radiant perfection. Meditation is simply a process of moving your awareness field from the awareness of this world, from the awareness of time and space, into eternity, into the eternal dimensions.

The world you see around you is largely physical. It's perceived through seeing, tasting, smelling, touching and feeling. It's also analyzed through thought, it's felt through emotion, it's remembered through memory, anticipated through projection and experienced as now. But there are different modes and levels of perception that most people are not familiar with. There are different universes, astral universes, and above the astral universes, the planes of light and beyond the planes of light, nirvana itself—perfect enlightenment, the essence and nexus of all things.

Meditation is about becoming conscious of who you are, becoming happy, relaxing, slowing down, chilling out and learning to smile. It's also about very profound things that are hard to express in words—about beauty, about being most excellent at everything, finding the perfect part of yourself, overcoming your self-destructive tendencies, overcoming depression, anxiety, nervousness, fears of all types and descriptions. It's about being happy, being conscious, being free, and most of all about being who you really are, which is something that most people don't have any consistent consciousness of.

Meditation is eternal awareness. The height of meditation is normally symbolized by the Buddha, a person who yokes their mind, through the practice of yoga, meditation, Buddhism, with the highest light in the universe. They experience it in a state called samadhi. Samadhi is a complete cosmic consciousness experience. It's like climbing to the top of the Himalayas and seeing the ranges, the mountains up there—an experience that really is unparalleled. It just can't be expressed in words.

Meditation is a journey, a journey to the other side. The other side can't be explained—the mystical worlds, the timeless, miraculous worlds of light. But they can be certainly, most certainly, experienced by you. So this tape is about how to meditate.

Meditation is essentially a wonderfully easy process, unless you live in this age, in which case it's hard. Oh, maybe it's hard. Meditation is about making your mind calm and quiet, and if the earth was not so overpopulated and toxic, this is a very easy thing to do. The mind is not naturally so active. But there are two factors you have to take into consideration—a crowded planet and the fact that we're all psychic.

Each human being has an aura. An aura is the energy body that surrounds your physical body. Your body of energy gives off impressions just like radio waves—short wave, long wave—and you feel those impressions. You feel the thoughts, the feelings of others, particularly people you are in close contact with, either physically or emotionally. You're very open to them. But you also feel the vibrations of the people in your neighborhood, at your school, where you work, where you drive your car, your town, your state, your country and your planet. Most particularly you feel the vibrations in a radius of about 100 miles from where your physical body is.

Everyone is psychic. People just don't know that. They think so much; they worry so much. They are so caught up in unhappy emotions. They're not still enough. They're not wise and silent enough to see that 90 percent of what they think and feel is alien to them. Ninety percent of what they think and feel, 90 percent of what you think and feel, are not your own thoughts and emotions. They're somebody else's, a lot of other people's.

I always remember an adventure of "Star Trek" where Spock is explaining to Captain Kirk that people come to Vulcan from other planets not so much to learn to be psychic, but people who come with

4

psychic abilities learn to block out psychic impressions. That's what the advanced psychics teach them. At Vulcan, they teach them how to keep other people's thoughts out of their minds. Kirk thought they went there, of course, to learn to be psychic. That's not the problem. Everyone is psychic. The difficulty is just having your own thoughts and feelings. Because if you don't, you can't possibly know who you are, what you care about; and you end up doing things, thinking things, wanting things, fearing things, that have nothing to do with you. They are somebody else's ideas, thoughts and feelings. It's absurd. But everybody does it.

Meditation is a process of not doing that. It's a process of not doing. It's about being still, being centered, being clear, being happy, being organically in touch with the universal light, developing parts of yourself that are unknown to most people, very powerful parts, very beautiful parts, very strong parts. The billions of people on this overcrowded planet put out so much energy and so much of it is unhappy, that it makes everybody's minds active.

Everybody is thinking all the time, stressed out, can't slow down, can't feel what lies beyond this dimension. Normally it's very easy to do that. If you don't believe me, take a walk in the woods. Find a nice wooded path that not too many people have been on, where there are not a lot of impressions. Take a walk. Take a hike. And you will notice that your mind, if you monitor it, becomes very quiet. You don't think much.

Now let's leave there and go out and walk down a city street. Drive on a highway and walk through a building. If you begin to examine your thoughts, you will observe that they change from where you are to the next locale. In other words, they're influenced. Go into a room with unhappy people and you'll find you get depressed, pulled down by their energy. Go into a place with happy people and you'll find you are brought up.

If we lived on a planet in which everyone was happy and progressive and it wasn't so overcrowded—getting more so every day— it would be very easy to meditate, very easy to feel infinity, to be in tune with our spiritual self. But that's not the case. And when you meditate, in particular, and you slow your thoughts down, you actually become more sensitive. You become more psychic because you are clearing yourself of thoughts and impressions of this world so you can feel the other world and feel the perfect worlds of light that exist beyond this plane.

It is kind of tricky to meditate in this age, in short, and I've figured out a way to do it, to make it easy for you. It's to meditate to music. I have created a number of albums, two in particular, which are designed for meditation. There's one for morning meditation and one for evening meditation. There are 15 songs on each album. They're about four minutes each. And each album is designed to provide a morning or an evening meditation. The "Enlightenment" tape is for morning meditation. "Canyons of Light" is for evening meditation.

To meditate, all you need to do is sit down, either in the cross-legged position on a rug or else out on the grass or some place that feels good to you, or sit in a chair. Your back needs to be straight, though. Don't lie down. When you lie down, it's almost impossible to meditate because your body relaxes too much and you just kind of get sleepy. It's best to be very alert when you meditate. It's a nice idea to wash your hands and face, or, if it's a morning meditation, maybe to get up and take a shower, have a cup of tea or coffee or whatever wakes you up. Sit down, relax, and if it's a morning meditation, put on the "Enlightenment" tape.

Each of the 15 songs has been composed around a dimension, and they're in ascending order. The morning tape offers you an experience of 15 different higher dimensions of light that provide the energy, the insight and the power to go out and have a wonderful day. The evening meditation tape, "Canyons of Light," references 15 other dimensions that are easier to get into at night, and you'll go very high in them. It's easier to meditate at night because in the evening people shut down. They get kind of quiet. They go home, fall asleep. And the dimensions that are available—some are easy to get to at night, some in the morning. The "Enlightenment" tape is an hour long. If you are new to meditation, you might just want to meditate for half that time until you get your pace and your stamina built up, and then do the hour. The hour is great.

So you might sit down in the morning, put on the tape and listen to Zazen, which is the name of our music group composed of myself and three other students of mine. Zazen is a Japanese word. It means to sit in silence, to listen, to be aware of everything and nothing and what's beyond both. Zazen is also sitting meditation in Zen Buddhism.

If you sit, if you make your mind quiet, if you're still and you listen to the music, the music will do two things. One, it will provide a kind of an auric blanket. The energy in the music is very high. I've gone to very high planes of consciousness, into samadhi, to bring a certain power into the music as a whole. When you put on the tape, the energy is so high in it that it will simply block out the thoughts and impressions of the people in this world so you will just be—safe. It's as is if you're sitting in a pristine environment in a beautiful power spot with no impressions. It's very easy to touch the other worlds. But, secondly, all the songs are in groups of five. In other words, there are three groups of five on the first and three groups of five on the second albums. And the songs reference particular chakras.

A word about chakras, energy centers, the subtle body and the doorways to infinity. There are three primary meridians in the body. There is a body of light, also known as the subtle body or the astral body, that surrounds your physical body. It is composed of a network of filaments or fibers of light, and those fibers join at places that we call chakras. There are seven primary chakras, and they run from the base of the spine to the top of the head. They are connected by three astral nerve tubes, the largest of which is the shushumna, and then there is the ida and the pingala. The base chakra, the root chakra, which is where the kundalini energy is at rest, is at the base of the spine. Around the area of the sex organs there is a second chakra. The third chakra is around the navel area and a little bit below—about an inch below the navel.

Chakras are not in the physical body, but they correspond to these spots. They're in your energy body. The three lower chakras are the power chakras, and when you start to meditate, you should meditate first on the navel center. By meditating on your navel center you'll bring up the ki, the kundalini, from the lower centers. It will come up from the lower two centers, and it's very easy to enter the navel center and bring the power up to that spot.

So for the first five songs in the morning or evening tape, meditate on your navel center. Simply hold your attention—feel the area around your navel, about an inch below. If you have never done this before, if you are new to this process, simply place your fingertips of the right or left hand about an inch below your navel and press very gently.

Now close your eyes and feel the spot. The first few times you meditate like this, you can keep your fingers there if it helps you. It's not necessary to really visualize anything. You don't have to hold a picture in your mind. Simply feel the spot. As you become adept at meditation, you'll have no trouble feeling the spot because there will be tremendously beautiful surges of energy, of kundalini energy, around that chakra. But in the beginning, sometimes it's helpful just to put the fingers there—very gently.

Hold your attention on the navel area and listen to the five songs. Each of the first five songs is very different and they are designed in an ascending order. They reference different planes of light, and you move from one to another and climb up the ladder of light just by listening to them. Then, when those five songs have ended, move your attention to the center of your chest. The next chakra up is called the heart chakra. It's in the center of the chest. If you hold your attention there—same thing. If you want to, you can put your fingers there and apply a little pressure. Hold your attention on the center of your chest, gently press very lightly and listen to the next five songs.

The chest center, the heart chakra, and the chakra above it—the throat center at the base of the throat—are the centers of balance, of happiness. The best chakra, the easiest to activate, is the heart center, and it will also pick up the throat center for you. If you hold your attention there for five songs, you'll feel tremendous happiness, brightness. You might see vivid colors. You might feel sensations of lightness. But if you just listen deeply, you'll stop thought. The same thing will happen with your navel center and with the third eye.

After you have listened to the five songs—now you have gone through ten, you've moved up to a much higher plane of energy, climbing up the latticework of light, of dimensions—hold your attention on the third eye. Your third eye, which is between your eyebrows and slightly above, the agni chakra, is a center of knowledge. The third eye and the crown center, which is at the very top of the head, are the knowledge centers.

The three meridians are power; balance, which is happiness; and knowledge, or wisdom. When you bring all three together, you are complete.

There are five songs, of which the last five reference the higher chakras. Simply listen to them and keep your attention on the third eye. When thought comes in and out of your mind, ignore it. Simply listen to the music. Don't get frustrated if your mind is restless. There's a lot of energy in the world, and it takes patience to learn how to meditate.

What's happening as you listen to each song—the first five songs for the navel center, the second five songs for the heart center and the third five songs for the third eye—is you are bringing the kundalini up through concentration. The chakras are doorways to different dimensions, to different planes of enlightenment. As you hold your attention on them, the kundalini energy at the base of the spine will gradually rise, first to the navel center, then to the heart center, then to the third eye.

The crown center is a little bit different. It's not connected to the other centers. When you open it, you go into samadhi, into very advanced states of attention. It takes many, many years of practice to be able to activate the crown center, so I wouldn't be too concerned about it at this time. Just bringing the kundalini eventually up to the third eye will release a tremendous amount of energy, brightness and beauty into your life. Your mind will become clear. Your life will become centered. You'll be able to use higher aspects of mind, have inner dimensional experiences, and learn to be a little bit silly and smile about even very difficult things. You'll gain knowledge and power. All kinds of wonderful things will happen just from meditating on these three chakras to the music.

As I said, there's an album for morning meditation and evening meditation. Optimally, you will do an hour of meditation in the morning and an hour in the evening—not necessarily at the beginning. In the beginning, you might just try meditating in the evening for half an hour once in a while or every day or in the morning. But as you have progressively better and better experiences with meditation, you will find that it's good to meditate in the morning. When you meditate in the morning after you first get up, you energize your body, you wash out all the energies you picked up when you were very sensitive and your defenses were down, during sleep. You clarify your mind. You gain mental power, control, and you release a lot of energy through the chakras, have inner-dimensional experiences—and you'll gain tremendous happiness.

Then during the day, you might say your auric immune system will be very powerful. You'll find it easier to keep thoughts and impressions that are negative out of your mind. Your mind will be clear and sharp. You'll do real well at school, in sports, at work, or just in having fun. You'll become more creative, balanced—instead of the person who just goes through the day without all that energy and all that clarity and just kind of makes it, you can be on top of things, in charge, and happily so.

Then, during the day, after your morning meditation, you should practice mindfulness. It's a fun game that you can practice all day long. All day, after you've meditated in the morning, as thoughts come in your mind, emotions, feelings, realize that most of them aren't your own. And just bounce out anything negative, anything unhappy, angry, jealous, suspicious, anything that would make you unhappy and destroy your inner calm, your inner equilibrium that you gained from your morning meditation. Just blow it out. Push it away. You gain the inner ki or power to do this from your morning meditation. If you keep doing this, eventually you'll find that you'll just be happy all the time. After a while, your mind will automatically filter these thoughts out and negative impressions that you pick up from others, without even having to think about it very much.

So we charge up our auric battery in the morning with a good meditation. Then in the evening, around sunset or whenever you get home from the day, meditate again. Take a shower. Maybe go for a run, whatever works for you, and meditate. Put on the "Canyons of Light" tape. It's a beautiful tape. Each of the songs references a power place in the Southwestern United States, an inter-dimensional vortex of power.

During the day, of course, you will have used up a lot of the energy from your morning meditation, picked up impressions. So sit down. Meditate. Relax. Chill out. Be calm. Be centered. Be beautiful. Eternity is around you and within you. Don't be afraid. There is only happiness beyond this world—the happiness, the endless happiness of nirvana and of the spirit. Relax. Trust life a little bit. What we see here is just a blink of the eye, this life. It comes and goes very quickly. There's much more to all of this, and it's much better.

Listen to the "Canyons of Light" tape. Allow it to guide you and take you through the 15 higher dimensions that it references. Start with the navel center—five songs there, the next five for the heart center, the next five for the third eye. Remember, the key to success in meditation is to enjoy it, not to fight thought, but just to listen to the music.

You would normally learn to meditate, if things were ideal, with an enlightened teacher such as myself. You would sit, come and see your teacher twice a day and sit with them in the morning and evening. In the morning, you'd meditate together, and when an enlightened teacher meditates, it's very powerful. Their aura gets very charged up, and the pure power of their mind as they move from one chakra to another, from one dimension upward into the planes of light and into samadhi and enlightenment and nirvana—as they do that, if your mind is at all subtle, if you practice meditation a little bit, the power of their aura will lift you along with them, from one plane of mind to another.

That's how you really learn to meditate. I mean, you just can't know where these planes are, how to get to them, just by trying by yourself. Enlightened teachers are there so you can meditate with them and they move your mind from one plane to another. Then you can practice on your own and learn how to get back to those stages of attention, those wonderful worlds of light.

Normally you'd meditate with your teacher in the morning and later in the evening, and they would lift you into these higher planes. By doing that repeatedly, day after day, month after month, you would learn—just as repeated motions in martial arts teach you the motions and the movements of martial arts—you would learn how to meditate.

What I have done is created two albums—there are others, but these two in particular, the "Enlightenment" tape and "Canyons of Light" on tape and CD—that are like having a private enlightened teacher. I have infused each of the albums with the light of enlightenment and with a tremendous amount of kundalini. The composition of the work actually came out of 30 different dimensions. Each song is actually—I can't explain how it is done, but let's just say that it's hooked up to a certain dimensional access point. So when you listen to the songs, the level is actually there of a particular universe, a very high plane, and it will lift you up if you can just listen to it, into these higher dimensions, the same way it would if you were meditating with me or with another enlightened teacher.

So when you put on the tape or the disc, essentially you're sitting down with an enlightened teacher and meditating with them. They're holding a plane for four minutes and you experience it as you focus on a chakra and you shift to another and another. Gradually, the kundalini rises from the base of the spine to the third eye, opening up the chakras, in the morning and of course in the evening.

After you meditate, after you finish the session, always bow. If you're sitting in the cross-leg position, if you can, touch your head to the floor. If not, you better lose some weight and do some exercises and limber up. If you're sitting in a chair, just bow slightly. We just like to offer our meditation to the universe. And sit still for a couple of minutes. Relax. Never judge or analyze a meditation. Just do it. Focus as hard as you can on the chakras while you meditate.

Handy tips—avoid eating much before you meditate. Your body will feel heavy. It's like eating a lot before you exercise. Yuck. Relax. You're not going to learn how to do it in a day, but every time you meditate and simply listen to the music you'll go very high. You'll have a very beautiful experience. When thoughts come in and out of your mind, ignore them. If you have experiences, see light, colors, sensations of lightness, that sort of thing, if cabbage grows out of your ears, don't worry about it. Just ignore it. (Rama laughs.) Experiences come and go in meditation, and, you know, let 'em go; let 'em come. What matters is that you just focus on the chakra undistractedly. Another hint—disconnect the phone before you meditate. Everyone

12

always seems to call you when you start to meditate. Put on the music and listen.

Zazen means to sit, to listen. You are listening to enlightenment, to the universes, to the planes of mind. You're sitting with an enlightened teacher, with enlightenment, more specifically. Let that enlightenment flow through you, purify you, clarify you. With practice, you'll find that you get a lot better. In the beginning, the music may actually distract you a little bit. The music is very pure, though. Not only is it played by some of my students and produced and composed by all of us, but in addition, after the music is done, I take my aura and go through it and take out any human impressions, so it's absolutely clean. It's perfect music in terms of its consciousness. And it's not bad, overall. We work hard on it; we really do, to make it for people, so they can have a beautiful experience.

So listen to the music. Meditate. Relax and just let it take you into the world of light, past other people's thoughts, other people's ideas and even your own. There is nirvana. There is enlightenment. Beyond this world and beyond all worlds, there's something perfect and real. The comedies, the tragedies that we see played out before us on this earth don't last. We do. We are eternal spirits. These events will come and go, but the planes of light and nirvana will always be there.

If you'd like to learn more about meditation and enlightenment, then you should find a teacher who you feel is balanced, powerful, knowledgeable, enlightened and funny. If they're not funny, they're not enlightened.

Trust life. Trust that it will always guide you to the right thing. And be kind. Be compassionate. Take time to help others and help yourself. Be patient. If you meditate or, what Rama always says is—if you meditate each day and run each day, you can do anything. If you run a few miles and meditate every day, you're OK. That's in my opinion. But even if you miss the running, just get a little exercise any way you want to. Meditate each day, and your life will get better. You'll be happy, free, successful, and eventually you'll grow into pure and perfect light, into the world of enlightenment, and there is simply nothing better than that.

So please enjoy the music. We made it for you. Enjoy the tapes. Grow, develop and always be optimistic. Always be positive. And ignore those who aren't because they're obviously confused and out of touch with light.

If you're meditating, if you're practicing every day, you don't necessarily see the changes that are taking place in your life because you're so close to them. You don't remember how limited your awareness field was six months ago or a year ago, let alone yesterday, before this morning's meditation. The real miracle, obviously, is the transformation of consciousness from limitation and pain to enlightenment and ecstasy.

— *Enlightenment Cycle*: Miracles

Enlightenment Cycle:
INTERMEDIATE MEDITATION
1992

We find ourselves in the world. We're born here. We don't know why. We look around and we see life. We feel it. Sometimes it hurts. Sometimes it's pleasurable. Sometimes it's boring. Sometimes it's exciting. Sometimes it's frightening. Sometimes it's beautiful beyond comprehension.

Our bodies grow and develop. Our mind develops. We have experiences. And then something more happens for some people, and they begin to develop spiritually. It's an ache at first, a longing, a feeling for another time, another place, another condition. We want more. Or less.

We can feel the earth on a sunny day, feel the heat on a rainy day, the wetness, the wind. In the city, we have the traffic, the noises; in the country, we have the sounds of the forest. We can make love, make money, go to work, feel fatigue, be excited. These are the things people do. One day melts into the next. And all you have for the days that you've gone through are memories, for the days that have not yet occurred, anticipations.

All that truly exists is this moment. This moment you're experiencing now.

Yoga is a science. It's the science of consciousness. It suggests that there's more, more or less—that outside of what you experience there are other realms, other dimensions that go on forever. They're just beyond the portals of your vision. There are dimensions of light, perfect light, on the other side of sense experience and mental experience. There are dimensions of ecstasy, worlds where time does not exist, and there's nirvana, the central nexus from which all this comes, the creator, enlightenment.

Meditation is traveling. It's a journey. It's a process by which we go from here to there with our minds. We see that the mind is infinite.

It's not relegated to the brain or to thought or to emotion. It's made up of an endless series of realities that stretch on into infinity. You can come to know these realities. You can experience them directly yourself. This is the essence of Buddhism. This process is the gaining of self-knowledge, of the awareness of life or its many awarenesses.

I'm a teacher of meditation. I've been teaching meditation for a while—many, many lifetimes. I'm also a student of meditation. There's always something new to learn. And I've observed a very interesting thing—that most people who meditate don't meditate. They think they're meditating, but they're not really meditating.

Meditation is concentration in the beginning. It's a focus. Then, in the intermediate stage, it's an opening, a deepening of one's awareness but with a focus towards the planes of light. In intermediate meditation, you're touching light more deeply than in introductory meditation. In advanced meditation, you become light. You transcend self, ego, time, space, dimensionality. You merge with the clear light of reality or return to samadhi, and you go beyond this world.

Your ideas, your feelings, your needs, your wants, your loves, your hates, your ups, your downs—you go beyond it all and you become God. You become nirvana. You become enlightenment, for a while, for a timeless time. You merge with the ecstasy of the clear light of reality. And it changes you. It remakes you. It reforms you. It shifts you, and then you're that.

Your awareness returns to the world brighter, different, less solidified. And repeating this process endlessly or in many years and many lifetimes eventually will culminate in the experience of enlightenment where you will always be in a state of light, in a condition of limitless awareness. It goes on forever. As Bilbo tells us in his story in *The Hobbit*, in his little song he sings, the road leads on forever. That's the good news. There's no end to enlightenment. There's no end to incarnation. There's no end to infinity.

And then there's the world of pain and discouragement and frustration that most people live in, where they watch their bodies age and their hopes fade, and the things they believe and love destroyed. There are moments. Good moments. But there are a lot of bad moments, if we're going to be real about what human life is for most people.

So people who meditate seek good moments forever. They know that there are other worlds beyond this world. They feel it. It's true. It's not imagination because it's something that you can experience directly when you sit to meditate. I experience those worlds when I meditate, and I teach others to experience them. But as I said before—it's amazing—I've observed that a lot of people who profess to meditate don't meditate. They sit, they engage themselves in some kind of concentrative practice, but it's not what I would call meditation because they allow too many impressions into their mind. So our topic is intermediate meditation.

In introductory meditation, you learn to focus on the three chakras—the navel chakra, the chest chakra and the third eye, which is between the eyebrows and a little above. These are the three primary doorways that take in the three primary meridians of power, balance and wisdom. You learn to sit for 15 minutes, half an hour or 45 minutes, maybe even an hour, and focus in turn on these three chakras. If you're a student of mine, of course, you meditate to music that I've composed, and it's played by some of my students in our group, Zazen. [It is] music that comes out of higher dimensions, that's extremely pure, and if you focus on it during meditation, it will make the mind quiet. It ensures that you will touch worlds of light and brightness, that you'll be headed in the right direction, as opposed to the wrong direction. It also acts as an auric block—the energy in it—to block out the billions and billions of auras from the people who live on this planet, so that you can just sit in your own aura and then direct your mind to infinity and move from this world to infinity, experience the ecstasy of infinity and come back, better for your journey, more conscious, happier, wiser, hopefully sillier.

Now, that's meditation as I've come to know it; as it was taught to me by my teachers over many, many lives, and as I teach it. It's always the same, yet it's always new. But the process involves stopping thought—first slowing it down, detaching yourself from it, but eventually stopping thought and then directing yourself towards light.

This is the key—directing yourself towards light, not towards other people, not towards places, things, but towards light. So what is light? What is the light I talk of? Light is awareness—awareness without mental modifications. If you can stop your thoughts and allow nothing else into your mind, you will experience light. If you stop your thoughts just for five minutes, you'll experience a very deep light. That light is on the other side of the sense perceptions—seeing, tasting, smelling, touching, feeling. Just on the other side of sense perceptions is a beautiful, perfect light. It's so close to us. It's always around us, yet we're relatively unaware of it because we're distracted by the images of life, by the world of physicality.

There's nothing wrong with the world of physicality. There's nothing wrong with existence. It's perfect. But it's terribly transient. Your body—its cells, its longings, its wants—are terribly transient. These things don't last very long, and very often they leave a great deal of pain and frustration in their wake.

Enlightenment is the alternative, to enter into a condition of perfect light, to have complete peace and stillness in your mind, to not be frustrated when things don't go your way, to go a different way, different than the people of this world. People of this world, who knows where they're going? Every day, they're going someplace else.

I see them driving cars, winding down the streets. I don't know where these people think they're going. They're all going to the local funeral home, that's about it. Between where they are today and this local funeral home, they're going to have experiences that are going to be forgotten really fast. I love it.

There's a sign—I'm sure you've seen something similar on the highway—near where I live, and it's from my local funeral home, and it says the name of the funeral home, then it says in huge letters, "Slow down! Enjoy Life!" No really, that's the essence of it. Then it says, you know, local funeral home.

That's it, isn't it? Slow down. Enjoy life. Chill out. It's tough to slow down if your mind is going a million miles a second. It's tough to slow down if you think what these people do here matters. I mean, you need a form of government; you need a place to live, you need something to eat, you need some entertainment, yes, OK. But what else do you need? What these people do here is obviously not working. They're unhappy. They sit in their commuter traffic hour after hour, or they make the earth a toxic waste dump. They've got lots of theories, lots of books, lots of sciences. I've read a lot of those books. And you know, most of them are pretty unhappy.

There's an alternative. It's an old alternative. It's not for everybody. It's only for people who are smart. Limited market. It's enlightenment—to become aware that there's more to life than television, to stretch your mind and touch infinity, to feel eternity around you. Not as an idea, not as a nice intellectualization, but to really feel it; not to be a religious fanatic who's strung out on some weird idea of salvation to the exclusion of common sense. I'm not talking about that.

The real religious experience is the experience of life, but to experience life, not as an ideation, not as a bunch of thoughts that are whipping around in your head and explosive emotions that are out of control, desires that are endless and unrealistic, frustrations that just don't matter. If we really come down to it, what's the purpose of life? To be happy. What else could it be? And happiness does not come from other people. It doesn't come from places. It doesn't come from things. It's inside your own mind. All happiness is inside your own mind. Chances are, you have not discovered that yet. That's an interesting phrase, but chances are, you haven't experienced it.

Intermediate meditation is about experiencing the happiness that's inside your mind. If you're sitting, practicing meditation on a daily basis and you are not experiencing a greater happiness every day, then you're certainly not meditating.

It's not hard to do, to be happy. It's not hard to experience that happiness, but you must meditate correctly. As I said before, I observe many people who say they're meditating, but I sure don't see them meditating. They sit and they touch a lot of people, places and things psychically, but they sure don't meditate.

To understand what I mean by this, let's consider what meditation is and is not. When you sit to meditate, you become very psychic. You're focusing on the navel center, chest center, third eye, something like that. You're listening perhaps to music. Or you might be doing a different type of meditation, another type, that another teacher might teach—focusing on the breath, focusing on posture; the eyes might be open, focusing on a yantra.

There are different ways to meditate. They're all leading to the same place. They're all ways of focusing your attention, withdrawing it from the senses so instead of looking through your physical eyes or through these things, you're bringing your awareness into one place and then you're directing it towards unlimited light, towards the planes of light. There are other planes, there are planes that are not light, there are planes that are shadowy. But that's not our interest in meditation. We want brightness. We want ecstasy, brilliance beyond comprehension, to merge with that ecstasy of life and go into the stillness and dissolve the ego; to be the totality, to be all things. Not just to gain power over things—how infantile. If you even care about things, that means they have power over you.

Not only to be at peace, but to be a bright field of light— intelligent, endless light—that's what makes the universe. That's what we are. But you've got to get to that deeper part of yourself, to that deeper part of life. The mind must be made calm and still like a lake without any ripples, and then it's aimed at the sky, at the brightness, at infinity, at that infinitude of being that stretches out endlessly in every direction forever.

Intermediate meditation, the way I teach it, is sitting, focusing on a chakra, let's say for an hour meditation session—20 minutes on the navel center, 20 minutes on the chest center, 20 minutes on the third eye. Just 60 minutes, but each of those 60 minutes divided into the three 20-minute units must be directed towards light. Because when you meditate, particularly when you've been doing it for a while, your meditation is a very powerful time. Very powerful. And you're very psychic. When thought slows down, when you're focusing on these chakras, you become very psychic. It is most important during that period of time from one minute to the next not to allow your attention, your mind, to wander towards anything but four primary areas of focus.

You can focus on the chakra to the exclusion of everything else. You can focus on your teacher to the exclusion of anything else, if you have an enlightened teacher. You can focus on music, if you're listening to enlightened music, to the exclusion of everything else, or you can focus on light to the exclusion of everything else.

Let me give you a little template here of what I mean. If you're sitting to meditate—let's say the first third of the meditation, you're going to spend focused on the area of the navel, the power center, to bring up raw power. The second section, you're going to bring it up to the chest center, and that raw power will transmute when it gets up there into love, into an ecstasy of oneness. And then we're going to go up to the third eye, and once it's been transmuted, bring it up higher on the chakra scale into wisdom, into knowledge, into pure and perfect seeing of worlds of light and experiencing. That's our plan.

So let's start down in the navel center. You've got 20 minutes— 15 minutes or 10 if you're just meditating for 30 minutes or 45 minutes—but let's say you're doing the hour. You're down there for 20 minutes in the world of power. Now for that 20 minutes, you have to keep your mind on light. If your mind does not focus on light, then whatever it focuses on, because you're in a highly psychic state, you're going to take through your aura in a way that you would normally take almost nothing through your aura.

Normally your aura is like an immune system. It keeps things out. But in meditation, that immune system is removed, consciously. We want it removed. Because not only does it block out things that are negative, it also blocks out things that are positive. So we're going to consciously move it to the side for a period of time and then, of course, during that period of time, have a complete focus on light, brightness, spiritual oneness, God, infinity, eternity. You know, silly things. By doing that, we are going to bring that into our aura. We are going to touch it psychically, and it's going to touch us. We're going to merge with it. We have to move the protective aura aside for a time to do that. Then, at the end of meditation, the protective aura will be even stronger because we're energized, and it will block out everything negative. We've filled ourselves up with so much light, that we're set. We're satisfied, so to speak. We've come back from our journey, and now we've closed the door.

It's not—you know, some people have a kind of paranoid feeling. They say, "Well, when you meditate, when you're outside of your body, can something get in your body?" No, this is nonsense. I'm talking about keeping your awareness pure. You don't leave the body— that's a way of talking. You become a little less aware of the physical side of your being because you become more aware of the spiritual side of your being. Nothing's going to get in. You're there. But in an intensified period of focus, when your mind is locking onto something, it's most important that it only lock onto something bright, beautiful and perfect.

Now when a lot of people meditate, what they do is, the whole time they're there, they're thinking about other people, sometimes even psychically talking to them, telepathically. This is a terrible mistake. If you do this, stop. Or if you're new to meditation, make sure you never start. Because during the period of meditation, when you drop that auric immune system shield, if you focus on another person, if you feel different people, you take their energy in your body completely. You completely absorb their energy, and you experience a kind of a psychic overload. All their thoughts, their desires, their impressions, their restlessness, their unhappiness, their confusions—all enter you. So if you were to think of ten or 15 people in a row for a few moments even during meditation, you're in such a psychic state, it's so powerful, that each of those person's minds will enter your mind, and you'll just be completely gummed up psychically.

In other words, in meditation, what you're trying to do is simply get rid of your own junk. You're trying to move all the confusion out of your mind, all of the heaviness, the emotional upsets, the impressions that you've picked up since your last meditation. It's kind of like taking a shower, where you're just going to wash all the dirt off that you've picked up since your last shower and be clean. Then from there, we can move into the world of light.

In meditation, if you start picking up other people's impressions while you're meditating, then instead of clearing yourself, you're just going to completely glom yourself up to the point where there's going to be no meditation. You're going to end the period of meditation in a much lower state, lower vibratory state, than when you started. Now a lot of people do that, and they get very dissociated because they sit and they think of other people. Or they focus on things that vibrate very slowly during meditation. And because you're in such a highly sensitized state during meditation, because you're so open, you just make yourself really sick, psychically.

The way to avoid this is to have things to focus on during meditation. And as I said, there are four things you can really focus on that are very healthy. You might come up with something else, but these are four that are for-sures. You can focus on a chakra, to the exclusion of everything else. You can focus on your teacher to the exclusion of everything else, if you have an enlightened teacher. You can focus on enlightened music or you can focus on light itself.

Now let's get basic. The first 20 minutes of your meditation session, if you're meditating for an hour, sit down, put on a meditation album. I have three meditation albums at the moment. The "Enlightenment" album is for morning meditation, "Canyons of Light" is for evening meditation and "Samadhi" can be used for morning or evening.

So let's say it's morning and you have the "Enlightenment" album on. You just got up, took a shower, drank some tea or coffee, if you need that to wake up—if not, water or juice will do. You're feeling pretty good, a little tired. Sit down, sit in a cross-legged position, sit up nice and straight. Focus on the navel center.

This is intermediate meditation, so you're used to doing this. You've been doing this for a few months or maybe even a year. So it's no longer a big deal to sit down, focus on the navel, the chest center, the third eye. You've gotten used to that. You've met me, perhaps, an enlightened teacher, or maybe some other teachers, so you've experienced to a certain extent the feelings of meditation. If you've been with some enlightened teachers while they've meditated, just being with them, their aura expands you, and you've gotten a sense of what meditation is—that feeling of timelessness, of perfect beauty, of endless awareness.

So you plomp on down, meditate—sit on down, meditate—close your eyes, focus on the navel center. You've got 20 minutes; the music is on. Now, the key issue is, what are you going to do during that 20 minutes as you focus? OK, well great, let's focus. That means that you're going to bring your attention to the area of the navel or a couple of inches below. You're going to feel that area. Not just casually, or vaguely, but you have to hold your mind there. It's like doing pushups. It's a complete focus. You're going to hold your mind on the area of the navel to the exclusion of everything else. There's a chakra, an energy center, there and it doesn't activate unless you're focusing intensively.

So you focus your attention around the navel area. You feel that spot. Visualize it. Do whatever it takes. Once you're there, just keep focusing. When thoughts come in and out of your mind, you pay no attention. Pictures, thoughts of people, feelings, you don't pay any attention. You just stay right on that spot. You can probably only focus on that spot for two or three minutes at a time, unless you're a very strong meditator. It's hard to keep your focus there.

Now when I say "focus," I mean to the exclusion of everything else. It's so intense that there are no thoughts. There are no feelings. You're not aware of anything else. Usually you can only do that in short bursts in the beginning, the beginning being the first few hundred incarnations of practice.

So what do you do?

Well, most people—if they focus intensively to begin with— after a few minutes they'll relax, they'll stop, and their mind will drift. Now they're in a highly charged psychic state and they're going to absorb whatever they think of, and it's going to screw up their meditation. There are alternatives. You're sitting, listening to enlightened music. So after focusing as hard as you can on the navel center, and when you simply can't do it any more, accept that, don't fake it. Now, shift your focus. Keep a general feeling of the navel center, that is to say, kind of feel that area of your body. Always keep part of your attention there during the first 20 minutes. But now focus on the music.

When I say focus on the music, I don't mean listen to it as if it's a song on the radio that you sort of hear, sort of don't, while you think of other things—your mind drifts, you imagine people, you imagine places, you imagine things, you think about tomorrow, you remember yesterday—all that sort of nonsense. Don't do that. Absolutely not. Bring your attention to the music. Listen to every note. Go into every feeling. Focus on it so you don't hear anything else. Now you're doing a hearing, a listening meditation. Focus completely till there's nothing but that pure and perfect sound.

Now that you've done that as long as you can, maybe three, four minutes, maybe one song—but you listen to it perfectly—when you're doing that psychically, just like with a chakra, you're entering the chakra, you're entering this music. This music is composed in other dimensions. That's where I go to compose it. Then it's brought here into this world from the planes of light. And it's played by some of my students. I go through the music that they've played with my aura and wash out anything impure aurically, so there's only light in the music. It's perfect music on an auric level.

So focus on the music. Go into it. Meaning, feel where it's coming from and travel with it. Travel to those emotive places that are described in musical alliteration through the songs. When you can't do that any more, be real about it. Now you've saturated yourself that way, now focus on, perhaps, your teacher, if you have a teacher who's enlightened, a teacher who is no longer in the body, but they were enlightened—Ramakrishna, somebody like that. Or if I'm your teacher, you think of your teacher. You have to be careful when you do this because the teacher's aura is very powerful. But first you have to make sure you're even connecting with the teacher's aura.

If, for example, you've only seen your teacher with hundreds of other people around and you've never had a moment with them, a private moment, you might be making a mistake. Because when you sit with a lot of people and your teacher is present, you might not be feeling much of the teacher's aura; you may be feeling simply the auras and impressions of all the people who were there to see the teacher. You may begin to associate that with how the teacher feels, but maybe that's not the case. You have to get a sense of what it [the teacher's aura] feels like. Now, listening to me on this tape, if you listen very intensely, you can feel the emptiness, the perfect emptiness of my mind. There are no thoughts. There are no impressions. There's only light, the light of enlightenment. It's perfect. It's pure. It's pristine. It's endless.

I meditate and have meditated very, very hard so that there's nothing but light. There's no human confusion. There's only perfect light. Now feel that as we pause for a moment. For a moment, I will meditate here—and feel this light.

(Silent pause.)

Now, that's the emptiness. That's the light. It comes in endless forms. So if you have had a personal experience with me as a teacher, a moment when we were alone, and you've felt that perfect light, or you were out in the desert or whatever, but it's a moment that definitely is not associated with other people's minds, then you can focus on that, or you can focus on just a moment like we just had together. In other words, it's a tuning fork. It's a mantra. It's a key. It's a template to other universes. But it has to be pure.

Some people see teachers, and they associate the feelings of the other students who are present with the teacher. So when they sit to meditate and they imagine their teacher, they're really imagining all those people who were there, and psychically they connect, at the moment they imagine them, with all those hundreds of minds— wherever they happen to be today. They pull all that stuff in, and they get completely dissociated and they don't key to the teacher at all. So if you're going to focus on a teacher, it has to be done properly. You have to be focused very much on the teacher and not peripheral vibrations that might have been around them, or it will totally screw up your meditation.

There is always a sense of being alone, a beautiful aloneness to meditating. Not a loneliness, but a beautiful aloneness. You're sitting in the middle of infinity or some far-flung corner, and you are merging with it. It's an alone feeling. You can't have other people there. If other people come to you psychically in meditation, push them away. Don't see their faces. Don't think of their minds. Push them away with your power. It has to be alone.

Only alone can you go into eternity. Only alone can you feel that transcendental light. Only alone will it purify you and perfect you. It is not a shared experience because if it's shared, you're down in duality. You're not up there. You're down in the world of bonding realities where there are multiple minds and multiple forms and multiple confusions. And that is not meditation.

Meditation is a pure experience. By pure, we mean undiluted. It is not something that you can share with others. It is something that you experience alone. You by yourself were born into this world. You may have come through your mother's body, but you have nothing to do with her other than that. Your spirit is ageless, timeless and immortal. That spirit may have taken physical form and come through a physical body, but you come into the world alone and when you die, you will die alone, even if you die in the company of another person, if you both die together. Yet in your own mind you are alone, and you will leave this world alone and go to the next world alone.

We are alone. It is our condition as perceivers. We can experience others, and others are a reflection of the universal mind, yes, and that's fun, of course. But the period of meditation is a time when we go back to the source. We go back to what we were before we were born. We go back into essence.

We have lots of time and substance. But we need to renew ourselves. We need to regain our purpose, to discover who we are. These aren't things you can express in words. They're feelings, knowings, intuitions that you can experience when you meditate. So meditation is quite a complicated thing. It's a return to the source. We're going back into the light, into the perfection, into the unborn, uncreated state. And as long as we can sustain ourselves in that state, we will be renewed, transformed. All our pain will be taken away, our frustration, all of the aggregates that we pick up in the human plane, in this dimensional reality, will be washed away, and we will be spirit, pure spirit, pure light, pure love, pure ecstasy. Then we can come back into this world and address the tasks of our life brightly and happily.

Our work, our play, school, relationships, wherever our karma takes us—we can live fully because we're not confused. We know that we're infinite spirit. We know that we can't die. We can go through the experience of death, but we see in meditation that our experiences are endless, that we're an endless, eternal spirit. Not as a thought or an idea you read in a book. You had the experience yourself. Every day.

As you get better at meditating, you have that experience more strongly and more profoundly, and it changes everything for you. But you have to stay to the center, if this is the sort of thing you like.

You've got to go for it. Or you can drift. You can meditate once in a while and just have a lot of other experiences. Then you're in what we call the samsara, the world of illusions, the world of human experiences—the emotions, the feelings, the passions, the loves, the hates and all that good stuff. You're in that world and you're moving around in it. But you will not be in the transcendental reality. That is to say, you're in the world of time and space and dimensionality, and you must accept the conditions of that world. You have no choice.

On the other hand, if you meditate, you can experience that world, but you can experience the other world and the far-flung eternities and dimensions, and you're not stuck in any one of them. So if the physical world gets to be problematic, you can easily slip off into worlds of brightness and spirit and reinterpret your experiences in the physical world and not know suffering and pain from them.

You decide. You don't have to meditate. It's not necessary. You don't have to practice self-discovery and Buddhism. It's not necessary. You can just go live. You should only experience ecstasy when you meditate, and you should only practice self-discovery if you have really had it with the human world. If you feel that there's a bright, beautiful world out there with nothing but wonderful experiences every day, you don't need to meditate, I guess you're there. (Rama laughs.) Either that, or you need a good psychiatrist.

On the other hand, if you're like most of us who have lived a little bit, maybe you're a little wiser and you realize that life is complicated. It has its good moments, it has its bad moments, it has its ups, it has its downs, its in's and its outs. And there's usually a lot more pain than pleasure and a lot more unhappiness than happiness. Otherwise, you've been watching too many TV commercials and too many sitcoms. Get real. Life is heavy. It's difficult. It's complex, even for the wise. Examine your experience of the incarnation so far and realistically add up the moments of happiness and unhappiness, and you tell me, oh somewhat vaguely nobly born, you tell me, what has it been like for you?

People who are drawn to meditation have had lots of incarnations in the world of experience, and we know the score. We know that experience is great, but it's not enough. We have gone around the loop enough times. It's like relationships. You start a relationship with someone and everything is wonderful in the beginning, and then it's not. You might work it out. It might have more moments that are positive than negative. But only people who haven't had relationships think that they're just always wonderful and carefree. We're in the world of Stayfree MiniPads where everything is perfect all the time. I'm afraid not.

Grow up. Get a life. Life is pain, and anybody who tells you something other than that is trying to sell you something, absolutely— life in the physical world. Then there's ecstasy, the ecstasy of enlightenment. But if you're going to experience that and it's not just going to be a phrase, you've got to work during meditation. So—back to the navel center!

In the navel center, you're focusing on the chakra as long as you can, and then maybe focusing on music as long as you can, then the teacher—but the teacher in a pure way, not just the feelings of hundreds of people who might have been there when you saw your teacher. Because whatever you focus on during meditation, you psychically actually travel to and touch. It's not just a thought. You might think of a person in your normal waking consciousness and not necessarily touch them very deeply. But in meditation, when you think of somebody, you actually go into their aura at that moment and you pull it into your aura. That's the issue. So it's most important to keep your meditation pristine, unalloyed.

Now after you focus on the teacher as long as you can, then try pure light. Just feel or imagine an infinite field of white, bright, perfect light or any color you choose, and just go into it. Hold the image in your mind very strongly. Then once you can't do that any more, if your time for that chakra is not up, go back to the chakra. In other words, have a number of things you can move your mind to, each of which is bright and perfect, that connects you with light—not human aura or anything lesser—during the experience of meditation.

It's not enough to just say, "Well, I'm going to sit down and focus on a chakra for 20 minutes. And then the next chakra, and then the next chakra, and that's an hour of meditation." You're not going to meditate. You're going to drift all over the place in a highly empowered state and touch many, many auras and pick up a lot of negativity. You must have a number of focuses, or call them shields, if you will, during the experience of meditation. Because you're in an empowered state, and let's be realistic—unless you have total control over the mind, the mind wanders. But you can't let it wander.

Every time your mind moves toward something, don't be uptight, don't be afraid that you're going to get sick or pick up too much aura; that'll only happen if you don't then move the mind. And of course, the fun part is you're developing a new neural track. You get better at this. It becomes a habituation, a habit. And good habits are as hard to break as bad habits.

Try and break a good habit sometime. It's not easy—if you have some good habits. If you have good posture, try and slouch. It doesn't come naturally. If you have good habits, they're your friends. You can develop a positive good habit, which is called meditation—meditating properly. It will take about a week or two to get the track laid well. And if you've been doing it incorrectly for years, then it will take a month or two to redo it.

The real issue is to use the full power of your concentration. If you find that you're drifting and drifting, and you can't do an hour meditation, then just do a half an hour meditation. But it has to be done intensively. Better to do the hour, if you can. I think you can, if you do it in small, incremental modules. That's the method that I think is preferred. So as I've suggested, now that we've moved up to the heart, the chest chakra, perhaps what you'll do here is start with the chakra, focus on it as long as you can, as hard as you can. And of course, you pick up energy doing this, [it] makes everything brighter. Now focus on the music for a few minutes. Now focus on your teacher for a few minutes. Now focus on light. Then go back to the chakra—or in any order you prefer.

Focus on something bright and beautiful. But you must keep your mind occupied at every moment with that which is bright and beautiful. If you do, then there will be nothing else. There won't be people, places or things, the future or the past in your mind.

You can't just sit in emptiness. Even the enlightened don't sit in emptiness. We call it emptiness, but we move our mind into a world of light. Meditation is not emptiness. That's a way of trying to talk about something that is impossible to put into words. It's not that it's empty; it's a world of fullness, if anything. So meditation, in other words, is not really thinking of nothing. In the beginning, it's just replacement thinking. Instead of having the usual negative things that kind of wander around in your mind, or limited things, certainly— people, places, things, past, future, emotion in most cases—you are replacing those things with very bright images. Now those bright images, when you're in an empowered state, in a highly psychic state, are not just images. They're doorways.

Whatever you focus on, you become. That's the key line, you know. Meditation is the bow and concentration is the arrow. Whatever you focus on, you become, particularly during that highly charged state when you let go of that auric immune shield intentionally because you want to go beyond it into pure brightness and to pure light. But you must be very, very careful not to allow other images to come in your mind. Just fwak them right out. It's like playing a great video game. Every time another image comes in your mind, just push it out. Don't focus on it a lot when you push it out, or you'll connect with it.

The way you push it out is by refocusing onto something bright. This is the good habit you will develop. You're sitting there meditating, and every moment you're focusing on either a chakra, the music, light, or your teacher or something else that will connect you with the dimensions of light. And every time something else comes in your mind for a moment—you think of a person, an experience, whatever it is—you consciously must pull your mind back from that image by substituting an image of brightness. If you try to sit in emptiness, you're creating a vacuum. It'll be filled by something. It'll be filled by thoughts and images from your memory or just things that you're feeling psychically. Uh-uh. You have to substitute something and refocus.

Meditation, in other words, is a refocusing, in the intermediate stage, on symbols. And through these symbols, you will come to know your own mind. It's not emptiness. We're using symbols, doorways to step from here to there—from one world to another, from darkness to light, from death to immortality.

Think of meditation on the intermediate level as a substitution. We're substituting a bright thought for a dark thought, a happy moment for a sad moment, an infinite feeling for a finite feeling, a cosmic awareness for a mundane awareness. What you're doing is learning to retrain your mind. For one hour, or half an hour, 45 minutes, when you sit to meditate, you're retraining the way your mind works. You've never trained it; it just sort of happened growing up. Now you're actually training the mind to focus on brightness to the exclusion of all other things.

If you do this during the period of meditation, then it will more readily occur the rest of the time when you're not sitting in a postured meditation, as you go through the day and the evening. You're setting up a template, a good habit. When you first get up, and hopefully again in the evening, you do another equal period of meditation, and you're pulling up power and energy to allow yourself to do all kinds of things and use more of the mind and be in multiple dimensions and all that good stuff. Of course.

What you're doing is re-routing the way you perceive. You're taking a limited perception—which is the sense world and the mental world and the emotional world, which is what most people have—and you're expanding your perceptual ranges so that you can perceive more ranges, greater ranges, all of the time, not just during the period of meditation. Of course, you will experience the normal ranges of perceptions, actually with a lot more clarity and depth because your mind will be clear and sharp and it will have a lot of energy and all the junk will be out of it. So your physical tasking will be tighter and brighter. And of course, you'll be happy.

So what have we learned thus far? In other words, hopefully we're redefining, or perhaps defining meditation for you for the first time. What have we learned? We've learned, essentially, that meditation—intermediate meditation—is a refocusing, a retraining of the mind. To just think that you're going to do what you did in introductory meditation for a longer period of time is incorrect. You're not just going to plop yourself down to meditate and focus on a chakra, meaning once in a while you'll focus on it, most of the time you'll drift all over the place. That's introductory meditation. You're just getting used to sitting, focusing; sometimes you feel some energy, sometimes you don't.

What we have learned is that intermediate meditation is the use of symbols, not abstractions. A symbol is something alive. It's a connector. It's a hyphen between one reality and another. We're in one room. We have to go to another room. We need a doorway to go through. We open the door. We pass through, and we're in another reality. These symbols are doorways to other realities. Focusing on an enlightened teacher is a doorway. It's not a person. We're focusing on the light that passes through them. But our mind is holding the physical image of the person. As we hold that image, our psyche is connecting with the light within them, then we are moving not to them but through them into that field of light, into the planes of light that stretch on forever, and eventually to nirvana.

The chakra is a doorway. When you hold on the navel center, it's the chakra leading you to the planes of power. When you focus on the chest center, it's leading you to the planes of emotive feeling, of spiritual oneness, of ecstasy and happiness. When you're focusing on the third eye, you're going to the planes of knowledge and vision. These are doorways that lead you to these other dimensions. But you have to focus on them completely to the exclusion of everything else. You can't just vaguely hold onto them. Nothing will happen. Or worse yet, you will empower yourself to a degree, become highly clairvoyant, and then, if you allow other images—particularly of people, places and things—to pass through your mind during that state, you will pull in all those other auras, and you will be much more confused and much more dissociated than you were prior to your meditation experience.

Intermediate meditation is learning to use the mind in a new way. And eventually we will develop a habit, a good habit, that we will use not only during the period of meditation but 24 hours a day. The answer is not to try and sit in emptiness and just have the good intention that you're going to hold your mind in a perfect state. Nonsense. Get real. Get a life. That's not going to happen.

Good intentions are not enough. You have to know what you're doing. You need the techniques. By having a number of symbols, doorways that you can focus on from one moment to the next, there will never be a gap during the period of meditation. At times you may go through the doorways and enter into light. Then there's only light in the mind, there's no thought, there's no images, there's no psychic connection with other people, places, things, times, or all that sort of stuff—beings, whatever. Then, naturally, that's fine.

If you're in light, the only time you then have to refocus is when the light fades, gravity pulls you back to the mind and suddenly the images are coming up of the world again. So then, jam ahead. Focus on another symbol. You will find that these symbols work better and better and are easier to focus on as you meditate each day.

The key to meditation is focus on the intermediate level. Not just focus, as a vague abstraction, but focus, or focusing, on specific symbols. The symbols are the chakras, an enlightened teacher, enlightened music or light. Now, there are other alternatives. Sometimes you focus on a yantra with the eyes open. But then again, it's the same thing. You can't be sitting there focusing on the yantra or colored pebble or whatever it may be, vaguely—vaguely looking at it and allowing your mind to drift. If you're using the visual sight to still the mind, you must focus to the exclusion of everything else.

I like music better because the music, in particular the meditation albums, are designed for meditation. If you focus on a yantra, it is a geometric representation of other vortexes of energy, but still, it's a bunch of lines. (Rama laughs.) It's not charged the way the music is. Music is more engulfing. We're dealing with the rhythms, substructures, tonalities. A visual focus is OK, and I recommended it until we had the music. The music is superior, definitely, to the visual focus.

That's why I now recommend that you close your eyes during meditation, if you're using one of the meditation albums. I've put so much energy into each song, so much bright, brilliant, beautiful energy, and the compositions are all based around other dimensions. Each composition references a particular plane of light, so that by focusing on the music to the exclusion of everything else, you'll just pull beautiful, bright light and go through the music into that light as far as you can. And you'll go a little further each time. Then, when you can't hold on to the music, focus on the teacher in a private way, if you have an enlightened teacher or know one.

It's sort of like the feeling that's between us now. Focus on that energy that's coming through my voice or on any enlightened teacher, be they embodied or disembodied—but not on a bunch of their students or not on one of their students who teaches. Bad mistake. [Focus] only on the enlightened. Again, we're not staying with them; we're going through them into the light itself. Or focus on just light. You can imagine light, feel it, hold it in your mind. It can't be vague because then your mind is drifting. So it's through substitution that we meditate.

Advanced meditation, which we might talk about another time—it's pretty hard to talk about—is different. It's not substitution. It's transmutation. It's another step, another stage—that's samadhi, the superconscious. But intermediate meditation will do you, I think, quite well for a while. My recommendation is to know the symbols of your mind and through those symbols to become fully conscious and fully aware, to focus on the chakras while you meditate, to use all three in each meditation. You'll be bringing the kundalini up from the root chakra to the crown center by just focusing on those three. It'll take care of it for you.

Spend a third of your time, starting with the navel center, a third of your time on the chest center, a third of your time on the third eye. But during those periods of time, which should be equal, hopefully you'll be listening to enlightened music which will block out the incredible number of vibrations on an overpopulated planet that you would otherwise be picking up, because you're in a highly psychic state when you meditate. The music will act as an aura block. It will help. It won't do it all. Then you should start each part of the session by focusing on the chakra.

If we're doing the navel center, focus on the chakra as intensely as you can for as long as you can. Then, when the mind tires and you just can't do it, be real about it. Keep a vague feeling of that area throughout that period of that chakra meditation, and now switch to the music. Focus on the music for as long as you can. When you just can't do it, focus on your teacher. Then focus on light. Then go back to the chakra again. Do this in any order. You can mix it up. But for that entire period of that chakra, always have a symbol in your mind that you're focused on. Whenever a person's face, an image, a memory, an anticipation comes in your mind, fwak it out. Push it out by returning your mind to the symbol, by returning your mind to light, to the music, to the teacher, a bright moment with the teacher, a pure moment, a beautiful moment of transcendence, or to the chakra.

In other words, substitute. Don't just sit there and push the thought out because then another thought will just come in. Or you'll focus on that thought as you push it out. Instead, move your mind to the symbol. Eventually this gets easier, with practice. Then move to the next chakra when it's time, and [then] the last chakra.

What we're really keying to or looking at is the time you spend sitting there. We're looking more specifically into the moment-to-moment experience while you're focusing on a chakra. It's not enough just to say, "Sit and focus on a chakra." That's introductory meditation. Now we're making sure that it's "quality time," as they say in the 90's.

And keep your sense of humor. Stay funny. Decide if you want to do any of this. Maybe you don't need to do this. This is a lot of work. It creates ecstasy, liberation and a fine life, sure. But maybe this isn't your moment. Maybe you should just go and do something else. But if you do feel that pull to the eternal, then you can't stay away from it. Then it is most important that you meditate properly. Otherwise meditation will do you a disservice. It will confuse you more than clarify you. It will bring tremendous impurity in you, if you're allowing your mind to wander during the empowered experience.

Keep your mind centered on that which leads to light. Intensively. That's intermediate meditation. Accept no substitute, and/or have a nice incarnation.

Your life is either getting brighter from moment to moment or it's not. If it's not getting brighter, it's because there's no risk. There's no risk in sitting thinking instead of stopping your thought. There's a lot of risk in stopping your thought. You might experience ecstasy. You might enter new dimensions. You might see yourself or reality differently. There's no risk in doing a lousy meditation or not meditating at all. There's no risk in being convenient and comfortable. There's a lot of risk in the world of enlightenment. There's the risk of perpetual freedom.

    – *Tantric Buddhism:* The Natural State

Tantric Buddhism:
The Awareness of Meditation
1990

Meditation is the art of breathing—breathing out and breathing in. The universe, which is beyond understanding and description, is always breathing out and breathing in. It breathes in our lives and then it breathes them out. It breathes in dimensions, beings, feelings, understandings, mind itself. It breathes it in and breathes it out. We could say that life is a cycle, but that implies there's something that is observing it or that's outside of the cycle. There's really only breathing. It's very simple, really.

Meditation is a process in which we're essentially, at first, breathing out. We're exhaling. We're taking all the thoughts, impressions, feelings, vibrations, understandings, all the self-importance, attitudes, desires, loves, hates, passions, dispassions, meanings, lack of meanings, confused states, illumined states, bored states. We're taking everything—the concept of everything; that which perceives everything, that which is beyond perception, that which is beyond perceiving—everything must go. We're exhaling existence, taking it out of the mind, and the mind out of the mind.

After meditation, we inhale. We experience life. But we've changed. We're different because in the purification process of meditation we have touched a deeper threshold within ourselves, of eternity. Mind appears to exist because of the diverse attributes of existence that it perceives as itself. Mind by itself is nothing. It's colorless. It doesn't have a substance or a form. Mind only comes into apparent existence through the action of perception. Mind appears to exist because it perceives. It perceives the perfection of existence. As it perceives it, it is that. But by and of itself, mind not separated from mind is qualityless.

The action of perception is inhalation. The action of perception is mind perceiving something as other than itself. The qualityless mind cannot perceive itself in that there's nothing to perceive. Mind is an essence. It doesn't take a formation. In other words, we tend to think of mind as who we are, "My mind, it's what I think with, it's what I experience with, it is my mind." Some people are a little further in their understanding of mind, and they think, "Well no, mind isn't a tool, it isn't a case tool. Mind isn't something that I think with. It's not like my foot that I walk with. Mind isn't just an appendage, it's not brain, but I am mind. I am the mind. I who can think or perceive or even construe that a mind exists, that is mind. All that can be said to be existent is mind. There's nothing else but mind."

Someone a little further along in their cosmology would say, "Well, there is only mind. But truly, mind is qualityless." This is the Tibetan Buddhist realization, that mind does not have any particular qualities or attributes of its own. It's clear. We say that the mind is composed of clear light, "clear" indicating that it doesn't have a definite shape, color or destination or point of origination. It is always existent. It is beyond cycles of existence. It will always exist. There's only one mind, and that is infinity.

The perception of mind in its variegated states, the perception of mind as different roses—yellow rose, red rose, black rose, primrose, various roses—variegation, coloration shifts, subtle or great changes in intonation—that is mind perceiving other than mind. Mind, if it were only perceiving itself, cannot do so since there's nothing there to perceive. It's qualityless.

Now, this is hard to begin with; this is not easy. You've got to strain yourself a little bit to understand what I'm saying. This is not the easy course in meditation that gives you mediocre results. This is the hard course in meditation that gives you outstanding results. You have to follow along with me.

Now your mind has to follow my mind, which is qualityless. Your mind has qualities because in its apparent perception, it's involved with a differentiation process that is not yet completed and it still perceives itself as other, whereas my mind does not perceive itself as other. It doesn't perceive itself at all because it's clear light. Intrinsically they're the same. But in the act of working out perception—which we call structural being, or living, taking a body, incarnation, existence, multiplicity, duality—we perceive mind as separate and as having qualities.

One person's mind is different than another's. Bob and Sally are different because their minds are different. Their bodies may be different, but their minds are real different. But if mind is truly perceived as mind, it is qualityless; it doesn't have form or shape. There's no difference between anybody's minds because there's only one mind.

But yet we all have a sense of having a different mind. Your mind is different than somebody else's mind. It isn't really different. We are perceiving it as being different because the mind is perceiving qualities. It's identifying with things that are not mind. And in doing so it makes a mistake; there's an error in judgment. It perceives separativity, the mind as separate, and qualities appear to have a validity that they really don't.

Now, we could get into a discussion, I guess, of the difference between that which can be perceived—in other words, if there is mind, and mind is qualityless, what the heck is that which we're perceiving, which has qualities? If there is only mind, then how can there be anything out there to perceive? You see? But that really is tangential to our discussion. We just take it for granted that the universe is complicated and we're not going to get it all in one night or one incarnation or one infinity. The universe doesn't have to be sensible and doesn't have to work out to our pleasing. It's complicated; it has variant sides. And to try and think that in one unified field theorem of mind you can get it all is ridiculous, because it's just not that way.

So we try and perceive it a section at a time—the section that we need, by necessity, is the section that we're in. That's karma. Karma relegates us to the reality that is currently extant for us because that's where we are in our perception. In other words, we're born into a world that's suitable for where our mind is at, for what we're working on. That's the assignment that we've gotten.

So we perceive that action, an orientation of reality that is self-sufficient for us at any given moment. To go worrying about what we're going to do next month when it's not next month yet is kind of stupid. We stick with one thing at a time. We're not going to worry about the qualities that are beyond perception or that are perceivable and confusing. Our aim is to have mind in its primordial, basic, perfect, pristine state, which is meditation.

Meditation, in other words, is mind perceiving itself as mind, without qualities. That's perfect meditation. It's simply perfect mind. Meditation is not an action. It isn't something that you go and do. Rather, what it is, is just mind in its perfect state, without qualities, without confusion. You don't have to go and meditate. That is mind. Mind is meditation.

Meditation is a word that we're using to suggest something other than our normal perception, which is confusion. Confusion is the mind confusing itself and thinking that it's something at all. It can only do that through the function of ego, the sense of "I am." "I am" is the confusion. "I am" implies a quality or series of qualities, which we call self or being. That suggests that being and self are separate from qualityless mind, and this is where you get all screwed up.

So to start with, as I said, this is the hard course. To start with, to understand mind directly and meditation directly is to see that meditation is not something that we do. It's not an action. Susie meditated, OK. Meditation is in that sentence a __? (Rama asks audience. Audience responds.) It's a verb. Right. OK. Meditation can never be a verb because meditation is qualityless. It is mind in its primordial state, and there's no grammar in nonexistence. Grammar has qualities, shapes and forms. As a former English professor, I can assure you that grammar is the qualitative interpolation of language. Adjectives, pronouns, predicates, past pluperfect indicative—ridiculous. It has to do with qualities, shadings, differentiations, rhythmic structures of symbolic meaning. Curiouser and curiouser, if you will.

So then, mind has nothing to do with any of this. Mind is the world of Alice In Wonderland. Alice is sitting up on the bank and she's learning her lessons and she's bored, and this little rabbit goes whipping by and down the hole and Alice says to herself, "Hmmm, wonder where the rabbit's going?" So she slips down the hole and she ends up in Wonderland. Now in Wonderland, if you've read the book or seen the film, you know that nothing is the way it appears to be or it certainly wasn't like it was before you fell down the hole following the rabbit. Caterpillars talk, Mad Hatters have tea parties, all kinds of things go on that don't make a whole lot of sense to the rational mind that likes to work in the field of qualities.

The study of meditation is the entrance into the world of Wonderland. It has nothing to do with how you'd like it. You want a nice neat little study that's easily understandable, that can be laid out with start, middle and end. But the end might be the start, the middle is all the time and there's hardly ever anything but a beginning in meditation. You're in Wonderland and it's just not going to make sense. It's just not going to do it. So you will either reject it, or you'll go study TM [a form of meditation]. TM is logical, scientific, and will do very little for your complexion. It's watered down meditation; it's designed to pacify the mind. In other words, it's very sensible, scientific—it makes sense. If it's that, how can it be profound? Profundity suggests that the simple mind is immediately excluded from the audience.

Meditation is profound. It is mind and it is essence. So then, meditation is not a verb. It is the way mind is. That's why in Zen they call it the natural state, which means that you don't have to go and do anything to meditate. In effect, a person who is trying to meditate is doing something that's impossible since meditation is not an action. Yet at the same time, if you don't do something, you know you're not going to be meditating. That's the catch-22 of meditation.

In the Zen monastery we used to pound people on a regular basis whenever they thought they understood anything. If you think you understand, obviously you don't, since mind is by its very essence qualityless. In qualityless, things are not understood. You can't understand. You can't understand since there's nothing to understand and no one to understand, and understanding itself is a quality principle that is invalid. This is why not too many people meditate. Or if they do, they do TM, which is simply repeating a mantra over and over that has nothing to do with meditation.

In other words, they practice some form of meditation that is simplistic and not really meditation. It might someday lead to the awareness of meditation. Ah! There's a key phrase—the awareness of meditation, the awareness of mind. We're in Wonderland and sometimes a thing is the way it appears to be for a few minutes, and then it changes into something else. Nothing is the same in the world of mind.

At best we can say that mind does not have qualities. And what it appears to have as qualities—it's confused, it's identifying itself with something other than mind. That's not up for debate, it just is. If you debate the issues and the principles, that's great, but you just get caught up in more qualities and there's no meditation.

So then, in order to meditate, all we have to do is stop. If we stop, it's perfect meditation because it's perfect mind. That's it. We just have to stop. Now what do we stop? Thought. Impressions, desires, aversions, states of consciousness, ideas of being, essence, substance, predicate adjectives—everything has to go. Final clearance, everything must go. Exhalation—we're going to exhale everything, all qualities, all perceptions from mind until there's only the perfect, pristine, clear light, which does not perceive itself as other.

Since we're in Wonderland, that doesn't imply that it doesn't perceive. Just because it's qualityless doesn't mean that it doesn't have qualities. This is Wonderland where anything can happen. Because it's the essence of the void doesn't imply it's a vacuum. That's just an idea that a person has.

Qualityless simply means that there's no way to discuss it. There's no way to pin it down. It could be anything at any given moment since infinity is not bound even by itself, nor by the words that human beings choose to try and talk around it. We're dealing with something that's very big here. It's mind. It goes on forever. It's endless. It's perfect. It's radiant. It's enlightenment. Mind is enlightenment.

There are numerous ways to get into Wonderland. Once you're in, it's very hard to get out, fortunately. That's the good news. Once you've become enlightened, it's almost impossible to become unenlightened. There are as many ways to become enlightened as there are many roads that lead to McDonald's. Once you get there, there's the drive-up window or you can go in for the full experience, you see. So meditation comes in many and variegated forms. The product is the same—when you go to the drive-up window at McDonald's or whether you go inside, the product is the same. The double cheeseburger is going to be the same, the shake is going to be the same, but you might feel different in your car or in the McDonald's. That's a whole different issue. It doesn't have much to do with what we're talking about, but I just thought I'd point that out to you. You can get real lined out in the McDonald's—I mean the aura of the people who have been there before you, well, you understand. Of course your car, who knows? It's hard to say.

So then, if you perceive meditation as something that you don't have to do, it's easier. It's breathing out. What you have to do is simply breathe out everything in your mind. When everything is gone and there's only mind, that's meditation. See how easy that was? Whereas if we had done it any other way, you wouldn't have arrived at this understanding. That's why I had to go through all of that. It's not that I don't understand, it's just that I'm qualityless, immaculate, perfect mind.

This is not easy. You want it to be easy. You're Western. You want it to all fit in the microwave. You just want to mic it up and it's done. No effort. Kick back. Sure, meditate. Sure, nothing to it. That's why TM was such a big seller. They said it was effortless meditation. That doesn't—I mean there's no connection—effortless meditation! Effortlessness is a quality. Meditation is qualityless. You think I'm just fucking with you. You're right! (Audience laughs.)

But we're also discussing perfect meditation. It's Wonderland; we can do both simultaneously. That's the good news. We only have good news in Wonderland. We don't print anything else.

All you need to do to meditate perfectly is to eliminate everything from mind that has a quality, and when there's only mind, it falls back on itself and there's no perception of other—which is why in true meditation there's no perception. There can't be perception. If you're meditating and there's a sense of the passage of time, if there's the sense of otherness, of self—even if there's no thought and there's a sense of anything—you're not meditating perfectly. There are still some qualities in the mind and you've got to get rid of them. You've got to breathe out more. When there's no perception, mind is perfect—in its perfect state. It's not confused. So meditation is simply the elimination of everything—in mind, in your mind. Everything that is in your mind goes.

Every time one thing leaves the mind, mind is more pure. It has one less quality and it's more correct. So it isn't really a hard thing to do, to meditate. It isn't really something that we do. Rather, what we do is sit, and we allow the mind to fold into itself and to become perfectly still. Then, as the kundalini energy increases, as the energy of the psyche becomes more pronounced, which it does as thought becomes eclipsed by silence, all the variant mind states and all the stuff burns away. It just goes away, it breathes out.

In other words, we don't even have to force it out. It'll go by itself. All we have to do is to make the mind completely silent. If we stop thought, then everything will go away. The breathing out will be done for us by the stoppage of thought.

What meditation really is, is the science of stopping thought. When there's no thought, it's meditation. When meditation is meditation, then there's only pure mind. Pure mind, of course, is ecstasy. All pain, suffering, difficulties and general life problems come from the confusion that occurs in mind of perception, where mind is perceiving itself as something other than pure mind—of itself as a body, a person, a state, a plane, a being, a rock, frog, cosmic deity. This is all confusion. This is the duality of existence where we believe that we have a separate existence other than pure and perfect, immaculate mind.

Pure and perfect, immaculate mind, which is also referred to as nirvana, is not something, by the way, that's cold, unfriendly or in any way related to what you call death. Death is simply a doorway that we go through in our experiences. In other words, mind is still confused. If you can die, you're confused because death is a perception of something ending and something else obviously beginning, which means we're still hung up in the qualities.

The wonder of immaculate, perfect, pure mind is that when it is in its perfect, extant state without confusion, it can be anything it wants to be. In other words, the riddle is that mind can still manifest itself forth in qualities but remain qualityless. Mind can perceive itself as qualityless in the middle of the qualities. But if you're perceiving yourself as qualities, that's the difference.

So the enlightened person, or whatever they are, enlightened shrew or anything, perceives itself as immaculate mind in the valley of qualities and can move through the qualities and even experience the qualities, but knows that it is not of them. Whereas non-enlightened simply means that you perceive yourself as qualities and enlightenment as something other than qualities. Enlightened mind simply means that you are enlightened mind. That's all there is, and that's all there could ever be. But you can be in the valley of qualities—in the valley of the Jolly Green Qualities, right? And that's fine, that's not a problem.

In other words, to be pure, immaculate mind does not mean that you don't exist. It doesn't mean that you're in a can somewhere on a shelf with some big guy who is green on the label. It has nothing to do with green giants and green valleys or anything that's green whatsoever. It's qualityless. Green is a quality.

You're very serious people. I noticed that right away. I can tell that you're people because I can see that you're identifying with the body and the mind of humans. If you weren't doing that, then you'd be enlightened, you see? Or you'd be asleep, dreaming. That's different, of course. Then you're simply seeing the qualities and identifying with the qualities in the astral as opposed to in the physical and the awakened mental.

When you're enlightened or when the mind is void, vacuous and perfect, it doesn't mean that you can't sort of zip around, drive your car, read a newspaper, walk and have experiences. You can. Void, immaculate mind is all there is, so obviously it can do all those things. In other words, there's an objective correlative to infinity that is a good trick, which suggests that (Rama talks like a nervous person), "Oh God, if I, if I was just void, immaculate mind, I wouldn't be any more, Harold! It would be awful! Oh, I don't want that! I just want, like, better everything! Who wants to get involved with all that cold nirvana? Oh, not good. I won't be anymore. And who will feed the cat?" (Back to normal voice.) Well, since the cat is truly void, qualityless mind, free of all catness, I'm sure the cat is capable of finding a mouse.

This is the peril of mice. This is why it is good not to incarnate as a mouse. Exactly. That's the truth. You can choose these things.

So then, the key perception that we're getting to here is that meditation is not what you think. Meditation is not an action; it's not necessarily difficult. You just have to be very patient. It's something that's natural to all of us because we all are that. But it's not easy to understand. You have to work at it. Meditation is coming back to your original self, if we can use self without a sense of self. It's perfect, clear light; radiant, infinite mind of the universe, as it is, without identifying with qualities. That's something that you already are.

It's like amnesia. A person has amnesia and they walk around and they think that they're somebody other than they are. They've forgotten who they were and they take on a new identity. They wake up one morning in the hospital, they just can't remember. Somebody gives them a new name, they go out to get a job, pretty soon they have family, friends, and they've forgotten that before that hospital they were somebody else. That's what birth is. Birth is a forgetting—not death. As Wordsworth said, birth is the forgetting. We forget who we were before birth, that we were in another body in this world or another world with another identity. Life is eternal.

Meditation is remembering. Meditation is not void. It's not empty. It's simply perfect, qualityless, clear light, which is the essence of all existence, and the substance, perceiving itself as such without anything else. That realization, when the clear light perceives itself as such, without qualities, which isn't really a perception, it's a way of trying to talk around it—then that existence always is and it can do whatever it wants. So really, what we're just saying is that enlightenment, meditation, is really a shift in perception. It's not a thing that you go and do or become, since you're already that. But rather, what you are doing is becoming aware of something that you're unaware of.

You're waking up from the amnesia of birth, the forgetting of life, and you're remembering. And remembering is a flood. Suddenly you remember billions of lifetimes. Suddenly you remember the perfect, immaculate nature of the clear light of mind. That's what meditation really is. It's not a state, it's not a condition, it's not an ecstasy, it's not peace. Those are things you go through as you eliminate qualities, as you eliminate qualities from mind. It's the identification. You experience ecstasy, peace, perfections, bliss, naturally, pain, and all those—frustrations, desires. Everything goes away. All the things that are negative go away and then all the things that are positive go away until there is just clear light.

But don't think that clear light is just clear light. In other words, you have a mental concept of what that is and it has nothing to do with it. That's just a mental concept. Clear light is the extant, radiant, perfect knowledge that is reality. It takes all forms, which are all of us and all things that are extant in any universe, in any reality, in any dimension, in any samsara. And yet it's beyond and above all these things, what you would call God, I guess, unless you think of God as having qualities—masculine, feminine, mean, friendly. But if God does not have qualities, if God just is beyond all consideration of the mind— God's really big, you see, and your mind can't quite—God does not have qualities. That's the clear light. But that's what we are.

That's the message of all enlightened beings to all unenlightened beings, that we are God. We are the clear light and you really don't have much to worry about. You just don't know that right now. Someone who is enlightened has shifted their perception so that the clear light is aware of itself as such, without qualities. Yet it acts and exists and takes form. And that's what you already are, but you just forget that.

Meditation is a remembering. And each time we meditate, we are remembering that simple thing. But it's not a remembrance in the sense that it's an intellectualization. It's an actual experience. You the experiencer meld yourself with the qualityless, perfect light until there's only the qualityless, perfect light, and you do that as much as you can, and that determines your advancement in meditation—how much you can melt into the light.

So meditation is melting into the light, but what I'm suggesting is, the confusion is—you think that you are the person who is melting into the light. That's what this whole explanation was about. Whereas truly, you are the light that is being melted into, but you don't know that now, and I do. I don't just mean know as a phrase meaning, "I accept that idea, I believe in it." I mean it an actual, visceral experience. You know it. Not just as a thought that, "Yes, I agree with that concept" or, "No, I don't." But knowing implies reality in Buddhism.

The thing that increases your power the most is first and foremost meditation—in other words, disciplining the mind so that you can stop thought for protracted periods of time. At the stoppage of thought, a doorway opens to infinite mind and you are empowered. And the longer you can stop thought perfectly, the more power flows through you and the further you extend yourself into other realities, into other you's.

— *Tantric Buddhism:* Peak Experiences

Tantric Buddhism:
Focus and Meditation
1990

The practice of meditation is emptying the mind. When the mind is empty, completely empty, it's perfect meditation. It's really that simple. There are a variety of different approaches to emptying the mind. All of them work equally well. We can just stay with one; we can use a number of them. It really doesn't matter; it's a question of personal choice. What we're doing is stopping thought. But really, before that, we're learning to control thought. And really, before that, we're learning just to sit down and focus on something.

I have a simple prescription method for learning how to meditate, which, if you do it, works very, very well. The main thing that you need is not really creativity but consistency. Creativity is a nice quality but it doesn't have much to do with learning to stop thought. Consistency does. Consistency really involves just doing something once, each time, and not thinking about time or space or repetition. You just live it once. Forever. And that's consistency. That's perfect consistency.

To meditate, what I suggest a person do is, of course, they sit in an upright position—if you lie down you relax too much and you don't really have the focus of concentration necessary to meditate. You can sit in a cross-legged position on a rug, you can sit in a chair. All that matters is that the back is relatively straight, the spine is straight. What I suggest a person do for their practice is to focus on something with their eyes open for half the meditation, and for the second half of the meditation to focus on something with their eyes closed. The length of time depends upon how long a person has been meditating. If a person wants to start meditating, I recommend that they meditate for fifteen minutes a day, once a day. After they've been meditating perhaps for a few weeks, then I would suggest that they double the time and go to half an hour. After several months, I would suggest that they increase the time to 45 minutes and then, that they stay at 45 minutes for a while, until they've been meditating about a year, every day consistently. After a year, if a person chooses to, they can increase the time, perhaps to an hour—maybe for another six months or a year. Then maybe after two years, go up to an hour and a half, ninety minutes.

The primary meditation, which is done in the early part of the day, after waking, is the meditation I'm discussing. It is nice to have a second meditation in the early evening, or about halfway or two thirds of the way through the day. It renews the initial meditation. It renews our contact with the divine, with the infinite light. That meditation should be of fairly short duration unless you're just very inspired— maybe 30 minutes, 15 minutes if you're new. But the important meditation is the meditation that you do to start the day because when you wake up from sleep, the mind is relaxed and you've not yet set it into motion. It has the motion of the astral dream experiences, but they're slight. Whereas, after you've started to have conversations, act in the world, perceive things in a sensorial way, the mind gets very stimulated; it picks up a lot of impressions and it's harder to move into the qualityless state of no thought.

The best time to meditate is when you first get up, whether it's morning, evening or afternoon, depending upon your schedule. It's nice to be clean; it wakes you up and just takes a lot of the energies off. Water neutralizes strange energy, unpleasant energy. So if you can take a shower before your—we'll call it the morning meditation, regardless of when you do it—that's a good idea. Or at least wash your hands and face. But water takes a lot of the strange energies that you've picked up in dreaming and the human aura of the planet Earth and washes it away and it makes it easier to meditate.

Then sit down. If you're terribly hungry, you should have just a little something to eat. If you're terribly sleepy, you should have some coffee or some tea or some kind of stimulant that will keep you awake. But if you eat too much, you'll be too aware of your body and you won't meditate very well, and if you use too much of a stimulant, too much caffeine, caffeine makes you think and it makes it harder to meditate. Ideally, I suppose we'd wake up in the morning and take a shower and just meditate. But sometimes a little bit of food or something with some sugar in it is helpful, just because there's so much impure aura on the planet Earth and it raises the blood sugar and kind of gets us going, and sometimes some caffeine or whatever you use might be helpful. You don't want to fall asleep, and you don't want to sit there being hungry; it'll interfere with your meditation. Nor do you wish to satiate your body with too much food because you'll just get very sleepy, and too much of a stimulant, too much caffeine does the same thing—your palms sweat, your adrenaline starts to rush a little bit and you don't meditate well.

Then you want to sit down and for whatever period of time is apropos for your level of study, you want to practice concentration—focus. All meditation involves focus until we enter into the qualityless, thoughtless essence, when we perceive ourselves as the thatness. So really all you're doing is learning to focus. Let's say you're going to be meditating for 30 minutes. I would suggest for 15 minutes that you meditate with your eyes open, focusing on an object of some type, hopefully an object that's beautiful or powerful. You could find a pretty colored stone that you just feel good about. It's a little rock that you found somewhere, life drew you and the rock together—your karma. It has a nice energy, and you could place that in front of you on the ground or on a table at eye level, if that's more comfortable. And you could focus on that. You could use a flower, a candle flame, anything you want that's bright and suggestive of beauty and eternality. Then with your eyes open, you'll focus on that to the exclusion of all thought.

Naturally in the beginning, if you're undisciplined, which everyone is mentally when they start meditation, you'll think a million thoughts, a lot of images will come through your mind. But if you focus on the object and you keep focusing, gradually the thoughts will become quieter and quieter, gradually the images will disappear from the mind. What's happening is, through the power of focus, as you look at something and concentrate on it, the kundalini energy which is situated in the base of the spine, in the astral, begins its long journey up through what we call the shushumna, which is an astral nerve tube that goes from the bottom of the spine up to between the eyebrows and a little bit above, which is the agni chakra. And as that energy begins to radiate and rise, it causes the mind to become quiet, and the further that energy goes up, the higher we go into different planes of consciousness.

The planes of consciousness are correlated to what we call the chakras, which are located along the shushumna. There are six of them. Then there's one other chakra of the primary chakras, which is not directly connected to the other six, that is located approximately at the very top of the head or an inch or two above it in the astral body, and that's the seventh [chakra].

Each of those chakras really are dimensions. We think of them as objects, but they're not really. They're dimensional access points whereby we can enter into different levels of mind, and that happens automatically. It's kind of like the mercury in the thermometer rises as it gets hotter. As that mercury goes up, it hits little plateaus and when we hit those plateaus, everything shifts. We pop into a different dimension where we perceive ourselves, the universe and mind completely differently. When we get to the top one, if we do, we're in very high planes of attention. And the higher we go, the less physical things are, the less time and space exists. But there's a big transition from the sixth chakra, or the agni chakra, to the seventh, because it isn't exactly a pathway—we do it another way. And that's the chakra of illumination, the planes of enlightenment. That's a little more complicated.

But for now, we're back in the first chakra again. We are in the earth plane, very much in time and space, very much in a body, very much identifying with all kinds of qualities, and we have no sense of the mind as being pure light. If anything, it seems like it's the opposite. So we sit down and we focus. And as we focus on something, the more intently we focus for longer and longer periods of time, the kundalini rises and the kundalini is hot, it's a hot energy. Sometimes you feel it cascading up your spine, and it's kind of searing or it's tingling. It almost feels sexual, but it doesn't arouse. Sexuality arouses, and it causes a physical arousal with the glands in the body. This feels sort of like that, but there's no arousal of the sexual organs. It's that same sort of tingly energy, but it goes up the spine in the astral body. It goes up the shushumna. You don't have to be aware of this, it just happens. You're not necessarily aware that your blood is flowing. but if you go running, your blood flows a lot more rapidly, even though you don't feel it coursing through your veins—but it's happening. There's no need for it to flow rapidly unless there's an escalation of the heartbeat, which occurs in motion.

Normally, kundalini is always flowing through all your chakras, through your subtle body, subtle physical body, what we call your astral body. Kundalini is the blood of the astral. And it's doing everything it needs to, but it doesn't need to flow much more than it is, unless there's reason, unless there's demand, unless there's activity. So in human life, unless there's something very major that happens of an emotional nature, there's very rarely an elevation in, kind of, the seratonin level of kundalini. It doesn't change much. But when you seek to enter into other states of consciousness, that requires more energy, and so the kundalini flows. Of course the more complete your concentration is and the less thought, awareness of self in the mind, the more the kundalini flows and the higher you go beyond body, mind, time and space and so on. It's hard to talk about some of these things; you have to really experience them.

When we meditate, then, what we're doing is not just simply concentrating. We're raising the kundalini through focus, through concentration. There's a metaphysical astral process that's taking place. What I would recommend is, if you're meditating for half an hour, sit down with the eyes open, look at your little power rock or flower or candle flame or anything—yantra, geometrical design. Focus on one point and hold your attention there. The mind will waiver, you'll think a million thoughts, but each time you do, bring your mind back to the point of concentration, seeing it visually. If one were blind, one can simply focus on a feeling.

Sight is not absolutely essential for this process, but we use sight because sight is the dominant sense. We can use hearing and do the same thing. We can listen to a tone. We can feel something physically. We could smell something and do it. But sight is the dominant sense. It takes precedence over all other senses unless one is blind or has been trained otherwise. So it's easiest to interrupt the flow of thought in sense perception and move the mind beyond sense perception with sight. That's why we do something visually to start with.

What we're seeking to do is internalize perception. Perception is very much involved with the senses and the mental processes and the emotional processes. That's what 100 percent of our perception is usually engaged in. But what we're going to do is gradually remove our perception from the sense world—seeing, smelling, tasting, touching, all those sort of things. We're going to remove our awareness from our thoughts, the thinking cognitive process. We're going to remove our awareness from feeling emotions and we're going to take all of our awareness and take it someplace else—into luminous realms, into inner light, into the very thing that we are that perceives. We're going to take perception into itself, into the perceiver, and see that what's there is perfect, qualityless, endless radiant light, which is a way of talking about something. It's not really just qualityless light; those are human abstractions. But it's nirvana; perfect perfection, beyond comprehension—ecstasy.

What we're learning to do is really change a lifetime of habits of taking our perception and having it go into the senses or into thoughts or into emotions, and we're retraining our perception to go into the void. It sounds a little nebulous at first, so what we do is, rather than just focus on the void, which would just be an intellectualization and wouldn't really occur, what we're doing is changing the course of a mighty river, and we do it in steps. We're creating a new pathway for it. And we do that first by focusing on something physical.

By disciplining and training the mind to focus on one thing, we gain control of our perception; we learn to grab it and put it someplace we want it to be rather than just in any sense that happens to be operating, or in any thought that happens to be passing through, or in any feeling that just happens to be going through us—who knows why, or even if we do know why.

We're learning to take our perception and place it in one place. By focusing on something, we do that. And be not discouraged. Everyone goes through the process you're going through. Takes a while to do it. Takes a number of years to learn to hold the mind perfectly in one place. But each day we do a little better, and in the doing of it we're releasing energy that is taking our mind into higher, diffuse planes of attention in which we're seeing life more as it really is. And if we do that every day, there is an add-up process. It's kind of like—as we release more kundalini, we use a little bit of it but we also save it; we store it; it resides in our awareness field, so that as we meditate; it isn't just that we go up and come back down, we come down a little bit less each time.

"Come down" isn't really the right phrase because that implies we're getting high; high implies that it's an abnormal state and low is the regular state. The opposite is true. Our current perception is very cloudy and all screwed up and as our perception increases through meditation, we're seeing life more correctly. The higher our perception, the more kundalini that's active and being properly focused, the more correct our perception is.

So, really we're in the darkest darkness now and we're moving towards light. And light frees us and the mind is perfect and we feel ecstasy, and we don't have any suffering and any mental aberrations; we're not in weird planes of consciousness perceiving ourselves as a self that's in some kind of pain or struggle or whatever it is. We see that we're the perfect light of existence that has always been and will always be. And we live that. It's not just an ideation.

Meditation is the freeing of ourselves from all mental states and concepts of self. But it really begins with a focus, with a retraining of the life force or the life energy. So you look at your object of concentration for, say, 15 minutes. Put a watch there, take out a clock, time yourself. Then, after you've done it for, let's say, 15 minutes, if your time period is half an hour, and you've really tried just to see that one thing, to look at it—you can blink, you can shift your position a little bit if you need to—but then after you've done it for half your meditation, close your eyes and now do the same thing focusing on one of the three chakras—either the navel center, around the navel; the median center, which is in the center of the chest around the heart; or the third eye, which is between the eyebrows and a little bit above.

You focus on one of those three centers, focusing on the physical area in the body that's near where it is in the astral. And if you focus around the navel center, or around the center of the chest by the heart, or between the eyebrows and slightly above, you will elevate the kundalini and you'll be releasing different types of energy into the astral nerve system. I recommend that you focus on these three centers in rotation. So Monday morning, do your navel center; Tuesday, the center of the chest; Wednesday the third eye; Thursday go back to the navel center. Rotate them because they take in the three basic meridians.

There are three lower centers. There are two intermediate centers, the throat center and the chest center; and then there are really two higher centers, the third eye and the crown center. You're accessing all three meridians, which creates the development of a balanced being, if you rotate them that way. If you just always meditate on the navel center, you get too heavy, you get too into certain energies relating to the lower three centers and you don't have enough will, you don't have enough power to deal with life and the world and the forces you have to deal with as you go through different dimensional planes and access points, in more advanced meditative states.

If you just meditate on the intermediate states, they're beautiful and pleasant, but you develop the psychic chakras a lot, a lot of the emotional body develops—but without the other centers there's a lack of balance. The upper centers are wisdom; the central centers are feeling, emotion, identification, beauty, the perception of life as beauty and truth; the lower centers are the power centers. So we put power, wisdom and feeling together and we have a good package in development. Otherwise, we're just developing without balance, and without balance our meditative practice will not continue to escalate.

Balance is the most important of all qualities. We don't want a little bit of rapid growth and then to stagnate. We want continual growth, continual development, which implies balance, always.

To begin with, you would focus for fifteen minutes, if you're doing half an hour a day, on a physical object; then you'd close your eyes and focus on one of the three centers, chakras, for the same period of time. If you've never focused on chakras before, the first few times you can actually put your finger around the navel center and apply a little bit of pressure until you get used to a feeling there, the same with the center of the chest or the third eye. After you've done it a few times, you'll find that you can just feel that area.

Now, interestingly enough, as you practice, you'll begin to feel the centers more. You'll actually feel that part of the astral body and you'll feel the energy releasing, and you'll notice that meditating on the navel or the center of the chest or the third eye really brings you into different mental states, to different planes of mind. Each one makes you feel very different after meditating. They're quite profound.

What we're really trying to do, then, with practice, is to spend more time in a complete focus. We do reach a point, however, when, while we are focusing, if we focus very completely, thought will stop. And when that happens, it's no longer necessary to focus—we can just let go. It's not as if in an hour and a half of meditation you're going to be sitting there, straining to focus on one thing the whole time. Rather what will occur is you will perhaps meditate for ten or fifteen minutes very intensely with a focus, then you'll find that your energy will rise sufficiently so that thought will stop for a while, and then you don't have to focus—you can just kind of let go. And then, when you start to think again, you go back to focusing again and releasing energy.

It's kind of like getting away from gravity. They develop a lot of momentum [for rockets] to get beyond the gravitational pull of the earth and then go into outer space. Then they shut off the rockets. They don't have to keep them on. Then you just float, in the light. Then, as you continue to travel, there may be some other great object, there may be a gravitational force that starts to pull on you, so you put on the rockets again until you're floating free again.

When you're floating free, of course, you are in the light. There are less qualities that you're apprehending, and then the transmutation takes place. Then the magic takes place. When you go in the light, and the longer you stay in the light, the more you transmute. The light washes out all the impurities of mind; it clarifies why we are, who we are, what we are, and it evolves us. It makes us more complete. It makes us more like the light and less like other.

You don't have to do anything when you get into the light. When you stop thought, it's not necessary to go anyplace or do anything. You've arrived. Nor is it static; it won't stay the same. But you've just gotten to a country where everything is done for you. You don't have to know, you don't have to not know. When you've gotten up that far, you just let go. There's complete consciousness, but then at that point the light does what is necessary for you. If you get in a shower, you just have to stand there and once in a while you turn around. If you get in a shower where it's hitting you from every angle, you're all set. So the light hits you from every angle. You just have to get there.

At the end of meditation, at the end of the period, we always bow and we touch our head to the floor – "Buddha's name be praised." That's our way of acknowledging our contact with all of life, thanking the universe, and it's just a letting go. It's realizing that there is something higher and deeper and more profound than our current self, and we're just acknowledging that and thanking it. We know that that is us. We know that we're not fully aware of that as "us" yet and that we hope to be some day. And we will be. Even though we already are, we don't know it. We have amnesia.

So what we do is shift our attention to a realm that's so wonderful that it really doesn't matter what happens here. And that's what the practice of meditation is. The practice of meditation is when we shift our mind through the use of the will to a realm of pure and perfect light. We learn to sustain ourselves in that realm, which actually exists. We go to another place, just like you physically walk from one room to another. We walk with our minds from the habituation of the senses that takes us into the sensorial world or the thought world—habituations of the mind or desires or aversions or the egoistic cravings. We learn to take our mind to another place that most people don't know about. It's a place of perfect purity, peace, light and ecstasy, happiness beyond your comprehension that never ends. We call it the clear light, nirvana.

— *Tantric Buddhism:* Buddhist Yoga

Tantric Buddhism:
Professional Meditation
1990

When a person has become used to meditating on a regular basis and the practice has become a part of your life, we reach a kind of threshold that some people don't cross. Initially, when you begin to meditate, it's challenging, it's difficult just to get yourself to sit down once or twice a day to do it. Then you begin to see results. There's more energy in your life, your mind works better, your body feels better, things appear to be brighter, you have more enthusiasm, your awareness shifts, you start to become a little bit clairvoyant, you can see inside people, see inside yourself and you just see there's a rise of your power. Everything in your life begins to come together.

Then what happens is the practice becomes a practice. It becomes something that is a routine, and each meditation may be fulfilling and you don't stop because if you did, you'll notice the days are not as bright. So meditation becomes something that we have to do because the loss of it reduces our energy level. But it's not something that we do because we are making continuous breakthroughs. It develops a kind of functional autonomy.

There was a time we didn't meditate, and we obviously got by. Now we start to meditate and there's a brightness and an addition, but now the reason we meditate is not because we seek a greater brightness but simply because the loss of meditation will bring us to a lifestyle, an energy level, an awareness level that we find unacceptable.

So then, once we're meditating on a regular basis and that's become part of our life, if not the main focal point of our life—the meditation and all that implies—the issue is how to continually make breakthroughs in meditation. How never to let meditation become just a routine in our lives, something that we have to keep because we fear the loss of it as opposed to something that is each day taking us into realities of mind, taking us into warp drive, taking us through dimensions, changes, dissolutions of the self and so on that are each day more amazing than any day before.

Now that's realistic when you get into advanced practice. In the beginning, that's not realistic. You can't say, well, each meditation is going to be five times stronger than the day before because you have not yet developed the consistency of reaching a singular level. One day you'll do well, one day you won't. It's sort of like in sports, there's amateur and professional. An amateur is someone who one day is brilliant, the next day they're not. A professional is someone who demonstrates a consistency in brilliance. And their worst day will be about the best day of the amateur. They have their off days and their off seasons. But even when they're bad, they're consistently good. They're just not amazing.

Meditation is similar to that. In the beginning you're an amateur. This is once you're consistent and meditate once or twice a day for an hour, hour and a half a day. You're meditating consistently, but one day you'll have a great meditation, and then maybe for three days it'll just be so-so. And what I mean by that is not how you'll feel during the period of meditation, but how you will feel after you've meditated. During the period of meditation, it's not a good idea to evaluate your meditation. When you're running, you don't say, "Gee, this is a great run" or "This is a bad run." You just run.

When you meditate, you just focus. And if you're evaluating, that means you're not doing a good meditation because you're not focusing or dissolving, depending upon your level of ability in meditation.

So then, we'll have one great meditation, then four or five that are just so-so. Meaning that afterwards, one day after we've done what we would call a great meditation, we know it's great because everything shines. The whole world shines, everything is bright, we're flooded with optimism, new ideas, enthusiasm, or maybe there's just a perfect peace and stillness, a sense of self-transcendence, and it's a day like no other day.

It's kind of like a perfect spring day, when winter fades, and there is such a thing as a perfect spring day when the whole world is awake and alive after winter. And the breezes that blow, these just kind of gentle little breezes, when they touch your body, your body is alive in a way that normally it isn't. There's an energy present on certain days in spring that's not available at other times. Each season has its special days. We call them days of power when certain energies are available in our locale or on the earth that are not available all the time.

So when we do meditate well, when we're able to stop our thoughts for a long period of time—or if you're not at the point where you stop thought, yet you are able to concentrate intensively on one point and you really hold to it, you really just put a lot of effort into it—then the day will be very good because you've released a lot of kundalini energy in that process. That energy will flow through you all day and all evening. Your personal power is up; you'll just zig when you should zig and zag when you should zag. When your personal power level is up, you see better. So you'll know, "Oh gosh, I'm not going to take that exit today, I'm going to take this exit," and get a whole different day. Everything works out. The days that our personal power level is low because we haven't done a good meditation, we don't see well. Then we don't meet the right person, we don't attract the right energies to us. Things don't work as well in life.

So the trick in life, of course, is keeping your personal power level as high as possible, and that's what meditation does. But in the beginning, we don't necessarily have the consistency to make that happen no matter what. You may wake up one morning and you feel kind of sick, and you can't necessarily meditate very, very well. You may wake up one morning, and you're just nervous or you're depressed or something's bothering you, and it's just hard to bring the full power of concentration into your mind. One day you just—your thoughts won't stop; they're incessant. And every time you try and concentrate, you forget that you're supposed to concentrate and you get caught up in your thoughts.

A professional is someone who is able, no matter what the state of their mind or the state of their life, to sit down, meditate, stop thought, enter into a state of deep concentration and shut the world off, bring their mind back from the senses, back from the thoughts and back from the feelings and enter into a quiescent state. When we stop thought, when we don't feel the senses or ignore them, when we don't feel feelings, per se, when we shut off the emotions and the thought processes and the sensorial processes, all of our awareness is free. And then, if we don't direct it, it directs itself. That's when we really begin to meditate. At that point, the mind enters into deeper spheres of its own being and we start to touch the radiant spheres. And of course, there's no way to talk about it at this point because we go beyond words into actual, occult, metaphysical, meditative, enlightening experiences.

The trick, then, to keeping your meditation practice alive—not simply consistent but wonderful—is you need to bring a certain will or force into every meditation. For the person just starting, I wouldn't be concerned. It's just enough to get yourself to the point where you meditate every day and then you see meditation as indispensable. That's a good place to get to, where it's just, it's like breathing, when you just get up in the morning and you meditate. You can't conceive of a day when you don't do that because the day would just be horrible. It wouldn't be a day; it would be a nightmare. And it's not that you've become addicted to meditation, it simply means that you want to be in touch with eternity and life at every moment. It's just an intelligent way to live.

I suppose we could say a person is addicted to food, and maybe they should give up eating for six months or a year. I don't think we get addicted to meditation. I think we just realize that it's an innate, natural process. To not meditate is very unnatural for a person who's evolved.

So then, once you're meditating every day and you see it as something that's indispensable, it usually becomes a routine. You sit down, you focus, you go through the usual states of mind that you go through. You may have pleasant experiences. But you're just driving down the highway at 55 [miles per hour]. You don't even have to pay much attention to your driving. You're fairly reflexive and usually nothing unusual occurs, so you just kind of drive. You get to where you're going, but it's not remarkable. That's not meditation. That's just a boring state of mind. But a lot of people call it meditation.

Or you have a certain power of concentration, you do increase your energy levels so you have more energy during the day, but there's no white light, there's no ecstasy, there's no smile on your face that's so big while you're meditating that it hurts after a while. There's no sense of brilliance, the world flooding into a thousand lights, your mind cascading through a billion dimensions and then going completely clear and entering back into the qualityless state—that's a hard word to say, "qualityless." That'd be a good tongue twister.

So you're not meditating. If it's not ecstasy, you're not meditating. I don't know what you're doing. Ecstasy comes in many forms, in many shapes and colorations. But you're not meditating if you're not experiencing ecstasy. You may be learning how to meditate but once you're meditating, once you're a meditator—one who meditates daily and who sees it as indispensable, as part of their life— you should be experiencing ecstasy every time you meditate. Not necessarily during the meditation—maybe at the end, maybe afterwards. But you can't be satisfied with anything less.

You concentrate so intensely, you bring your will to such a singular point that you break through all the limited mind states. You bring in so much kundalini because your focus is so intense that you snap out of the limited mental states into higher mental states, and then, of course, you experience the pure, shining void in whatever form you're capable of experiencing it and seeing it as, from your sentient mind state, and that in itself is ecstasy.

In other words, the universe is ecstasy. Now that doesn't mean much; that's just a phrase. What does it mean, "the universe is ecstasy"? I mean, you experience the universe and you do not necessarily experience ecstasy. How could plants, trees, stars, quasars, black holes— what does that have to do with ecstasy? Ecstasy is a personal experience. Those are—the universe is filled with things. Not true! That's how the universe appears through the senses.

But if you rise above the sense level, if you don't view life just through the senses, if you view life through the emotions, then the universe is made up of feelings. If you view the universe through the mind, it's made up of understandings. If you go beyond the mind that thinks and analyzes and understands, if you go beyond the senses that see, smell, feel, touch and hear, if you go beyond the feelings of pleasant, unpleasant, love, hate, I like it, I don't like it, attraction and repulsion—there are other levels of perception within us.

Meditation is a process by which we go beyond the senses, the mind and the feelings, and we engage the other levels of perception, other forms of perception. It's like sense perception, or mental or emotional perception. We have many other ways of perceiving infinity. But most people, of course, are completely unaware of them. And when you perceive life through those other modes, that's when you see that the universe is ecstasy. That's when you experience its ecstasy.

There is physical ecstasy, something sensorial. A great food or a great lay, or whatever it is. There is emotional ecstasy, the feeling of oneness, of love, of kindness, euphoria, joy. There are feelings of mental ecstasy where we just understand something, we just grasp something, we intuit something—a higher beauty, an intelligent understanding of life, of ourselves or of a project.

There is ecstasy in the body a little bit, in the mind a little bit and in the emotions a little bit. But there is also pain in the emotions— unhappiness, depression, disillusionment. There's pain in the mind, in the thoughts; there's a lot of pain, discouragement, confusion. There's pain in the body, physical pain. But in the other modalities for perceiving infinity, there's no pain. There's only ecstasy. And the mere fact that most human beings—out of the five billion people that are currently extant on the planet Earth, maybe several hundred, maybe several dozen, maybe a dozen, experience life in its true pure state— maybe a dozen. Maybe there are several dozen who experience it on and off in its pure state. Maybe there are several hundred who touch the pure state once a day. Maybe there are several thousand who touch it once a week, and then the rest only have heard about it or don't even know it exists. Or don't believe it if they hear it.

Maybe there are just a dozen people who live in the pure state all the time, a dozen fully enlightened people on the planet Earth. Maybe that's all. But because there are only a dozen, doesn't mean, because the number is few, that their perception isn't much more correct than the billions who don't perceive that way. There were very few men who framed the Constitution of the United States. A lot of people couldn't read and write back then. More couldn't read and write than could. Hamilton, Madison, Jay, Jefferson, these people—there were very few well-educated people—they put together a Constitution which has created a framework for millions. Just because they were a minority doesn't mean that they didn't see much more clearly than anyone else.

So there are very few people who are actually enlightened, who live in the higher spheres, in this particular world. There are worlds where everyone is enlightened, where everyone is in touch with that qualityless essence of existence, mind perceiving itself without coloration, and that's normal and natural. In this world it's normal and natural that most people perceive life through the three primary bands of attention. And when someone perceives life through the senses, that's a correct form of perception. It's not incorrect; it's just limited, limited to the senses. When someone perceives life through the emotions or through the mind, they're not perceiving life poorly. But let's say you're looking at life through a glass darkly. You don't see much through the senses, you don't see much through the emotions and you don't see much through the mind. They're very distorted levels of perception—distorted in that they don't show you the whole picture. They show you only a fragment. But the illusion is that when you see life through those three modes, you see life completely.

When you go beyond those three modes into the other levels of attention, perceiving life through other aspects of what we would generally call mind, you realize that all your life you've lived in a tiny village, maybe three tiny villages. And you would visit them. But there was a vast world with continents, oceans, mountains, things you never knew about, cities, that were outside of that. And it's only when you leave your three-village area that you go and see the universe. It's fun to live in a three-village area. I like it. But sometimes you need to leave to get a proper perspective, and there's pain there, and suffering, but there's no pain and suffering beyond the senses and the mind and the emotions. There's only ecstasy in variant shapes and forms.

So then, we would say that your meditation is quite excellent when you are able to, each time you meditate, go beyond the senses, the emotions and the thoughts. Not into a sleeplike state where you're just kind of unaware, but into states of complete awareness where you're perceiving life in other modalities, other than the three I've alluded to.

The way you do that, the way you become consistent, I think personally, is unexplainable. I mean, it can be explained but I don't think the explanation will change anything. I can say that, "Well, when you've suffered enough, and you see that the mind is wonderful and the senses are wonderful and the emotions are wonderful, but yet you've had enough suffering in them and you realize that they can never fulfill you completely and you seek that—then you'll go beyond them." Sure, I can say that, and it's true. But it doesn't really explain anything. I don't think you can explain life. It just is.

So if a person were to say to me, "Rama, how can I become consistent? I mean, I meditate every day, but I want that ecstasy level, that deep understanding of life, the dissolution of the selves, and you know, all the things that happen in the upper gradients." In other words, 99 percent of meditation occurs in the upper gradients, one percent is just getting started and getting above those three things and that may occupy a few years of a person's time, but real meditation occurs beyond thought, beyond emotion and beyond sensorial perception. So how do you get up there, how do you do that? Well, I would say, "What really has to occur is a kind of magic. It can't be explained. I can explain why or why not, but that won't make you do it. Sometimes your life just puts your back against the wall and you've experienced so much unpleasantness in those three realms that it drives you further. That may happen."

You can explain that to someone but if that circumstance comes along, it'll happen; if not, it won't. The closest I can come to saying this is—meditate. Meditate and realize that when you meditate, no matter how high you go, no matter how deeply you perceive, that you're only touching the bare surface of infinity. Just hold in mind the fact that beyond your perception is ecstasy. Not far beyond. Just with the stoppage of thought there's ecstasy—power, understanding, in limitless amounts. And no matter how far you go, you can never experience all of it. And if you dissolve the self completely, it doesn't end. The self is just a filter that prevents us from seeing completely. It has its place. Sometimes we need that filter, but sometimes we don't.

So I would simply say—meditate. Sit and meditate as deeply as you can. But when you meditate, don't get so caught up in doing it that it's kind of like the vitamin pill you take every day. You take it just because you assume it's doing a good thing, and maybe you didn't take it for a week and you noticed your energy was low, so you went back to it. That's not meditation. Meditation is about ecstasy. It's about the understanding of truth. It's about us changing ourselves and making ourselves God-like. Our mind melds with the mind of infinity and we become infinity. And we become perfect by virtue of the fact that the universe is perfect in its nonphysical aspect. It's perfect in its physical aspect, but it's transient, it changes. But the light itself is perfect.

So I would just say meditate on the light and merge with it. And always remember that you're only touching the surface of infinity. That it goes on forever, and that you have before you limitless ecstasy. Even the sage who's going into samadhi, and he's got all his terminology for nirvikalpa, salvakalpa, sahaja—you know, they divide it into a system, and maybe some of that's true. Maybe you can systematize a little of it. But even the sage who's doing sahaja samadhi, the great guru, I'd say, "Hey buddy, you know, I like the robes and everything, but remember, you're only touching infinity. And if you claim to be doing more, I think you're pretty much in the senses and the body and the mind because infinity is endless. None of us can compromise it or understand it."

But we can swim in it. It's like the ocean. You can go swim in that ocean. That ocean is big. It connects to other oceans and it changes all the time. And there are tides and currents, and even the very water that's before you today will be someplace else in the world tomorrow, and there'll be different water in your section of the ocean. And it's deep! The mountains under the ocean are higher than the Himalayas. But we don't even see them. There are many worlds there.

So when we meditate, we're going swimming in the ocean—the ocean of bliss, the ocean of ecstasy, the ocean of transmutation and personal refinement. Just remember that it's big and that every part of it is perfect and it's fulfilling beyond imagination. And if you do that, I think you'll find that you will be more likely to touch more of it, just with that simple understanding.

There's a resonance inside us, a sense of who we are. We're a multi-bodied traveler. We're an essence. We're a feeling, an awareness that has an ancient existence. The world of meditation puts us in touch with that being.

— *Tantric Buddhism:* The Mature Monk

Tantric Buddhism:
The Best Meditation I Ever Had
1990

The best meditation I ever had, I haven't had yet. It's in the future, which as anyone knows doesn't exist—anyone who meditates knows. But yet, I'll have it some day.

The best lifetime I've ever experienced hasn't occurred yet. I've had billions of lives. I've been around the universe almost as long as the universe, I think. I remember my lives; you don't. Or you remember a few. I remember a billion. And I've had wonderful lives. I've had wonderful lives, beautiful lives, lives of struggle, lives of battle, lives of ecstasy. I've had beautiful lives, and this is a beautiful life I'm in now. It's a hard life, as they go, but it's a beautiful life.

But I haven't had the best lifetime yet. It's around the corner, I know it is. It hasn't occurred yet because things get better in infinity as we get better. And in each lifetime we get better.

The universe is always ecstasy and it's always perfect. But we don't perceive it that well. And if we keep doing our yoga in every lifetime, we perceive it more correctly. It isn't that infinity gets better—I have no doubt that it could if it were in the mood, and maybe it does—but the real issue is perception in meditation. Meditation is the study of perception. What we seek to do in meditation is refine, which means, simply, make more accurate our perception of things. So I haven't had the best meditation I can have because there's no end to the refinement of perception.

Yes, I say that I am enlightened. What does that mean? It means I live in a condition of light. After many years of meditating, practicing, I've reached a point that can't be described or discussed—but one is always in a condition of light. There is really no primary self anymore. It comes back in every life without me seeking it. One has to refine it, but it just comes back unsought. I live in a condition of light inside my mind. Nice. But that condition of light can be refined.

There's no end to it because we perceive the universe through the universe. We perceive light through light, and there's no end to the gradients of perfect light.

So I believe that the best lifetime hasn't occurred. I don't think the most beautiful sunrise to be seen in the world has been seen on this earth. It isn't that the sunrise will grow more beautiful, it's that we will. And we'll perceive it more completely than anyone before. You might say, "Well, God, the universe is filled with a lot of slimy stuff. There are pollutants in the air, there hasn't been much aura on the earth from the time of Atlantis, and you could really see then." And I'd say, "Well, that's true, but you know, those chemicals create beautiful sunsets."

You see, Buddhists are optimists. We never saw sunsets in Atlantis like we do now. We didn't have all those great chemicals in the air. So what is beauty? Is beauty the acknowledgment that chemicals in the air create beauty or would beauty be to bitch about it and say, "Well, God, back in Atlantis it was much nicer!" And what does it mean? I would think it would mean you're further along in your perception of beauty if you can see beauty in things that other people wouldn't consider beautiful.

It's the refinement of our nature that is perfection. It's not a thing that we go and do. You're seeking a perfect town, a perfect car, a perfect wife or husband, a perfect teacher. You're missing it. The perfection is in your apprehension, not in the thing. It's in your apprehension, in your perception of things. You want a perfect job? Create a perfect mind and whatever your job is, it will be perfect. You want a perfect life? Create a perfect mind and whatever your life is, it will be perfect. You want to see a perfect sunset? Create a perfect mind and look at the sunset, any sunset, and you'll see a perfect sunset.

I've lived in worlds where there are three or four suns. We had incredible sunsets, beautiful. But they weren't more beautiful than here, if my mind is more beautiful in each life. Eternity becomes more beautiful as we age, if we age well—and I mean age not just within a lifetime but in a multi-life sequence. If we age poorly, then we don't improve our minds, we don't refine all the aspects of our being.

In other words, enlightenment is not static. You know, there's this sense of, "The Buddha was enlightened"—great good for him, and that's like some absolute—meaning that's the highest enlightenment. Or once you're there, that's it. It's sort of like a Ph.D.—you got your Ph.D. But what does that mean, when you get one? I've got one. It means that you've passed some comprehensive exams, taken classes, written a dissertation and done a lot of classwork and research and now you have a vague understanding of your field. And now your job is— now that you have your Ph.D.—you're going to go out and actually learn something about it. All the Ph.D. ensures is that you have some vague understanding of how large the field is, and you have some methods to approach it with.

So enlightenment simply means that you've gotten above the body-mind complex. You've refined the self, dissolved it in the white light of eternity and gone through all the gradient shifts. I mean, it's technical. But it doesn't end there. In other words, we have this view that enlightenment is, once you're enlightened, that's sort of it. That's the end of the show. You just kind of hang out in this quiescent state. You don't know that the quiescent state changes and moves all the time. It's never the same. If you become the quiescent state, which is what enlightenment means, it means that you're never the same. You move and shift as the quiescent state, in a body or out of it. And since the quiescent state is perpetual and endless ecstasy, therefore you are endless. You're not finite; you're infinite.

So the end of all meditation is the beginning of all meditation. It's the refinement of one's nature. The refinement—ultimately in advanced meditation—of enlightenment itself. Enlightenment can be refined, which may seem like a strange concept, but who cares about concepts? The reality of the issue is there's no end to it. Since infinity is by its very nature infinite, then enlightenment by its very nature is infinite and thus can be experienced in infinite ways, by itself or without itself.

So the most beautiful day hasn't dawned, the most beautiful lifetime has not been experienced. The most beautiful meditation has not been had, even by the enlightened. I guess that's the good news—it doesn't end. Enlightenment is not an end. Nor is it a beginning. It's just—there's no separation between the quiescent perfect state and anything else, inside your mind. Everything's inside your mind. Enlightenment isn't out there; it's just inside your mind. But it's not an intellectual understanding. It's not a knowledge that can be taught.

You can't teach someone to be enlightened. It's something you have to go and do. You can't teach someone to meditate well. It's something you have to go and do. You can explain, "Well, do this, focus on this, dissolve the ego this way"—there's a lot of technical material that you learn as you advance. A lot of it is very technical, as you go in and out of the different samadhis, as you learn to dissolve the self in a variety of ways—things that we don't teach to people unless they're very far along – [they] wouldn't make any sense, they wouldn't be understood—the motions of infinity. You have to learn the motions of infinity with your mind. Your mind becomes a perfect mirror to the motions of infinity.

Sometimes—you watch the Olympics and you see one of these people who are on the bars, you know the parallel bars, the uneven bars? They start to do these wonderful flips, spins. I mean they're moving so fast that you can barely see what they're doing, and unless you know their art very well, you wouldn't know the names for the ten different spins and shifts they just did. But each of those spins is quite technical. And of course they are judged on how well they technically execute very refined motions. But they're all put together so quickly that to you it's just, "Wow, look at that guy spinning around, that's amazing!" But it's even more amazing if you knew how many motions are in each spin.

In advanced meditation, we learn to do something like that with our minds. There are methods and formations of joining the mind with the various aggregate aspects of the universe, with the universal mind. Fusing it, dissolving it, things like that, that are done sometimes thousands of times in a microsecond, or outside of time. That's the tech of advanced meditation. But it's really all the same. Infinity is really all the same. Mind is really all the same. There's only one infinity, even though there are countless infinities. It's really all the same.

All of life is colored by your perceptual field. And whenever you're in a perceptual field, it seems like it's ultimate. It's a self-wrapping consciousness. There doesn't seem or appear to be anything else other than the attention field you're in. It's an ultimate view. So it's important to remember that there are countless views in infinity. If someone says, "Well, I am enlightened," that means they have a particular view. Maybe their view is above everyone else they've ever met, but that doesn't mean that it's ultimate because it can't be ultimate. Infinity is the ultimate view. And to have it, you can't exist. You can't be in finite form. No one could ever be said to have the ultimate view because all views ultimately are beyond perception, if they're at all advanced.

The study of advanced meditation, then, is the ability to undo the most impressive views there are. In other words, what you try and do in beginning meditation is to become consistent—meditate every day. In intermediate meditation, you try and always reach ecstasy—and deeper and deeper forms of ecstasy. But in advanced meditation, what you're really learning to do is to undo the most perfect perceptual states because every perfect perceptual state is seen as a trap. There's nothing wrong with it, but it's limited. And the game is, the more perfect the perceptual state, the less real it can be, the more you're drawn to the latest nirvana.

It's like restaurants. You know, you find the new wonderful restaurant in the city and it's just the best restaurant there is. You have to immediately leave it—after you've had dinner, by the way, and tried the dessert and gone through the whole experience. Then you have to leave it because the mere fact that it seems ultimate tells you that it's not, since there can't be any ultimate in infinity. You immediately have to leave it. But then you have to find the next ultimate. You're always looking for the ultimate. It's kind of like journeying to Ixtlan. You're never going to get there, but that's no reason not to try. You're never going to eat the best food—somebody must be hungry, I'm feeling all this hunger psychically—you're never going to eat the best food that there is because maybe it hasn't even been discovered yet. But that's no reason not to try, you see?

In advanced meditation, what we're always trying to do is avoid illusions. In intermediate meditation, we're trying to create illusions, the illusion of perfect meditation. But once we've achieved perfect meditation, we're terribly trapped because that's an illusion. There's no such thing. It's necessary to first reach the point of perfect meditation so that you can see beyond that. But ultimately, enlightenment is an illusion. Enlightenment, of course, is real. But what I'm suggesting is any enlightenment that seems ultimate is an illusion. There can't be anything ultimate.

So advanced meditation is a process of constantly undoing perfection. Because as soon as it seems to be perfect, we're trapped. We're stuck in an idea-form of perfection and all these idea-forms, of course, come out of the seamless void.

Advanced meditation is the study of the simple. That is to say, we come back to the most basic things and we see them as far more infinite than the most infinite things. So I can go shopping and pick up some Bounty Towels. Paper towels? The three-pack? You know the one. I can go home and open those up and look at them and see more infinity in them than in the Buddha's best meditation—in the three-pack. If I can't do that, that means I'm wrapped by the Buddha's best meditation. That means I see it as ultimate. And if I see it as ultimate, of course, that means I'm stuck in a view that can't possibly be, since nothing can be ultimate in the universe. There can't be anything ultimate in infinity because infinity is boundless.

So, advanced meditation is a continual process where we come back to the beginning. In the beginning we reject the senses, we reject the mind, we reject feeling—meaning, we feel that they're limited. We don't reject them, but we just don't spend all our time in them. In intermediate meditation, we hardly ever utilize those forms anymore. But in advanced meditation, if we happen to be in a body, we come back to those most basic things and we see infinity in thoughts, in physical things and in emotions.

It seems very strange to see—you see a very advanced master who's got a girlfriend, who listens to rock and roll, who thinks about things that are very earthy. And you say, "Well, how can this be?" Yet they glow. You say, "Why would they be interested in these things?" You don't understand, the advanced course has to do with coming back to everything that you had to reject in the beginning and seeing it as a far greater infiniteness than everything that you've attained.

But what you see is not the same as what everyone else sees, of course, because you've already mastered samadhi or been mastered by it. You've already mastered all the quiescent states in the universe and infinity, or enough, anyway, and you've refined the being out of existence. So it's perfectly possible to come back to the most sensorial level of perception and see all the infiniteness of all the endless, quiescent states in breadcrumbs—what are those things? Croutons! You see croutons, Pepperidge Farm Cheese and Garlic. Yeah, I go to the supermarket, I buy the pack and in one of those croutons is all of nirvana. In that physical, sensorial apprehension, is infinity plus.

You come back to the beginning. That's why in the "Searching for the Ox" sequence, at the very end of that sequence of the Zen paintings, we're back in the world again. We go around the circle. We go back to where we started, and we're back in the marketplace—in the picture, the block print, in the "Searching for the Ox" sequence where they're depicting the enlightenment experience in Zen. And we're right back where we started. We're hanging out again. We're in our Levi's and doing or going to work, but the thing is, we're doing something different with our mind than we were at the start. We've already become enlightened. But now we're seeing if enlightenment really exists in everything like they say it does in the books.

We've gone back to being very common. But not really. We're in different infinites all the time. So, consumer goods become enlightenment. Relationships—anything! It doesn't really matter because infinity exists in everything. "Greater than the greatest, smaller than the smallest, the self dwells in the hearts of all." That's in the *Upanishads*. If that's really true, then infinity is everywhere, but of course, you have to develop the mindlessness to perceive it in its infinite perfection, in all forms and formlessness.

Advanced enlightenment is really the apprehension that we have not seen the most beautiful sunset or the most beautiful sunrise or the most beautiful life or death. Then, in all things, in everything and in nothing, there's God. There's nirvana. There's infinity. While we have to leave a lot of things originally to purify our perception, in the end we just realize there's no end. It just goes on forever, in countless new forms. That's what's wonderful about the universe. It's not finite; it's infinite.

Naturally, real winning and losing all takes place at the meditation table. This is where the battles are, and of course, in daily thought. Winning is stopping all thought for protracted periods of time. Losing is sitting there and being subjected to all kinds of ridiculous thoughts. Every time you sit down to meditate, you have to sit down with a resolve to win. You're going to win at zazen.

— *Zen Tapes:* Winning

Zen Tapes:
ZEN: CONCENTRATION AND MEDITATION
1986

Hi there! This is Zen Master Rama. For the next 45 minutes, I'll be talking with you about concentration and meditation—zazen.

There is a wonderful continuity to life, isn't there? Continuity comes in different forms. There is the continuity of being, a sense of self, awareness of this world, of your life, the elements in your life, things that you think and feel, things that you desire and want to have or to experience, things that you'd like to avoid, unpleasant things— pain, frustration, depression. The continuous awareness of self, a sense of yourself continuing in time and space, is continuity—continuity of awareness.

One of the funny things about awareness, within that framework, is that it never assumes it will end. And in a way it does, and in a way it doesn't. When we're alive, we never picture ourselves dying, yet someday each of us dies. Someday in a room somewhere, perhaps a hospital room, in an automobile, perhaps outdoors, you will leave this world. You won't be here anymore and everything that you've known will fade from your view, and it will happen at the darndest time. You will be quite convinced that it couldn't be happening then, and yet you'll be powerless to stop it. Then another kind of continuity occurs, and that's the continuity that is beyond death.

Death is a doorway, but it's a very small, thin doorway, and only a portion of our being can walk through that doorway. The rest stays behind and is lost or transformed into something else. At the time of death, we walk through a doorway and our spirit, which is very thin, slides through into another world, another existence, another experience.

But for now, we are here. We are in this world. And in this world, there are limitations, and no one likes to be limited. We all want freedom. We all want to be limitless. Limitations exist in the mind. Freedom exists in the mind. Heaven exists in the mind. Hell exists in the mind. There are objective circumstances and situations. You can be in jail. You can be free. You can live in a country with restrictions on travel. You can live in a country where they don't restrict your travel. But happiness, awareness, consciousness has little or nothing to do with physical restrictions.

There are ten thousand states of mind, ten thousand planes of awareness. Most people spend their entire lives confined to a few of these states of mind. Let's imagine them in a scale going from the left to the right. Let's say that number one is all the way over on the left, and let's say that number ten thousand is way over on the right. Number one is very dark; it has almost no light in it at all; it's hard to distinguish it from complete darkness. Number ten thousand is bright light. It is hard to distinguish it from light, yet there's a subtle difference. And there are gradations in between—9,999 to be exact. Now naturally, since there are ten thousand, there's something more, beyond ten thousand. But the ten thousand states of mind are the place, the arena of experience, where you spend your time and your life.

Most human beings only experience a few of these states, and most of them are fairly far down in ranking, down around 100. Each state of mind is not simply a mood; moods will exist within the state of mind. But it's a way of seeing life and experiencing it, a way of knowing. And you are your state of mind. Your state of mind creates your view, or your window, on life.

You may live in Beverly Hills, in a beautiful house with a beautiful car, with a beautiful wife. You may live in a tenement in East Harlem, alone, in poverty. But your house has a window, and it looks out on something. It may look out on your swimming pool with the kids playing in it. It may look out [on] a gang down the street who are selling drugs to passersby.

You have a window and that window, which is your state of mind, will determine everything that happens to you, because it affords you a view on life. Opportunities, creative ideas or the lack of them, happiness, frustration, brilliance, talent, success and failure—all of these things are determined by the state of mind that you're in. You are the experiencer of states of mind. Yet your state of mind dominates your awareness to such an extent that you can't conceive of any other state of mind other than the state of mind that you're in. They're just mere words.

Concentration and meditation are practices that enable you to alter your state of mind. Within a state of mind, the state of mind you're in now, there are different possibilities. There's a higher end to the state of mind and a lower end. The higher end—let's call it the right side of that state of mind, which leads or borders the next state of mind that has a better view—has more light in it. The lower end has less light. If you spend enough time at the lower end of a state of mind and if you lose enough energy, you can drop to the next state of mind down. You might drop from 100 down to 99. If you spend enough time on the right hand side and you accumulate power and energy, you can kick up—maybe to 101. When you change a state of mind, your whole life changes. Nothing remains the same. Nothing looks the same because you have changed.

You yourself are a continuous awareness, but you don't really have a formation. In other words, we grow accustomed to thinking of ourselves as a personality with a history—I've been here and there, I've done this, I like this, I don't like that. All of these ideas that we have about self are an accumulation or an aggregate within a state of mind, and they chain us to a state of mind, to these ideas. Zen is about breaking out of your ideas and experiencing life and not ideas.

For example, when most people see a tree, they don't see a tree at all. What they see is an idea that they have developed throughout the course of their life of what a tree is. Only when they were very, very young did they see a tree. Only at that time were they at all aware of what a tree looked like, or perhaps it would be more precise to say what the tree felt like. Other than that, they have no idea of what a tree is. As they grow older and they accumulate more ideas and experiences around "tree" through associations with trees, experiences with trees, they no longer see what a tree is, or feel it. Instead, they have a much more limited view of what a tree is. They have an idea. This is true not just of trees, but of squirrels that live in trees, people, dogs, cats, jobs, the world, philosophies, everything. The more ideas you have, the less you feel and see life directly.

Zen—which means meditation, stopping thought—is about going beyond ideas to direct and immediate experiences. Inherent in this is a sense that there's much more to life. There is much more than the state of mind you're in. There are 9,999 other states of mind. And beyond that, there's something entirely different that is impossible to put in words, which we call nirvana, which is just a word to suggest that there's something else that's wonderful and amazing and fantastic that lies beyond the ten thousand states of mind.

A person who undertakes the study of Zen and learns concentration and meditation is like a gymnast. Most people can do limited things with their bodies. The gymnast can do a lot more. You become a gymnast of the mind. Very few people have any idea of what life is about, of what their minds can do, of the forces that affect them throughout the course of their life that cause success, failure, pleasure, pain, and awareness. In the study of Zen, through the practice of concentration and meditation, you will expand your awareness to gain knowledge and power and illumination.

You may just gain a little more knowledge, power, and illumination if you only practice Zen a little bit. If you practice Zen deeply, in a very, very in-depth way, then you will discover that you are limitless being, and you may attain what we call enlightenment, which means moving beyond but not excluding the ten thousand states of mind.

Enlightenment is the ability to freely transact within the ten thousand states of mind without a continuous self or awareness, without the limitations that are normally imposed by conceptual mind. There is no way to explain enlightenment. It's just a word to indicate something beyond, not just a little bit beyond, but something very, very far beyond the normal human condition—a state of knowledge, quiescent beingness.

Meditation, then, and concentration are practices that enable you to become more conscious and to utilize the moments in your life completely. Concentration and meditation are also taught in other forms of self-discovery, in yoga and in other practices. Zen differs from many other practices in that its emphasis is almost exclusively on concentration and meditation in two forms.

One is zazen, which is the practice of direct concentration and meditation, where for a period of time you are not active physically, and you sit down to practice concentration and meditation exercises. [Two is] mindfulness, which is a practice that an individual engages in at all other times, which is an advanced usage of the mind in a variety of different ways—to increase the power of the mind, to develop it fully, and to employ that development in direct physical, mental and psychic ways. In other words, when you practice mindfulness, you're able to accomplish basically anything you might like to within the parameters of your capabilities. But you realize those capabilities.

Most people are unhappy, let's face it. The reason they're not happy is not because they're good or bad, but they're in states of mind that are limited. In those states of mind, happiness is fleeting. Let's say there's a country that's filled with volcanoes and doesn't have any grass or pastures. If you're in that country, all you're going to experience are the volcanoes. There is just not going to be any grass or pastures. It is not that the country is good or bad; that's just how it is. Most human beings are in very limited states of mind. The states of mind they're in are not good or bad, but they have volcanoes. They are filled with unhappiness, desires, frustrations, jealousies, angers, lack of clarity, lack of awareness overall.

Some people climb a little bit higher up on the scale of consciousness and they seem to know more, feel more and experience more, and perhaps they are more successful. We say that such a person is deeper or more aware, more dynamic, charismatic. There are different formations of this. Sometimes it takes an intellectual tack, sometimes a spiritual tack, sometimes an artistic tack, maybe a physical tack. It depends. It varies. There is no way it has to be. These individuals have learned something. They may have just stumbled upon it, or they may have studied a type of self-discovery that gave them the knowledge to be more successful and more profoundly aware, to be happier.

Whatever they did, whether it was accidental or intentional, allowed them to stumble upon some higher states of mind. Yet very few of those persons could teach you how to do what they've done. They could give you a general prescription, "Well, I bought stock at this price and it rose suddenly to that price, and then I sold it and then I leveraged some real estate." Or they might say, "Well gosh, I sat down and I meditated for two hours a day every day, and after a while my awareness field changed." In other words, they could explain what they did in physical terms, but you have to be in the state of mind that they were in to experience what they experienced. You might employ the same prescription, and it might not generate the same results because you're not in the same state of mind that they were in.

A Zen master is an individual who is an instructor, specifically of the subject of awareness. And if the Zen master is enlightened, that means that they have the power and the knowledge to teach an individual who wishes it and who's serious about the study how to range through the ten thousand states of mind. Their ability is not simply to share their own experiences or to give a general prescription, but rather they are experts, not only at experiencing the ten thousand states of mind but also, since they are teachers, they are aware of how to express, or bring about, or transmit, that information to others.

I used to be a university professor. Before that, I was a graduate student and a college student. Naturally, after many years in academia, you learn that a lot of the professors in universities are wonderful scholars. The reason they are professors is because they have Ph.D.s, and they've written great papers and books. But they are terrible teachers. Their talent is scholarship.

Teaching, on the other hand, does not involve necessarily writing papers. It involves transmitting information and sometimes enthusiasm, methods of analysis and so on to another individual. It is a particular talent that an individual has. Such a person should be a teacher. They are good at transmitting something. Then there are people who can learn something and experience it. You might be a great real estate developer, but maybe you couldn't teach anybody else how to do it. It comes naturally to you.

There is a difference between knowing something and being able to teach it. Of course, there are people who are great teachers. They have that ability to communicate and transmit something. They can understand it and then look into another person's mind and see what that person needs to do to come to an understanding of the material. But a teacher may not be conversant in very many subjects. In other words, the combination of the ability to teach and scholarship is rare. That's why great teachers are always few and far between.

On the subject of Zen and meditation, a particular demand is placed upon the teacher. The teacher has to be first and foremost a scholar, in that it's really impossible to teach Zen, to teach about mind and the ten thousand states of mind and what lies beyond them unless one has directly experienced these things. Naturally, the laboratory is one's own life and one's own mind.

An individual who teaches Zen, if they teach the advanced formations as well as the introductory formations of Zen, is someone who must have personally experienced—through years and years of meditation, concentration, practice and engaging in dialectical situations of mind—varying states of awareness. And not just a few—if they've experienced a few, they can teach a few, and that may be more than someone they're teaching knows or has. But someone we call a Zen master is someone who is conversant, not just with a little bit of mind, a little bit more than most of humanity, but someone who is an expert in mind.

Also, in the study of the ways of mind, powers develop. A true master, a Zen master, a Tibetan lama, an Indian sadhu, if they're a real teacher and not just someone who's looking for a following, has developed, in their intensive inner practices and studies, certain powers. These powers, which are sometimes of the miraculous nature [and] sometimes of the nature of transmission of attention, are used strictly to enable the student to progress.

We hear wonderful stories about some masters who can walk on water and do all kinds of great things—do healings, things like that. These are true powers that can come from a person who engages in the study of mind. But the major power that a real teacher has is not the ability to do things like walk on water or heal. Those are interesting talents, and they're useful sometimes. But the real power that a teacher of mind develops is the ability to transmit power and knowledge directly to an individual. Because in the teaching of the ten thousand states of mind, particularly as one advances further—not so much in just learning basic concentration and meditation, basic zazen, but after a person has done that and they progress further—the teaching is done through transmission. This is where we differ from teaching algebra or calculus or English. Those things are taught through verbal instruction.

The majority of the ten thousand states of mind cannot be discussed. It is rather a question of teaching a person to step outside of the conceptual framework they have, showing them how to do a systems analysis continually of more progressive ways of their energy balance, so that more energy is coming into their lives than out of it, and transmitting directly blocks of attention or awareness to an individual psychically. In other words, once you've gotten your first-degree black belt as a student, which is just a beginning from the point of view of the master, or maybe the seventh-degree black belt, then at that point the instruction changes. Now it's not so much basic moves but advanced fighting.

Initially, when I teach a person to concentrate and meditate, I focus upon basic exercises that will cause a person to strengthen their mind terrifically, develop new talents and abilities, become much more successful and independent, overcome a lot of their fears and frustrations and gain control of their time, mind and life. But once a person has done that, if they do that, if they work on it, and it happens if you work on it—it will take varying lengths of time for an individual to accomplish this, according to the intensity of their practice and their own natural inclinations and abilities, the level of mind they start in— once a person has reached a certain level of proficiency, then the teaching changes.

In the teaching of concentration and meditation, the focus is more upon a transfer of awareness, where you will now give advanced lessons. Those lessons don't take place here. They take place in advanced states of mind. So a teacher will alter the balance of power by actually lifting a person into other states of mind, and then, in those states of mind, the teaching will take place in non-verbal ways through direct experience. Again, these are the mysterious ways of knowledge and power and enlightenment that I can only allude to in words. I can't possibly explain what this process is like. The only way to find out what this process is like is to advance to the stage of mental control that a person obtains after a number of years of practicing the basic disciplines.

The basic disciplines of concentration and meditation bring about immediate and wonderful results. But what I'm suggesting is that there's something beyond that. And that's when a person really begins to explore altered attention and awareness. That is when the most profound experiences of mind start.

That teaching process is lengthy because there are many, many states of mind to go through. And in each state of mind, there is a different aggregate of self to explore. Eventually, after you've led a student through all of the ten thousand states of mind, then the trickiest part of the study comes along, and that's moving from that knowledge and that level of fluidity and awareness to enlightenment itself, which is something very different than the knowledge of the ten thousand states of mind.

That's an overall glimpse of the study. In other words, we have our elementary school, our high school, our master's program and our doctoral program. Some people just go on through the college program. They don't go into the graduate school program, but they become teachers of Zen. And they are able to teach quite a bit. They are not enlightened themselves, but compared to your average human being, they have a tremendous, tremendous degree of knowledge. It is like learning to fight and you've been in a couple of fights, but suddenly you're studying with a third-degree black belt who, with one movement, can have you on your back. But the third-degree black belt is in no way near the level of knowledge of the seventh-degree black belt.

There is a certain point that you reach where the distance between the belts is much further. Some go through graduate school and they become teachers of very advanced states of mind. Some become enlightened. Those are the individuals who can teach individuals how to be enlightened.

Concentration and meditation is a practice in which you learn how to use your mind in ways that are foreign to most human beings. Most human beings have almost no mental control at all. Concentration and meditation are not taught in schools. In schools, we're taught subjects—how to read, how to write, things like that. But we're not taught about mind, states of mind, and how to use mind in a variety of different ways.

The study of mind is the study of life because all of life obviously interacts with mind. We can't dismiss aspects of our life, our careers, our relationships, our loves, our hates—all of these things are bound into the study of mind. The study of mind is the study of life itself. The study of concentration and meditation is not simply the study of exercises and focusing. It is that, but to truly engage in the study, you engage actively in every aspect of your life. And, of course, a revolution occurs in your being.

The average person who studies martial arts, even after a year or two, becomes amazingly proficient in self-defense. Were they to run into the common neighborhood bully who is capable of beating up most people on the block, they could drop him with one kick, because the bully's knowledge is simplistic. It may seem impressive, if you're just a kid on the block, because he's been in 50 fights, and you've only been in one or two. But after a couple years of martial arts, where you have studied the discipline of fighting and learned from an advanced master who learned from an advanced master and so on, you're studying such a high-tech form of self-defense that the bully, with all of his knowledge and all of his battle experience, will have no idea what you're doing when suddenly, that foot connects with his head and he's on the ground—and it's all over.

In the study of mind, you are engaging in a very high-tech study, the ultimate high-tech study, and that's the study of being. Even after a year or two of intensive study—let alone five or six years, or a lifetime, many lifetimes—you will possess a knowledge and power of mind that far dwarfs most human beings. Your ability to use mind in whatever way you choose is outrageous. Again, a lot will depend upon how intensely you approach the study and the state of mind in which you begin, and so on.

There are factors that influence progress. There are no guarantees, except that if you do it, your mind gets stronger. The high range powers and high range experiences come later. Oh, if you study with an enlightened Zen master, then it is possible to have high range experiences from the beginning, not because of your ability or your state of mind, but because the master is capable of generating, even in the novice, very powerful experiences through the transmission of awareness and mind. In other words, his power is sufficient to boost you up and give you experiences that you would not have yet on your own. The purpose of these experiences is to rapidly progress you through the states of mind and encourage you to work harder. It is another window. You are afforded a window.

You visit a wealthy person's home and look out the window and you see what it's like there, and that might inspire you to work harder, if you want a window like that of your own. Whereas if you've never seen such a thing, you don't know it exists, you might not try. That is why some teachers perform miracles. "Unless they've seen, they will not believe," they say in one book. The idea is that some people need proof.

I once went to a demonstration. This guy was opening a karate school. He had all kinds of medals and pictures of himself fighting and things like that. He was trying to get some students because he wanted to teach them the art. What he did, the way he was trying to get the point across was, he simply took a few concrete blocks and split them with his hand. Everybody quickly got the idea that there was something to all this karate stuff. In the same sense, sometimes the Zen master, or a teacher from another tradition, will perform miracles. Not just to delight and amuse people, but specifically to raise their awareness as a way of grabbing their attention and showing them that this miraculous occurrence, which is not the point, indicates that there is something more.

The study of mind generates a variety of different experiences, most of which are beyond the perceptual range of the average human being. Things that are impossible, that skeptics say are impossible, are everyday experiences when you live in advanced states of mind. You live in a world of constant miraculous awareness, only because you've learned to use your mind. The skeptics who say it can't be done are simply in extremely limited states of mind in which they can't even perceive the possibility of anybody doing anything that they can't do.

The real miracle is mind itself. Your mind. And your mind is capable of incredible things. But it is through the practice of concentration and meditation—zazen—and mindfulness, that you are able to accomplish so much, to succeed at what you would choose to succeed at, to be what you would like to be, to become aware that there are things that you can be that you're not even conscious of yet.

In short, the practice of Zen enables you to use your mind in an extremely effective and precise way. It allows you to succeed at whatever you would like to—within the parameters of possible success, owing to circumstance, and whether it's material success or psychic or spiritual success, or whatever. You can do it when you have mind at your disposal.

So, how do you meditate?

Well, the best way to really learn how to meditate is to go and study with a teacher. If you see a teacher on a regular basis, the same way you would see a martial arts teacher on a regular basis or a teacher of computer science or philosophy or English, or whatever it is—if you attend class on a regular basis and you practice what the teacher shows you, you'll learn, naturally. But for starting on your own, I have a simple program that I would suggest you follow. I would like to outline it for you in the next five or so minutes, maybe ten minutes. If you practice this program, if you don't have a teacher, it will enable you to make very steady progress in meditation and concentration. Then, someday, perhaps you'll meet a teacher for more advanced instruction, not simply someone who can repeat the things that I'm telling you, but someone who has the ability to transmit experiences and awareness, a master of mind.

The following are my suggestions for the practice. These are not to be taken in an absolute form as the only way to concentrate and meditate. This is just a simple approach. It will produce powerful results when properly employed. But this is not to be construed as a complete course in how to meditate. I can't teach that over a tape. That is something that I do in person, which is why I do seminars.

There are other methods of meditation, and you shouldn't be afraid to try them. In this business, it's not that there is a best way—it's whatever way works best for you. This is a simple program, but you should feel free to alter it in any way that you choose that you find beneficial. You don't have to be stuck with it, but it works very well.

If you are new to meditation, I would suggest that you meditate, to begin with, once a day for 15 minutes, then eventually, twice a day for 15 minutes. Once you're comfortable with that, I would increase your time to half an hour twice a day, then 45 minutes twice a day, then an hour twice a day. Once you have reached an hour twice a day, it's not really necessary at that point to add more time to the practice of concentration and meditation. Rather, at that point, you should increase the proficiency of the two hours a day. You should spend your two hours a day, an hour in the morning and an hour in the evening, with less and less thought. Don't increase the time at that point—increase the power of the two hours.

If you're a beginner, perhaps for the first few weeks or a month or two, practice 15 minutes once a day. After a month or two, add a second session. After another month or two, maybe after around four months or six months, or you may just find that you want to do it sooner, increase your time to half an hour twice a day. Then, after perhaps nine months or a year, increase the time to 45 minutes twice a day, and after about two years, increase the time to an hour twice a day. The time is not the key element. The key element is what you do during the time.

I wouldn't jump to an hour twice a day to start with, because you'll be wasting your time, because you will not be able to sustain high levels of awareness for that period of time. It is better to meditate for a short period of time intensely and go do something else with that extra time, than to sit there and space out and just think you're meditating and concentrating.

Very few people are capable of an intensive level of concentration and meditation for very long periods of time. You develop that ability the same way that you develop muscles, by working out. In the beginning, you can only do a few push-ups, maybe one or two, then five, then ten, then 50, then 100. So your mental agility and power will develop through practice. That's a simple training schedule for you.

Of course, the next question is what to do when you're sitting there practicing concentration and meditation. A few general suggestions—wear comfortable clothing, nothing that restricts you or makes you feel uncomfortable. Try to always be physically clean. If you can, take a shower beforehand—it helps—or wash your hands and face. If that's not possible, you can still do a fine meditation, but these things are helpful.

Most people find it helpful, if they meditate at home, to find an area of the house where they meditate on a regular basis—maybe a room, an area of the bedroom, perhaps outside on a porch on a nice day or on the lawn. You find a few areas that just feel right; they have a good energy. You sit there and meditate, and you build up a vibration and a force there that makes it easier to meditate. Sometimes it's fun just to meditate in a different place to break up your routine. Don't feel limited.

There are two practices—concentration and meditation. For the first year or two, you probably will be almost exclusively practicing concentration. You will try meditating, but it won't come until later. So I'll address mostly the practice of concentration.

When you concentrate, you're focusing on something. When you meditate, you're letting go and dissolving. You're losing awareness of anything in particular at all, even the awareness of awareness. In meditation, you are seeking to stop all thought. It is very hard just to stop your thoughts. Try it. Not to have one thought, image, idea, or associative feeling in the mind is difficult for most people. Rather than just trying to stop your thoughts, which is hard and frustrating, it's easier to concentrate and focus on something. As you focus completely on something, all other thoughts will be forced out of the mind because your attention will be dominated by the object of concentration. This develops your mental power exquisitely.

Let's take a simple session as an example. You're going to sit down. You're an absolute beginner, and you're going to meditate, let us say, for 15 minutes. If you're an absolute beginner, I suggest that you meditate with a watch or a clock, and what you're going to do is make sure that you sit there for a full 15 minutes. In the beginning, it's good to spend most of your time concentrating with your eyes open. You need to sit up straight. If you want to sit in a chair, that's fine, or in a cross-legged position on the floor—whatever suits you, but the back should be straight. You may be bothered by this initially. It may not be comfortable for you; that's because the muscles in your back are weak.

It is desirable to sit in a cross-legged position, but it's possible that's uncomfortable for you. If you'd like to be able to do this, I would suggest that you take some yoga lessons, where you will learn stretching exercises that will loosen up the leg muscles so that you can sit in a comfortable, cross-legged position. This is a well-balanced position whereby you can sit for protracted periods of time with ease and with balance. The main thing is to sit down, keep your back straight, relax and have an object on which to concentrate. You might use a candle flame; a brightly colored rock; a yantra, which is a geometrical design specifically for the practice of concentration and meditation; or something else.

Place an object within your view, hopefully at about eye level. You might have to look down a little bit. Some people have a meditation table on which they put an object of concentration—a candle, yantra, something like that—so they don't have to stare down at the ground where they have an object, which might be uncomfortable and would put your head in too much of a downward position.

Now you're going to concentrate. It's a good idea, in my opinion, to use a mantra before you begin a session. It's not necessary, but I think it helps. A mantra is a powerful sound which, when focused upon, clears the mind and helps bring you into a higher level of awareness. The most powerful of all mantras is "Aum" spelled A U M. You have probably heard it. If you repeat that sound several times with your eyes closed before you start the session, while you're sitting there, it will help clear your mind. It has a vibratory energy that helps eliminate thought. But you don't simply repeat the sound. You focus on it.

You chant the word, "Aum." (Rama demonstrates) A U M. When you chant that sound three or four times, or you could even do it silently within the mind—but it's easier for most people to focus when it's done out loud—that's a good beginning. Then, open your eyes and focus on the object of concentration. Now, for the next ten or 15 minutes if you're a beginner, let's say for two-thirds of the time you've allowed for the practice of zazen, you are going to simply look at the object, blink whenever your eyes become uncomfortable and focus on it. As thoughts come in and out of your mind, ignore them. Simply continue to concentrate. Then, about two-thirds of the way through, close your eyes.

I would like you to spend the remainder of the time focusing your attention on a chakra. A chakra is an energy center that exists within the subtle physical body. Our physical bodies are surrounded by a body of energy, which is not perceptible for most individuals. But as you develop your psychic facilities through the practice of zazen, you will be able to see and feel this body of energy around you. The subtle body has certain junctures or points of intersection that we call chakras. They are like windows that look into other dimensions. There are three that are useful for concentration practice. Around the navel area, there's a chakra. In the middle of the chest, there's a chakra. And between the eyebrows and a little bit above, there is a chakra. There are more, but these are the most useful for the practice of zazen.

Choose one of these three points and hold your attention there, just as you held your attention on the object. Let's say you were looking at a candle flame. You focused on a candle flame for ten minutes. Thoughts come in and out of your mind, but you just focus more and more intensely. Then, after about ten minutes, if you are a beginner, close your eyes and focus on your navel center. The first time you do it, or the first few times, you might even want to touch that spot for a minute or two. Hold your fingers very lightly against your navel, or in the center of your chest around the area of the heart, or between the eyebrows and a little bit above. As you press very gently there, it will be easier for you to focus. These are not random spots. There are windows here, windows that lead into other levels of mind. Each will generate a different type of experience.

The chakra around the navel area is the power chakra, and as you focus on this center you will develop tremendous will power. The heart center, which is in the center of the chest, develops the psychic centers, the psychic abilities, sensitivities, and also brings about a tremendous stillness within the mind and extraordinarily develops one's ability to experience love and beauty. It also develops your ESP and many other things. The third eye, which is between the eyebrows and slightly above—focusing in this area develops your intuitive wisdom, your knowledge, your higher mind, and gives you visions into other planes of reality.

Let's say that the bottom center is connected with power, the middle center is connected with feeling—feeling love, feeling awareness—and the top center has to do with knowledge. The combination of knowledge, power, and feeling creates a balanced individual. That is why I suggest that at different times you focus on each of these chakras.

Initially, it may not seem like you're doing anything and you are just thinking a lot. But you are doing something, as long as you're trying. It is like doing push-ups. You can be doing push-ups and all the time thinking it's not doing anything, but obviously, as long as you're trying and doing them, you're getting stronger. After you've practiced doing your push-ups for a while, after two or three sessions, you won't necessarily see huge muscles like Arnold Schwarzenegger has, but you will begin to see and feel a difference. It is the same with the practice of concentration.

Initially, it won't seem like anything is happening, but something is. Inwardly, your mind is becoming stronger and you're gaining personal power. After a while, that power will begin to manifest in your life. You will find it's easier to study. It's easier to do your job. Your mind is sharp, clear and defined. You are more aware. And a feeling will come after a while. You will just feel better. You are more in touch with everything in your life. Then knowledge and power will come to you, later, through these practices.

So for five minutes or so, focus on one of those three areas. Hold your attention there, and after your 15 minutes are up, chant the mantra again. Chant Aum or another favorite mantra, several times. Then, at the end of a session, we always bow down to the ground. That is our way of giving the meditation to eternity, of letting go of it, of letting go of our self.

If you practice this way, you will develop your mind. Practice 15 minutes once, twice a day, then a half-an-hour, then 45 minutes, then an hour. After you've practiced for a while, you might want to try meditating. This is all concentration, which is the most important to start with. But let's say you've been doing this for a year or so, or six months, or whatever, then you might want to begin to try something a little bit different. Perhaps you should spend half the time initially, instead of two-thirds, focusing on something outside—a candle flame, yantra, colored rock, whatever it is. Then take a little more time, maybe 25 percent of the time, and focus on one of the three chakras. Then take the last 25 percent of your time and don't focus at all, simply let go.

Now, this is not something that I recommend you do too much of because most people will sit there and space out. Their letting go won't have power. This is meditation. In other words, during the letting go phase, you want to strive to have no thought whatsoever in the mind. If you're just sitting there and zillions of thoughts are whipping around, it's not accomplishing anything. It is better, if that's the case, to focus. You will gain more from that than sitting there in a quasi-meditation, in which there are just a lot of thoughts kicking around.

I would suggest that you only do it for a limited period of time, after you've become fairly accomplished at concentrating. Once you've become accomplished at concentrating, you will discover that you can sit there for those periods of time without thought or with reduced thought. Eventually, after some years, you may find that you'll sit for half the period of time without any particular focus at all, and you're able to stop thought. Eventually, you may be able to sit for two hours without one thought. At that point, it's no longer necessary to practice concentration. When you can stop all thought, it is no longer necessary to concentrate, although it's still kind of fun, to tell you the truth.

If you follow this program, you will find a tremendous increase in your mental awareness—if you practice it faithfully. Again, it's a personal matter. There is no way to measure it. All I can tell you is that most people who do this see dramatic increases in their level of personal power and success. Of course, you will accrue more power, and higher levels of mind will start to open for you.

Once you're doing this on a regular basis and you're seeing progress in your life, then it's time to seek out a teacher, someone who can show you the next steps. Also, there are many other matters that enable you to meditate better. These are matters that I discuss on other tapes and in books, and that other teachers talk about. This is just the hard-core practice.

It is necessary to learn how to do a systems analysis of your life, to learn about the effects of places, people, jobs. There are millions of things that go into the study of meditation. This is the daily practice. Mindfulness and what you do with your attention the rest of the time, what you do when you're dreaming at night and so on, in order to enlarge the awareness field that you have, is a very vast subject. And that's not our discussion at this point.

So that's how to concentrate and how to meditate. If you practice these things, simplistic though they may seem, they will enable you to develop a great power in your life. Again, it doesn't seem very complicated when the guy just lifts weights all the time. There is not much to it—a bar, some weights, and he lifts them. But if he keeps doing it, he can quadruple his strength. It is the same [with concentration and meditation].

This is like working out. It is working out—working out with your mind. Most people don't do it at all. The only concentration they have is on the television set. That isn't very powerful or profound. If you do these exercises on a regular basis and you become consistent, then you will become a gymnast of the mind. And once you learn to concentrate and focus for extended periods of time, and then to stop thought, you'll be ready for more advanced lessons.

So I would encourage you to concentrate and meditate. There are thousands of worlds, thousands of dimensions. The beauty of life is incredible beyond belief. A clear and solid mind, let alone enlightenment, enlightened awareness, is the best thing. Life can be extremely wonderful. It is—when you're in a state of mind to see it. Practice, and new worlds and new vistas and new horizons will open to you.

So this is Zen Master Rama, wishing you well in your practice.

Meditation is always the key, regardless of the path that you follow. Meditation takes us there. It's a vehicle. Meditation is stopping thought. Stillness. Erasing the perceiver. The one inside who's watching, who's observing the personality forms. You are capable of everything. But to do that you need something that you don't have now. Power. The power of the kundalini energy which gradually rises through our being in the process of self-discovery.

— *Workshop with Rama:* Enlightenment and Self-Realization

Workshop with Rama:
MEDITATION AND KUNDALINI
1985

Tonight is not the end of the world. This our hot tip of the evening. Oh well. Tonight we're going to be talking about trigonometric ratios (audience laughs) and kundalini and meditation and music.

We're going to be doing three meditations tonight. You'll be learning three meditation techniques to use the kundalini, and essentially what I'm going to be doing with those techniques is using the kundalini, moving it through your subtle physical bodies to raise you into altered states of attention while showing you how you can do that yourself.

Tonight, three of my friends and three of my students, they're one and the same, are going to be performing some live music. As you see we have amplifiers, we have speakers, we have headphones, we have all kinds of things. Tonight we're going to have some live music for the meditations. We'll be doing three meditations of approximately 10 minutes to an hour each (audience laughs), about 10 minutes to 15 minutes each throughout the evening and we'll have some music to meditate to.

I like to use music in group meditations because it's harder to hear the megaphones (audience laughs); this is something they teach you in the spiritual teacher training academy in another world. So we'll have lots of music tonight. Lots of sound. The kundalini is music. It's energy, it's excitement, it's power. In the back someone heard that word, and they said (Rama amplifies his voice) "POWER." No, not that kind of power. Power, pure unadulterated power. Limitless. Mindless. (Rama laughs.) No, power. That's the kundalini. The kundalini is the life force, it is the essential energy of existence. It's the hidden ingredient in life. It is what makes it all work.

Tonight we're going to be talking about meditation and kundalini. How many of you, if any, are new to meditation? Could you raise your hand please? A few, a few. OK, great. Good. All right, well then let's begin at the beginning. That's usually a good place.

Meditation. Why do you meditate? I suppose it's different for everybody. Some people meditate because they need more energy and when you meditate you get a lot of energy, a tremendous amount of energy. Some people meditate because they are sick and tired of their lives, of the world, of the way people abuse each other in this world and abrogate each other's freedoms. And essentially they want out and sort of, "Stop the universe I want to get off." They just feel that there's more.

The life that we see on our small planet is not necessarily a great reflection of the entire universe. The planet is beautiful. The animals are beautiful. The people are beautiful. But they tend to destroy one another. And that's not necessarily an operative principle in all dimensions. So some people meditate because they want to get the larger picture on life because it could get kind of discouraging if this was all there was.

There are thousands of worlds, thousands of dimensional planes. Billions. Endless. Life is endless. It's discouraging. (Audience laughs.) It goes on forever. That's a long time. And you're eternal, which means that you have a great deal of time on your hands. Tonight I'd like to use a little bit of that time and discuss just about anything that seems irrelevant, and by discussing all things that are irrelevant we'll find that what is left over is relevant. What is relevant? That which you can't discuss, which is why we meditate, because when we meditate we enter into silence, stillness.

Meditation essentially means having a great time. Some people, they've applied a sense or a feeling to the meditative experience such that—I like that phrase, "such that" (audience laughs), yeah, just trying to loosen everybody up a little bit—such that meditation has become a quantifiable religious experience, which means that it's not any fun. In other words, meditation has been turned into a tool of the (Rama talks like a gruff French person) bourgeoisie. (Return to normal voice.) No, I'm sorry, wrong incarnation, I'm in different ones at different times and I've (Rama snaps his fingers) got to bring it around and get it straight; sorry, this is the, this is the, right—America.

Meditation is wonderful. It's just terrific. (Rama playfully imitates a Yiddish-speaking person) It's so wonderful, I don't know, why don't you do it more? It's just—it's the best, I mean, you know, it's the best thing since sliced kundalini, you know, it's terrific. How do you meditate? You should never ask. (Return to normal voice.) It's easy. All you have to do is stop all your thought and you're—that's it! (Audience laughs.) See, now you know. Admission seven dollars. Meditation taught, mission accomplished. That is the secret. Now you might, of course, ask, "Well, how do you stop all your thought Rama?" And I would say, "Well that's the art isn't it?

Tonight we're going to have three very talented musicians playing and I assure you that the first time they sat down and played, they never thought they would end up where they are tonight. I'm going to fry them with the kundalini. They're going to be within the 12-foot range, that's the kill range on the kundalini level (audience laughs). These guys have never been on stage with me. They have no idea what they're in for. But we'll all be very chic and casual and hip about it, you know, and just (audience laughs)—I like it.

So anyway, you're trying to meditate. How do you do it? Boy we're gonna learn. (Rama talks like a tough person) We're gonna learn how to do this meditation thing. When you leave here tonight—you won't. (Return to normal voice.) How do you meditate? Well, you have to learn to be very, very gentle to start with, with yourself essentially. Because meditation is not something that you force, you see? It's something that happens to you because, I don't know, life gives you a gift. There are billions of people out there walking around and they wear a lot of shoes. Have you ever thought about that? (Audience laughs.) But anyway. There are billions of people out there walking around and they don't meditate. You can tell. They're not having a good time with their lives. It's bad out there, friends. You know, it's just, people are not happy. It's just not working. One nation trying to destroy another, one race trying to destroy another, one religion trying to destroy another. It's the same old story over and over again. It's because they don't meditate.

Now I'm not suggesting everyone should meditate. Far from it. Meditation is for very few individuals. When I speak of meditation, of course, I'm speaking of something that's a powerful experience. Some people speak of meditation as kind of relaxation (Rama snores), then you do the mantra (Rama snores). OK. That's, nah, that's not what I'm talking about. Naah.

Meditation is the entrance into alternate planes of consciousness. Yeah, it's fun. The way you do it is by not trying to be too good at it too quickly. This is essential, because otherwise you won't have fun with it. If you expect anything in particular to happen—the stars to spin in the sky, light to flood your being, the kundalini to surge through you, give it a month (audience laughs). Don't expect that to start out with because you'll be very discouraged because it probably won't happen. At best at the beginning you'll just be kind of confused and you're not sure what you're supposed to do. You're trying to do the stuff that they say and you don't even know why you're doing it. And I don't know why you're doing it either. But I do know that if you do that for a long period of time, you will change in ways that I can't understand. But that's neither here nor there.

How do you meditate? The way you meditate is, well, there's not just one way. There are a lot of ways. That's why it's difficult to talk about because there are so many ways to meditate. A good way to start is with love. Love is perhaps the strongest force in the universe. When you meditate with love what you do is you feel love, and love is like a bird, you kind of ride it. You get on its back and you ride it up very, very high above the thought level. You're trying to stop thought but all your life you've been thinking. You've been taught to think, to analyze, to look at things, facts (Rama talks like Sergeant Friday on the TV show "Dragnet"), "Gotta have the facts, ma'am". (Return to normal voice.) Remember Friday on "Dragnet"? Yeah. So you've gotta have the facts, right? But here we're going to do something—the word "facts," I could care less. What facts? You call those facts? Where? I don't see a fact. You see any facts? I'm looking for a fact. (Rama sounds as if he is looking under things.) This is called fact finding? Ohhh. (Audience laughs.) Bad. Bad. I know.

I don't know anything about facts but I do know how to meditate. All you have to do is stop your thought, and if you stop your thought for a sustained period of time, you'll enter into other states of attention. But fortunately, the good news, I know this is ridiculous, but bear with me, I'll get through this phase—the good news is that you don't have to stop thought completely to be able to meditate well. Isn't that good? Whew! Because it takes a long time to be able to stop thought impeccably. What you need to do is to detach yourself from thought.

The serious part of the talk. There are essentially three stages in learning how to meditate. In the beginning you're simply sitting and trying to practice without any concern of what is happening, what is not happening, whether you're gaining benefit from it and so on. You're just trying to do it. This is the stage of ignoring thought. In the second part of the practice, we stop thought for limited periods of time and we don't stop thought, what we're doing is learning to think specific types of thoughts. In other words, thought control (Rama talks like a mad professor), mind control. Thought control. (Return to normal voice.) Sorry, it slipped again. (Audience laughs.)

The third stage is no thought. Now, no thought is not the end of meditation. That's the beginning of higher meditation. That means that you are about to experience the other aspects of your being. You are an endless conglomeration of awarenesses. You're not one singular self. You're a corporation. Inside you is eternity. Everything's there. A human being is not so simple. We're told that we're Ted or Sally or Willie or whatever and that we grow up and have experiences and we die or maybe we go to heaven, I don't know, but I do know that has nothing to do with what life is. You're eternity.

You have thousands of selves inside you, and meditation is a process of peeling back the layers of the self. We start with peeling back the personality form from this lifetime, your current one—the mental conditioning, the things that they told you. "Girls wear pink," you know, that sort of thing. Because these are ridiculous ideas that human beings have come up with, and in every culture they're different— there's no arbitrary standard of truth—and what they do is block you from being the totality of yourself.

Meditation is not for everybody, I'll grant you that. That's for sure. Because when you meditate you're going to become conscious. Most people don't want to be too conscious because they're afraid. They're afraid of awareness, they're afraid of life, they're afraid of being happy. Now that may sound ridiculous and I would have thought so a long time ago, but having been around the world a little bit I've seen that it's not ridiculous. People really don't want to be happy. They go out of their way to be miserable. So if you want to be that way I can't do a thing for you. Nobody can. Because you've already set the program and it's running, debugged, misery. (Rama sounds like he is sobbing) "Nothing's going to work out. Everybody's against me. Life has no meaning." (Return to normal voice.) You're right there, but (audience laughs), well, it doesn't need a meaning. A meaning is an arbitrary thought formulation that we affix to it because we're in the mood. Life is its own meaning. It's its own raison d'etre. It's exciting.

The kundalini is the energy, the energy of existence. Kundalini is the life force. It's given different names. Sometimes they call it prana. Sometimes they divide it into different segments—in Sanskrit it's the apana and the samana and all those sorts of fancy terminologies. Sometimes it's called shakti. Nice names, I like the sound of them. All it is is energy. It's the life force. The more life force you have, the more you can do, the more alive you are.

The kundalini is said to reside in the base of the spine. It's a bit of a misnomer because the kundalini really is not so much in the physical body as in what we call the subtle physical body or body of energy, also known by some as the astral body, that surrounds the physical body, the etheric body. When you see someone's aura, that's just the outer reflection of the subtle physical body. The subtle physical body is about the same shape as the physical body although it can change shapes. It can become thousands of different things. But it does have a basic structure.

The way it works is, as you all know, there are seven primary chakras or energy centers that run along, theoretically, the spinal column. The root chakra at the very base of the spine is where the kundalini is said to reside. The kundalini is thought of as a serpent, as a snake, it's something that's coiled, it means coiled. It's going to spring out. Kkhhuu! It isn't really like that. But it sounds good. It's much more intense than that. It's much more complete. The kundalini is not some little snap thing that goes fwip. The kundalini is the totality of the universe. All of the life energy of existence is going to flow through you. You will be in thousands of planes of consciousness at once or beyond all in nirvana, absorbed. Or maybe having a sandwich with a friend. Confronting an olive, and you can see the life in that olive. You can know what it is to be an olive. (Audience laughs.) You can! Because you can detach your attention from yourself and go anywhere. You can wander the universe. Big deal.

So to meditate what you need to do is to be able to free yourself from your ideas and your thoughts, which are probably wonderful— liar! (Audience laughs.) No, they're probably wonderful. Wonderful thoughts and ideas you have. Great. But sometimes there's something more, and that's beyond thought because all of the higher dimensional planes, the higher realities, the infinite cosmos itself is beyond thought. It's certainly something that you can experience and be, as are the other aspects of yourself.

Why are people unhappy? People are unhappy because they don't understand life. They're unhappy because—it's obvious why they're unhappy. Maybe it's better to look at why, what makes someone happy. By happy I don't just mean hmmm (Rama hums), but complete, aware, conscious, poignant, caring, loving, unaffected, cosmic, simplistic, humble, excited, passive, everything. You're everything.

We're a stage and there are players. And they come and they speak the speech, the loves, the experiences, the cares, the sorrows; it all passes through us. We're the audience. We're watching. We're the participant. We're the reviewer. We're everything. To know that, to know that truth, to know that awareness and still not get too stuck on yourself, so you're not "God's gift to the world," to avoid that, ecch. To be conscious of life, to love, to be free and yet to be able to deal with the world effectively. To be able to handle that freeway traffic, to be able to deal with pain and love and ecstasy. Ecstasy can be painful when it's intense enough, when the kundalini surges enough, the ecstasy is so complete it's overwhelming sometimes. Eventually you'll go into samadhi. Samadhi is a very advanced meditation. You dissolve in the clear light of eternity again and again, the experience of enlightenment—tomorrow night.

How do you meditate? We're going to do a meditation technique. I'm going to go through it now and we're going to do one. You will find that they will build over the evening. We're going to do three of them. This will be the first one. I'd like you to listen carefully. They seem very simple, and they are. That's why they work. But they're extremely powerful. Tonight as we meditate together I'm going to be moving in and out of different planes of attention and taking the kundalini and surging it through you in a lot of different ways to show you inside what it feels like to meditate.

Naturally when you're here, there are lots of wonderful people and they've got lots of wonderful energy, so you'll feel a lot of different things. But the true test of how the experience was, what it did for you, was how you feel when you get home. Go home, have a little bite to eat. Relax and look around you. See the energy. See how you feel tomorrow. If we did a good job, you'll be pretty gone.

What I'd like you to do, in a moment—stay relaxed—is to sit up straight. It's good when you meditate to sit up straight. Normally when you practice meditation you can sit in a chair, which I wish you would tonight. Please don't sit in the aisles because there are fire laws. I don't know. Fire has problems with it. But you can sit like this. You can sit any way you want, as long as you sit up straight and your back, the spine is straight. You should be comfortable. It's good to wear clean loose clothing when you meditate. You can meditate naked if that's what you're into. It doesn't matter. The main thing is to learn to be still.

Now, therefore why all this music when you're trying to be still? The music is used as a backdrop. We have a lot of people together, a lot of different energies, and it gives us something to focus on a little bit. I take the kundalini and I play against the notes with it. I kind of do a light show, inwardly and outwardly, with the energy, with vortexes of energy as you sit there. Opening you up. Opening up different parts of you that maybe you haven't felt since you were a child. It's no big deal. It's just what I do.

What I'd like you to do is a meditation. During this experience, the next 10 or 12 minutes while we're sitting here and feeling in new ways, new energies, you're storing something. Don't look for the flashy experience. It may happen. But if it's strong enough, you won't realize it's happened until much later when you start to come down from it.

What we're looking for here is storing power. You're accumulating energy, the kundalini. So I'd like you to begin this evening, just for a moment, by taking your hand and touching the area around your navel. Just take your hand and touch that area, OK? And you'll know how much weight you need to lose. (Audience laughs.) The holidays are always devastating. OK, this is one of the nadis. This is one of the places where the kundalini hangs out. So what I'd like you to do is, while the music is on, I'd like you to practice a simple exercise, maybe four or five minutes. Then you can stop the exercise and just go, and leave the driving to us.

What I'd like you to do is to focus your attention here, and you will feel surges of energy. You don't have to touch that spot when you do this. I'd like you to feel the energy moving. We're going to move that energy from here [around the navel] to the center of the chest. Now touch the center of the chest right here. This is the heart chakra. This is the navel chakra. These are two primary energy centers. The heart chakra is a very pure, luminous energy center. The shushumna is the tube that the kundalini passes up in the subtle physical body, and one side is the little guy called the ida and the other side is the pingala.

We're going to move the kundalini from the solar plexus region where it stores right up into the heart center, which purifies it and connects the two halves of the being. This is the central chakra. There are three above the heart chakra—the throat chakra, third eye and the crown chakra; [below are the] navel center, one halfway down, and then one all the way at the base of the spine.

To start with we're going to do a simple exercise, but it's strong. Focusing here. Then what I'd like you to do is imagine—because imagination is power in the inner world; when you use your imagination you are creating a movement of energy. It's not arbitrary. It's not daydreaming—well, daydreaming is energy. OK. What I'd like you to do is to sit up, relax, feel this area of your body and feel energy or just imagine it moving from here [the navel chakra] to here [the heart center] like a little surge, like a little fountain, going from here to here. If it goes further, fine, don't worry about it. You just sort of feel energy going from here to here.

Then you're going to come back down again and bring it from here [the navel chakra] to here [the heart center]. Little circle. Then you're going to come back down again and bring it from here to here. At this point we're not taking the energy so much in a circle as just bringing it up. I'd just like you to repeat this for a few minutes—four or five minutes. As you do, you'll notice your attention level changing. Thoughts will come in and out of your mind at this point, please just ignore them. Don't try and fight with them or stop them yet. Just ignore them, relax and just keep this focus. After doing that for a few minutes, stop. Let go and just let the music absorb you or the energy absorb you. The energy changes will be very (Rama claps his hands), very (Rama claps his hands) fast (Rama claps his hands again), very quick. I'll snap (Rama snaps his fingers) you through a lot of different planes of attention very quickly. If you feel uncomfortable, relax. It'll go away in a moment. You're trying too hard. Relax a little bit. Lighten up. Have fun with it. Smile a little bit. If it gets too intense just sit back. You might meditate with your eyes closed—normally that's the easiest. Once in a while it's fun to meditate with the eyes open and gaze forward without a particular focus. We'll talk more about that later.

To stop thought you have to go above it. So we're collecting energy and then that energy, when it's freed, it's like a flood and the water will rise and rise and will take us above a certain level. And then there's no thought. Then we're in altered states of attention. That's how the kundalini works, one of the ways.

I'd like you to focus your attention here and then just very gently as you sit there with your eyes closed, just bring the energy from here to here. Just imagine it. You don't have to see a picture in your mind. Just feel that, focus here, then feel here, then here, then here, and just feel it rising up, and as you do, you may feel a sensation kind of like you're floating. You may see visual colors, particularly if your eyes are open. You may see colors. There'll be certain light changes. Aside from that, you may see subtle changes in the subtle physical. Maybe no phenomena, it doesn't matter. You're absorbing energy. You're absorbing power, which you'll take with you when you leave this evening.

Let us begin. If you'd please sit up nice and straight. Relax. Close your eyes. Focus your attention on the navel center. Meditate for about 10 minutes. Just have a nice time. Don't fall asleep. Just let yourself go. Let yourself wander. You're thinking, "What am I supposed to do, what's going to happen?" Who knows? I don't know. That's what makes life exciting. Just let go. Ignore thought. Feel. Just practice feeling. Feel the energy shifts in the room. Ride the music for a while. Ride the energy. Go beyond thought. Feel love. Feel peace. Don't think about tomorrow or yesterday. They don't exist. Yesterday's gone, tomorrow hasn't happened. We only have this night and this night is eternity. Good. Let us begin.

(Music is played during several minutes of meditation.)

Please sit back and relax.

There are many, many ways to meditate. Essentially in the very beginning when you meditate, you're learning how to feel again. When we're very young children we know how to feel. It's innate. But as we lead a lifetime, we pick up so many thoughts, impressions, feelings, ideas, that our sensitivity goes away. Now little children don't meditate perfectly. Don't misunderstand me. Some children are perfectly horrible but their subtle physical bodies are perfectly intact. But as we grow up, as we're exposed to hate and greed and anger and jealousy and peanut brittle and all kinds of things, our subtle body erodes. The subtle body must be intact to transmit the kundalini, the life force. As the subtle body wears, we get sick and that's why eventually the body dies—it's because something happens to the subtle body.

The integrity of the subtle body is totally important. Think of the subtle body as the framework. The veins, capillaries, organs, everything is required for the body to function. The subtle physical body also is made up of many different strands of luminous energy, and energies are flowing through them constantly in the etheric plane that supports the physical body. Above the subtle body is the causal body and then, of course, the soul or whatever you want to call it—that which we are. We're the universe. We're all-intelligent. So what are we doing here? (Audience laughs.) Well, life is like that. You end up in the strangest places. They had a great brochure for this particular planet before this incarnation. You probably read it too.

If you're starting to meditate, I suggest that you set up a schedule for yourself. It's good to meditate twice a day. If you're an absolute beginner, meditate once a day. If you can't get yourself to meditate once a day, then try once a year. (Audience laughs.) Now you shouldn't expect as much, of course. Once a day is good to start.

The best time to meditate is when you first get up in the morning or evening or whenever you rise. What you want to do is get up, wake up, take a shower or whatever and sit down and meditate. Most people have a little meditation table they sit in front of when they meditate or sit in a chair. Sometimes they keep large amounts of cash on it (audience laughs), and they hope that through the process of meditation there will be more. I don't know. I myself have candles on my table and some flowers. The candles are nice because the light is very gentle. It's easy on the eyes. And sometimes I have a little incense burning, sometimes the rug, whatever (audience laughs) you're in the mood for. The flowers are nice, they bring nature into our universe.

Then what should you do? It's a good idea sometimes before you start a meditation to chant a mantra. A mantra is a very powerful word. It vibrates like music does, only not just on this plane but on other planes of reality. It creates a powerful force. It starts the kundalini moving. There are many different mantras. The most powerful of all mantras is "Aum," spelled A-U-M or O-M. It's usually chanted either silently or out loud. But it's stretched. So it's "Aaaauuuummmm" (Rama chants) stretched. All mantras are always elongated.

The mantra for beauty is "Sring," S-R-I-N-G, to enter into the states of beauty. That's "Sring," "Srrriinnnnnnnnng" (Rama chants) and so on.

If you would chant Aum either silently or out loud, maybe seven times—seven powerful numbers, seven higher worlds and seven lower worlds, according to one philosophy—if you would chant Aum seven times—sit down, OK, woke up (Rama talks like a stressed-out person), "Oh man, God, I gotta meditate. Man, I can't take it man, geez. (audience laughs repeatedly throughout foregoing passage.) Last night, man, that party, God I got so wasted. How am I gonna do it? Man, I don't know. Rama said I gotta do it, man, I'll do it. Geez, I gotta light the candles. Oh, I lit the flower man, God! Oh, bad karma, man, like I won't tell anyone. I'll just put it back together. No one will know. I'm gonna do this thing, man. I'm gonna sit here. I gotta do this Aum jazz, man. Sounds pretty jive but I'll try it, man. I think I'll do it. I hope no one will hear me, man, they'll think I'm sick. I'll go 'Aum'. That's good enough man, he'll never know. Now I gotta do this. What do I gotta do, one of those exercises he taught us, man. I got loaded before I went that night. It was pretty far out. I liked the music a lot. I don't know if I can remember. Let's see, what he said, something about the heart, man. I gotta like focus. Like right here. I'm gonna like put my attention. That's right. And sit up straight, man. (Rama inhales loudly) Oh, he didn't say I didn't have to breathe. No, no, you can do any kind of breathing." (Return to normal voice.)

What you're going to do then, to cut back to the present moment, is after you've chanted Aum a few times and gotten yourself basically together and put the flower out (audience laughs), you're going to sit there and focus your attention in a number of different ways.

Any of the exercises that you start out with will get the kundalini moving. You don't have to stay with them for the entire period of meditation. You want to go beyond them. We want to walk through the door. Once we're through the door we're outside. We're in another world. But we need to get up and walk through the door. A meditation exercise serves that purpose. It's not something to stay with because you'll fixate on it. We want to go beyond thought, beyond ideation, beyond feeling, beyond everything. But we start in the physical and in the mind. We use the transitory to go to the eternal because they're really interconnected.

So you'll sit down in the morning—if you can't make it in the morning, try the evening to start with. Do the late show. But you meditate best in the morning, even though you may be a little tired, the mind has not been active yet. Once you've been thinking, analyzing, talking, picking up energy, being active, it's harder to slow it down.

Even though you're a little tired, the mind hasn't been moving, it's easier to make it still. When you meditate in the morning you pick up a lot of energy, focus, awareness and that will be with you throughout the day. You'll have a shield of energy around you. It brightens the subtle physical body so you won't pick up as much negative energy from your transactions with the world. Your mind will be clear. You'll do everything well. Everything's better with Blue Bonnet on it. (Audience laughs.) Right. So if you smear it all over yourself before you meditate (audience laughs), nooooo, kinky, boy, I'll tell you.

So sit there and meditate. Practice one of these exercises that I'm showing you tonight or another one that you may know to start out with. Then what are you supposed to do? As I suggested, there are three stages. If you're very new to meditation, simply practice the exercise for a few minutes, say five minutes, or as long as is comfortable. Then after doing that for about five minutes or so, stop, just let go.

Letting go is the hardest thing, isn't it? Everybody's so afraid. They're so afraid of eternity. They're so afraid of life. They're so afraid of what's on the other side of death. There's nothing but light. Infinite light. Infinite awareness. God is everywhere.

Learn to let go. You do it a little at a time and you have small successes in terms of mental clarity, feeling better, deep perceptions about life, developing your psychic abilities, whatever it may be. The changes you go through. You become someone else when you meditate, you know. It isn't just a little technique. If you really pursue it, you change radically, constantly, because you evolve. You can go through hundreds of lifetimes in one. You can experience so much. Feel so much. Be so much. Or be nothing. Or everything. Or beyond both. And it all starts with that daily meditation practice.

How long should you meditate? If you're very new to meditation, maybe 15 minutes is fine. Set a minimum time. You'll sit there for 15 minutes. Don't expect anything in the beginning. Just to do it is enough. It's like jogging. The first few times you do it you're not going to suddenly be running marathons. But if you do it every day for a little while, you'll find that time will increase by itself. It won't be as hard. It'll feel good and pretty soon you'll be amazed at what you can do. Or in the case of meditation, not do or undo.

If you've been meditating for a while, after a month or so, if you're new to meditation, or two months, work it up to a half an hour. After six months or a year meditate maybe 45 minutes, twice a day. You'll sleep less, have a lot more energy and you'll begin to become conscious of consciousness, of awareness.

Meditation gives you personal power. You'll notice that people will treat you very differently as you progress because they can feel that power or that energy. Naturally it's the hope of those of us who teach meditation, particularly the release of the kundalini, which is a very powerful form of meditation, that you use that power wisely. If you search your heart, I think you will. You'll learn through experience like every one.

Experience is the great teacher. You'll have to go through the trials and tribulations and the ecstasies and abandoned moments of wonderfulness that all of us did on the way to enlightenment. It's a great, great life we lead but it causes substantial changes in the way that you see life. Because the way you see life is the way you've been taught to see life. You've been programmed, brainwashed to see life in very specific forms. Some of them may be useful forms but still they're specific forms. Life is endless and we are a body of perception. We're an awareness that's endless. As you meditate you experience different parts of that perception, and as perception alters, the universe alters because the universe is only perception.

In the beginning when you're sitting meditating, just ignore thought. Pay no attention. Shine it on. Then after you're comfortable with sitting there, you've been meditating a month or two, try selectively eliminating negative thoughts. By that I mean thoughts that draw you into the world of unhappiness, that agitate your mind. Rather than worrying about your exam that you've got to take, or your career, or the person you're in love with, or whatever it may be, begin to have thought control. You can practice it during the day also. But start in your meditations. Meditate and think positive thoughts. If you must think, think good thoughts, happy thoughts, constructive thoughts. You'll find that sometimes while you're sitting there, you'll get a lot of great ideas. Now granted, you want to go beyond ideas and beyond thought but that takes years of practice, if not lifetimes, to erase thought, even subconscious thought, completely for extended periods of eternity.

In the beginning we're just stopping thought for a while. But first just ignore it, then selectively work with your thoughts. Then you'll begin to move into periods of no thought. It'll just happen and you won't realize it's happened until you've started to think again and you'll think, "Boy, I wasn't thinking."

It's good to meditate in the early evening if you can. Ideally one would meditate in the morning. Clear yourself. Bring in a lot of kundalini, a lot of energy. Go out into the day. Have an exciting day. Come back slightly worn by the day but feeling good, having learned in the school of life. Come back. Meditate again and clear yourself again. It's very easy to meditate at sunset. There's a doorway that opens between the worlds at the time of the setting sun. It's very easy to still your thoughts. Sometimes it's fun to meditate outside. Be creative. Meditate at the beach. On a mountaintop. In the desert. Wherever you're comfortable. Don't get hung up in rituals or routines.

How do you end a meditation session? It's nice to chant a mantra again. Maybe repeat it a few times. It seals the meditation. You'll notice sometimes after a meditation, I bow. Wonderful for the stomach muscles. (Audience laughs.) What am I doing? You don't have to do it that way, you can just do it inside. You don't have to give it physical form. You're giving the meditation away. You have a meditation. You do your best and then you just give it to eternity.

Don't judge your meditations. Don't rate them. The mind, the physical mind, cannot tell how well you did. If you start to think, "Gee that was a good one, that was a bad one" —nonsense. There's no such thing. The only bad meditation is when you don't meditate. As long as you're sitting there trying, something will happen. But you will not necessarily feel the positive effect of your meditation experience perhaps for a half an hour or an hour after you've ended the meditation. Then suddenly everything will get very clear. You'll just feel very good, a sense of well-being. This is the preliminary, the beginning. You don't stay with well-being, you move to ecstatic consciousness, perceptions about life, eternity. You become the cosmos. It just depends how far you want to go with it. That's up to you.

Kundalini can be used in a lot of different ways. Essentially in the beginning you're just trying to get it moving within yourself. Everyone has kundalini. It's already there. But it's a question of waking it up. As I suggested before, the subtle physical body must be intact. If there are problems with the subtle body, it's very hard for the kundalini to flow.

A certain amount of the kundalini is always floating through the ida and the pingala, these two little subtle nerve tubes on either side of the shushumna, which is the central tube in the subtle physical body. That's what keeps us alive. When the subtle physical body is damaged you'll begin to notice changes in your skin, when your skin starts to get gnarly, dry, problems. Now I'm not speaking of acne. Acne is not necessarily a problem with the subtle physical body, it just means that you have a lot of kundalini, which stimulates the hormones.

But when you see deterioration in the skin or the hair particularly, you're having problems with the subtle body. You're taking in too much bad energy, usually from people, or you're thinking too many negative thoughts. You're just on the wrong circuit. You're pulling an energy that is not suitable for the human life form. The human life form vibrates at a certain rate, but all vibratory rates are not suitable for human life. So it's very necessary to meditate on higher octave energy, on the clear light, on joy, on happiness, peace. If you try and pull too much power through too soon, you'll injure yourself.

The kundalini can be transmitted. You're trying to awaken it, bring it through you; it brings you into other states of consciousness. But it can also be transmitted. A person who is very adept at the kundalini, who has a great deal of it, who's gone through this enlightenment process, can transmit it—and that's of course what I do. When you're sitting here I'm taking the kundalini and moving it through you. Some of you, if you're sensitive, of course, you'll feel it. If not, you won't. But it still has an effect. It's like radiation. Whether you feel it or not, it's affecting you in a very positive way.

You may notice during the meditation that sometimes I'm moving my hands and doing different things. What I'm doing is moving the kundalini in very specific ways. It's kind of like reaching into another dimensional plane and pulling the kundalini through and moving it through you in specific ways and forms. You can transmit the kundalini physically when people are there, and of course, long distance. It's energy, interdimensional energy.

It's much easier for women to meditate than it is for men, innately. And it has to do with the nature of a woman's subtle physical body. The subtle physical body of a man and a woman is slightly different. Both a man and a woman can meditate well. But women will just find it a little bit easier. They have to do a little less work, that's all, because their subtle physical bodies pick up the kundalini much more quickly. They vibrate at a slightly different rate that passes [kundalini] very easily. But that's also problematic because a woman also picks up bad energy or negative energy. It affects her more—hate, anger, things like that affect her subtle physical more. Sensitivity is a two-way street. When you're sensitive you can feel and appreciate, but you can also be injured more easily. But women find it very easy to release the kundalini and bring it through their beings.

The kundalini brings about changes, structured changes in the being. We're reordering the self. We're made up of a series of awarenesses. Beyond the subtle physical body we have something called the causal body. That's more what we are; we're a series of interconnecting awarenesses. It's possible—it's like a molecular bond, a DNA, a double helix, we can change that. That's what self-discovery is. Self-discovery is a very advanced art. What we're doing basically is screwing around with what you're made up of. We're taking awarenesses, feelings, ideas, impressions and changing them. We do that with ourselves. As you expose yourself again and again to the power of meditation, to the kundalini, you're changing that and refining it, enlarging it.

You have a house that has many, many rooms in it, but you've only seen a few. But there are so many. Then there's beyond the house. There's the outdoors, the endless universe. You are sitting on this little planet, spaceship earth, but the universe is very accessible to you. You don't need a spaceship to travel there. Most of the worlds are non-physical. And it's all God, it's all eternity.

I'm going to teach you another meditation technique. This one is very simple. It's a focus on the heart center. The heart center is the principle chakra. There are three above and three below. It's the central access of the being. What I would like you to do, it's very simple, is to focus on this spot and to feel love.

Now, how do you feel love spontaneously? Well you can think of someone you love or something you love, a nice experience that you've had, anything to get the flow started. The patient is on the table, not breathing. We're gonna pound that sucker—pow—to get him started. Once he's started, then the heart will get going again. But we can do it more delicately. What we're going to do is feel love. That's going to get something in us started. That's going to get our awareness moving, light flowing through our consciousness.

What I'd like you to do is simply to focus on this center. If you like, you might visualize a flower or feel that there's a flower there, but it's like a rose and it's all folded up. As you meditate, feel. You don't have to see a mental picture, but just feel that the flower is opening, that there are all these petals, they're closed up. And gradually they're opening up and there's set after set of petals. As each set of petals opens up, it's a little larger than the first set. The first set that opens up will fill kind of a small area. Real slowly and gracefully they'll open up and light will go through your being. The second set will open up and maybe it will fill the chest area very gracefully. A third set will open and fill the whole body. A fourth set the room. A fifth set the whole sky. A sixth set the universe. The seventh set all of eternity and so on. Endless petals opening up. Each time you open up a set of petals you're going deeper into the self, deeper into nirvana, deeper into eternal awareness.

When thoughts come in and out of your mind, just ignore them. You might try meditating that way with the eyes closed for a few minutes. You might try meditating then with the eyes open. It's good to learn to meditate that way. We call it "gazing," just looking forward without a singular focus, and you can see the kundalini actually moving through the air—other than the light changes, of course. There are other changes taking place. As you watch my hands you may notice energy flowing through them. It's going through you. It's the transmission of the kundalini.

We'll meditate for about 10 minutes, and you'll notice that this meditation will be quite different. Try to feel love. We're meditating on love this time. It's the strongest force in the universe. We're just going to open ourselves up to it and let it carry us. There are a lot of wonderful people here and we're all networking our energy together. We're getting high together. And they can't do anything about it. (Audience laughs.) So let's try.

Sit up nice and straight please. Focus on the center of the chest. Relax. Relax. Enjoy yourself. This is your life. Exactly. And imagine a flower there if you like, or just focus on that spot for a few minutes. Feel it unfolding. Let yourself go, ignore your thoughts and let's meditate.

(Music starts. Rama continues speaking when meditation has ended.)

Please sit back and relax.

It's a good idea when you meditate to avoid eating for a few hours before you meditate because otherwise you just feel your body too much. You really don't want to feel the body. If you're very, very hungry though you should have something to eat because otherwise you'll just sit there and think of food, which is not the worst thing to think of, granted.

Kundalini flows in different directions. Some people are under the assumption that the kundalini just flows from the base of the spine up. That's not the case at all. It flows a lot of different ways. Kundalini also flows downward. You can take the kundalini from the crown center, which is an access point, and bring it down. You can bring it up or you can stabilize them both. When you stop breathing in meditation, the kundalini is stabilized. When you go into samadhi, very often you won't breath for half an hour, an hour, there's no breath at all. The kundalini, the life force, is perfectly stabilized. Usually it stabilizes in the solar plexus area. You can stabilize it anywhere actually. But that's the most common.

The kundalini can be used for a lot of purposes—healing disease obviously, healing the mind. More importantly it can be used to help awaken someone to life. We're all asleep. This is a dream that we're in this world. We're trying to wake up. We have this recurring dream that we're human beings, that we have bodies, that we're in time and space, that there's birth and death. We keep having this dream day after day. To awaken from the dream of life or to see endless dreams, or to go beyond the dream to nirvana, to be conscious of eternity and yet to be here and to be aware of the moment—meditation. Never leave the body without it.

I'd like to answer a few questions about meditation and the kundalini specifically for a few minutes. We'll be doing another meditation after a while. It'll be our final one for the evening. But that won't be for a while yet. If you have a question I'd like you to raise your hand. If you could say it nice and loudly so I can hear you it would be helpful, and I'll repeat the question for everyone else because they probably won't be able to hear. This is such a vast area, meditation and the kundalini. You may have specific interests. When you meditate at home sometimes it's good to try very hard. You know, you just want to really do your absolute best.

Sometimes some people say when they start to meditate they get a headache. It's because they're trying too hard. You're pulling too much energy. It's like eating too much and then you feel sick afterwards. If you feel any ill effects, it means you're trying too hard. But tonight it's really not necessary for you to try very hard because there's just so much kundalini surging that if you try too hard you'll get in your own way. It's best just to let go and leave it this evening. That'd be the easiest. To try and not to try. It goes back and forth. To strive and not to strive. There are different ways of talking about something that's really beyond words. That's an experience, which is why we meditate together.

You see, real, higher meditation is not taught through techniques or words. These are the beginning steps. It's how we start someone. Everyone has to go through that process. Really. You have to learn the basics. One can never be too proud to learn how to begin again. But the real meditation experience is taught; it's learned, through practice naturally, but it's taught inwardly. In other words, you shift a person through different dimensional planes but they have to do the prep for you to be able to do that as a teacher. So it's necessary for you to meditate on your own and refine your consciousness.

Tighten up your life. Constantly examine your life and look for weak points. Are your relationships sloppy? Are your emotions sloppy or are they tight? Are you loving and giving, or are you being selfish and weird? You know what's going on in your life. As you meditate you get clearer on that. You get clearer on the fact that you can shape and mold your life. You can be an architect of your own destiny. Most people lead their lives like they drive their cars. You can be more precise, you can lead a life poorly or very well. Meditation gives you the energy and also the insight to do that.

As to meditation, how should we meditate—hard, easily? Every meditation is unique. There is no absolute rule. That's what makes it fun. You have to feel out each situation and try as you go. If you're sitting there meditating one day and you're meditating on the heart center; it's been great the last three times, this time nothing—don't stay with it, switch. Do something else. Be creative. Meditate on your navel center. Do another exercise. Switch it around. Don't be bound. Stop for a minute. You're sitting there, it's just not happening. Stop. Take a break for a moment. Walk around. Sit down, try again. Try a different room, a different energy. Every place has different energy. Be creative in your meditation.

Tonight if you're sitting there and you're trying real hard and it's just not kicking over for you, don't try so hard, obviously. You see, every situation is different. But there's just so much energy tonight that it's not necessary.

Questions. Yes. (Rama repeats the question.) How do you deal with the fact that you're meditating at home and sometimes you stop breathing. And your question is, how do you deal with that? (Rama holds his breath and pretends to asphyxiate. Audience laughs.) How do you deal with it? Well, I don't know. I can remember when that started happening to me about 15 years ago and I wouldn't breathe and then suddenly become real uptight because you're not breathing. Your mind says, (Rama talks like a terrified person) "I'm not breathing! I'm supposed to be breathing! God, I'm not breathing!" (Rama gasps for air then returns to normal voice.) Then you realize all you did was just bring yourself down from a nice meditation.

The trick is to meditate just a little higher and you won't even know that you're not breathing. Then it isn't a problem. As long as you're in the plane where you know you're not breathing you're going to think about it. You know, try not to think about an armadillo with a purple beret. Good luck! Here he comes now. (Audience laughs.) Right. So you're not breathing. OK. It's good you're not breathing. You don't need to breathe so much. People breathe too much. Listen, if everybody would breathe less there'd be more oxygen on the planet. Rama's suggestion.

You don't need to breathe. It's happening by itself. But your mind will tell you you do because we've been conditioned to think that we need to breathe. You don't need to breathe so much. I mean breathing is nice. It's OK. But it's nothing to get attached to. It's a matter of just ignoring that whole experience. It's just another place to get stuck. As you're meditating you're stuck to start out with. You're stuck in your thoughts. It's like your feet are in Bonomo's Turkish Taffy or something. Ughh. You're trying to get them out. You get one free and then you get the other one free and then finally you're going but then, along the way, there are little things that kind of, whoosh, grab you. Those are all your attachments. So you're having a great meditation, thoughts stop, you're cruising along and then suddenly the love of your life comes into your mind. He, she or it is sitting at home thinking about you. (Rama talks in a raspy voice) Reaching out! Throwing a lasso of occult energy around things. Don't go so fast there! Think about me! (Return to normal voice.)

Now, of course, if you're not experienced in the ways of occult power, you'll assume that you're just thinking about Susie or Bill or, you know, the armadillo or whatever you're into and you won't realize that they are—because human beings are very strong and they all radiate kundalini and energy—inserting themselves into your thoughts. It's true. It's true. It's a good idea if you're going to have a really good meditation to unplug the phone. You'd be surprised. Boy, that's one you learn early because just when it's finally happening, rrrring! "Hi, son." (Audience explodes in laughter.) You know, whatever it may be. And it's like, ah, ah, ah, ah. The energy crackles along the line.

Another question. Yes. OK, so your problem is, then, that you live in a, as you said, a multi-room dwelling where different people live known as a rooming house. And there's a fellow who lives in the room next to you who, as you put it very poetically, has a drinking problem. And that when he starts to rave and scream. as you said, he puts out a lot of bad energy and you're sitting in your room and you notice the flowers are wilting and stuff like that. So your question then is, I'm just repeating it for all to hear, your question is, how can you put out an energy that will protect you from that experience?

Well, the obvious answer is move, naturally. That's the easiest because when it's real serious, it's going to be a battle every step of the way. But if that just isn't in the cards, you really like the room or you're just determined or you signed the lease or whatever, and you're stuck with it, then you need to turn your room into a place of POWER. Power, ooohhhh! (Audience laughs.) It's a good idea to have flowers around, candles, incense, you know, happy things. Make your room a beautiful place. You should always do that with your house anyway. You should have beauty wherever you are because life is so pretty. Just make your room really beautiful and keep it very clean. Impeccably clean. All the closets in order, drawers. Everything in perfect place. And just turn on music when he screams. That's the best, I think, personally. A walkperson, headphones.

There's not much you can do except feel that he doesn't exist. Ah! This is the trick. What you can do—it's possible—now I don't know if you can do this, but I can do this. It's possible to block out any noise. Not by blocking it out but by expanding your attention level so that it's so vast that it's just another part of eternity and you do not apply a specific mental charge to it. In other words, that particular sound or those vibrations that person is sending out are offending you. They are offending your sensibility. They hurt your subtle body. But it's possible to go up high enough where everything's sort of a white noise. Everything just blends together, if you can do that.

In the beginning that's pretty hard though. I'd move. That's my advice. But if you don't do that, just make your own life as tight as possible. Don't think badly of the person. What can they do? This is his karma, right? He can't help it. He's got a weak subtle physical body so he drinks. Life hurts sometimes real badly. Who knows? We should never criticize or judge a person who does things like that because who knows what they've been through in their life. Some people have some pretty rough lives and he's just killing the pain. That's all he's doing. But naturally you're in a different place. You're vibrating at a different cycle so you have to do something about it. I'd move or just try to be very compassionate and understanding and play music. Little things. Little, practical applications. But if you can in your heart understand what's going on, it's easier to deal with it because obviously this person has had a tough incarnation.

Question. Ah, yes, OK. You're saying that sometimes when you meditate you're kind of going beyond the body and then you notice that your body is tilting or falling or something like that, yes? Right. And that brings you back. So that's not a good thing. What you need to do is learn to discipline your body to sit there. You can do this when you go into very advanced states of attention. The way you do it is just by gently correcting yourself. When you meditate your body shouldn't move. Some people get this kundalini sway business. You know, it's nauseating to watch them meditate. You get a whole room like that and it's like you bring Dramamine to the meditations. So the body should be kept still. If you find yourself leaning during a meditation, then just correct yourself. Just gently, don't worry about bringing yourself down, that's fine. Correct yourself. You just have to do it a few times. You make a little habit of it. As soon as you start to go off, bring yourself right back. You'll find after a while the body will know that and it will just stay that way.

The only time that there will be variances is in nirvikalpa samadhi. You go completely beyond this world, beyond the physical level of attention and the body just, poof. That's it. It doesn't stay; it's gone. Erased. Doesn't matter. You don't care. (Another question from audience.) Exactly. Your body's distracting. That's why I'm saying if you take the time to every time observe your body for a while and correct yourself—in other words, this problem could go on your whole life. Better you should take a little time and correct it early, now, and just pay a little attention to your posture. Every once in a while check yourself during the meditation. You might think, "Well that's going to bring me down." That's OK. If you do it just for a little while, for a month or so, it'll become a routine, you'll never have to do it again. Otherwise you're going to deal with this thing forever. See what I mean? Just use a little tighter physical attention on it and it will work out fine.

Question. Yes. There's somebody back over there. OK. If your subtle body is damaged, how can you tell where it's damaged and how do you repair it? I wouldn't so much worry about where it's damaged because usually it's not a specific place. It can be. But usually it's more of an erosion of the whole subtle physical body. It's just not healthy. What can you do about it? Well, first of all, naturally you have to stop the harm that's being done to it. But actually, even before that, you have to realize that there's harm being done to it.

Let me give you an example. Let's say that you go up in the mountains and it's real cold up there. You come into the cabin and it's just freezing, it's 10 below zero. Even some of the windows are open. They have to be boarded up. It's just a mess. The first thing to do is light a fire. Don't worry about the windows. Light the fire. Once the fire is going, that'll provide a certain amount of warmth. With that warmth you can then take your time and fill in the biggest holes to start with, the biggest losses. The heat will spread and you'll get warmer. Then you can gradually get the little ones until there's no heat loss whatsoever. Also you can make the fire larger, whatever. So with the subtle physical body and with one's attention field, we start first by generating energy, the kundalini. You've got to make yourself warm.

You need energy and life force to see and feel what you need to do. Otherwise you're in a dark room and you can't tell what's going on. To begin with, you just need to practice more meditation. That's the best thing you can do, and to meditate well. Some people, I talk to them and they say, "Oh, I meditate for four hours a day." And you look at their consciousness and it's like, ughh. You meditate for four hours a day? They're obviously not meditating for four hours a day, they're sitting there spacing out. They're not meditating.

There's a large difference between spacing out into the lower occult astral planes, just kind of this weird, junky, fuzzy energy, and meditation. Meditation is sharp (Rama snaps his fingers), clear (snaps fingers), precise, perfect, luminous, shiny, happy, etheric, cosmic, dissolute. It has various forms and formlessnesses. But it's not this kind of spacey stuff that then makes it difficult to orient to your life. If that's your experience of meditation, you're not meditating. You're tapping into the lower astral planes, which is not a healthy place for human beings to tap. You need to have good, clear, sharp, precise meditations that are filled with love and light and energy. Then you can address questions in your life. And you start with the biggest energy losses.

The biggest energy losses for most people are relationships, interrelations with other people. That's where we lose most energy, through our attachments. Or just by opening ourselves up to people who may be very nice on the surface but underneath they have a lot of problems. When we open our heart up to someone, that energy, of course, comes into us. So you just have to start to examine the people in your life and ask yourself if you're really having fun with them. Sometimes we keep relationships going with people who aren't what they used to be. They're not the people we knew and liked. They've changed. We've changed. But we keep up this association because we're afraid to make a jump to something new. And we die inwardly. When we're young, we were little kids, we change, we make new friends all the time, we're alive, we're growing. But we get scared as adults. We get too conservative. We die.

Begin by looking at your relationships and usually what you do is you just take out a piece of paper, two actually, and on one piece of paper put down all the people you know and associate with who you feel are adding more to your life than they're taking. Then on the other piece of paper put all the people you know, list them, who are taking more than they're adding. You should also include people from the past. Just because you're not physically close to someone doesn't mean that there isn't an interaction of energy. You may not have seen your ex-wife for 10 years, but there can be an interaction taking place. Then what you need to do when you find any that you feel are not happening, they're not generating energy, you need to cut those inside yourself.

At the umbilical region we actually network with people. What you can do, there's a little exercise, where you just can picture, if you want to, that you're cutting these cords that go out to everyone you know. As you do that you create a sense of detachment. It doesn't mean you don't love them, it just means you're cutting down on the negative energy pickup from people. The people who hurt you are the ones you love because you're most open to them.

Then of course you have to look at your own thought forms. Are you sitting around thinking a lot of negative thoughts? These injure the subtle body. When you hate, when you're angry, you bring that energy through you. Are you focusing too much on the lower occult? The lower astral? Are you contacting entities and strange low vibe beings in weird worlds? If you do that you're accessing energies that are very bad for the subtle physical. You should be focusing more on light, energy, storing personal power, whatever it may be. But there are certain neighborhoods that are not healthy to traverse.

Then of course it gets much deeper, naturally. Then we get into self-discovery. That's my specialty. That's dissecting someone inwardly, looking at the different selves, making changes in them and so on and so forth. It's what we call the Tibetan rebirth process. It's a very complex process of changing levels of attention, changing selves around and so forth. It's all done inwardly with the kundalini. That's the art of self-discovery, advanced self-discovery.

But first you have to go through all those preliminary stages, and also there are obvious physical things you can do. Spend time in nature. Get away from the city once in a while. Go jogging down on the beach. The ocean is a wonderful place to be, if there are not too many people around, to draw in a lot of prana, a lot of good energy. Have a lot of plants in your house. Happy things. Plants generate energy. Make friends with them. Transact with nature. Nature is energy. It's prana. It's healing. Drink lots of water, it has lots of prana in it. Things like that. Physical exercise, anything that's aerobic where you're moving a lot—jogging, tennis, swimming, long distance walking, hopping, you know, whatever.

Be very careful whom you love. Not how much, but whom, all the usual spiritual stuff. Then the subtle body will begin to return. A lot of people trash their subtle physical body with drugs, psychedelic drugs and things like that. While they do certainly give you experiences in altered levels of attention, you pay a price for it. They create some awakenings but they definitely screw up the subtle physical. Sometimes yoga is very good for that. Hatha yoga, that's good. Sometimes fasting, not excessively, can be good. Lots of things, whatever makes you feel good. You might be listening to music, things like that. Just find what makes you feel gentle, what makes you feel still, and people who have that effect upon you. Sometimes it's fun to just be crazy with energy and laugh and be silly. Don't misunderstand. That can be very regenerative. But you need the stillness too.

What is the relationship between the kundalini force and the sex force? The sexual drive is kundalini. Really any energy within us is a form of kundalini, so it's a particular fragrance or aspect of kundalini. Now, like all things, they're neither good nor bad, it's how they're applied. I wouldn't even say the effect is good or bad but there is what we call karma. Karma simply means that there's a reaction for an action. There's cause and effect in the world of duality. The sexual energy becomes problematic if you use it to enslave someone, to demoralize them, to hurt them, to wrap them up. In other words, the way most people use sexual energy is to hook somebody. They use it to wrap them, to get control over them. Some people use the sexual energy particularly during intercourse to take personal power from each other, or it's just a gratification of a physical sensation; there are lots of ways it can be used. But those ways don't engender a rise in consciousness. If you use that energy to love somebody then it works a little better in terms of raising one's level of attention.

Some people say that if you have sex you can't be enlightened. That's not my point of view. I think it isn't really so much whether you have sex or not, but it's what you're doing with your attention level during that time. That's the issue. In other words, if you can meditate and be very high regardless of what you're doing, then that's what you're doing. You're meditating. But you have to be able to slash through your desires to do that. Otherwise you get so caught up in physical sensation, you know, pleasure, this, that and the other thing, that you're distracted from meditating. You have to have a very intense degree of detachment and determination to do that, but then it can become a cosmic experience, as everything is.

The kundalini and sex are extremely interrelated, and sexual drive is part of the kundalini. That's why it's funny, because some people who have a lot of sexual energy think of themselves as being not spiritual because they have a lot of sexual energy. That's like, you know, tee-hee, how silly. They're probably more spiritually inclined. All that sexual energy is kundalini. That's all it is. They'd probably do really, really well in meditation. But because in certain books they say (Rama talks in a deep voice) "Well you know, blah, blah, you know, uuurrr" (return to normal voice), and you figure you're kinky, right? You figure, what hope is there for me? Well from my point of view, you'll probably do better because you have more life force, more energy and it's just manifesting. But what you need to do is take some of that energy and use it in some other ways in addition to sexuality. It's a very healthy sign. It means you're alive. You've got a lot of life force, so you're trying to give it away. Nice of you! (Audience laughs.) Such a guy!

Now if you're interested in developing the siddhas, the occult powers (Rama exhales rapidly with a powerful whoosh), all that stuff, you have to be a little more conservative, unless you're very, very far along, because there is the certain drop of a type of kundalini when you have sex. So if you're into developing the supernatural powers, then it's a good idea to be a little more temperate. Some occult teachers suggest celibacy. I don't know. But in terms of spiritual development, meditative development, enlightenment and so on, it's not a big deal whether you have sex or not, the question is more of who you have sex with and what their energy is doing to you. Because if you're having sex with someone who's not on the same frequency that you're on, it can be very problematic because the greatest transfer, karmic transfer occurs in—aside from meditating with someone—sex with someone. Particularly for women because women tend to open themselves up more, and just because their subtle physical bodies are so much more sensitive they pick up the total energy of the man they have sex with.

It's a real problem because a lot of men hate women subconsciously or just are very confused about them or are afraid of their power, or want to suppress them, or, you know, the usual, and so when they have sex with someone what happens is on the one hand they're having a good time or they're trying to do this or perform or whatever, you know, it's Ed Sullivan (Rama talks like Ed Sullivan), "He-ey!" (audience laughs), but, but, gotcha. But the problem is that it's not Ed Sullivan. That's somebody and you're affecting their attention level incredibly, and if you have a lot of problems inside yourself, they transfer. So it's good to be selective and to love a whole lot and not be attached. It's a very delicate balance. The further along you go, the more delicate the balance—it's the razor's edge that we walk in advanced self-discovery.

What I'm trying to say is, it isn't important what you do or what you don't do, it's how. And by how I don't mean kama sutra position number 95, you know, hanging from one foot from a large building while chanting the mantra, "fwam." (Audience laughs.) But rather the quality of your love. That's what I mean. The quality of your attention. Your ability to maintain a sense of love and giving without any ownership, without any possessiveness, without any jealousy, without any greed. A sense of the total sensitivity of this universe that you're colliding with and trying to be perfect for that universe without any egotism or vanity whatsoever. It's a very fine line. And if you don't do that, if you're not able to do that exactly correctly, it comes back on you, naturally. It's a very quick karma, and your level of attention drops. Afterwards you don't get along. You don't feel so good. Your energy's down. It was not a transcendent experience because you didn't care enough and give enough and you got lazy, sloppy and selfish. Like most people. But it doesn't have to be that way. You could be one in a billion. Why not? What the heck? It's worth taking a shot at, you know. Practice. Keep me informed. (Audience laughs.)

One or two more, then we have to meditate. Yes. Another one. Oh yes, you wrap them up with your second attention. Yes. Most people do. Right. It's a habit. Yes, women are very good at it particularly. Well, men do it too in a different way. But women have really developed it as an art. They've had to to survive. You can understand, in the world the way men have designed it, if you can't use that power, then what else have you got? But the problem with it is, it limits you. It puts you into a control situation. And even though you can control someone and it protects you to a certain extent, still you're in a controlling situation in duality. It brings you down. What you really need to do is, I would suggest, first of all watch how much you do it. It's fascinating; we're brought up and educated to do it. Then you need to be around people who aren't like that, I mean people who have decided that there's another way to lead their life and it's not necessary to wrap people up. The reason you're doing it is because you don't have enough power. If you had enough power, if you could unlock your own personal power, you wouldn't need to control others.

You need to be around people who've learned there's another way of leading life. And if you can find people like that, who feel good to you, and you're around them and that's how they lead their lives, you'll find that it's catching. It's a happy disease to get. You don't have to control people. And you can easily stop them from controlling you. But you have to be able to see to do that. You have to develop your psychic abilities and increase your personal power and all the usual things. Yes, it can be done. But I don't have a simple technique for you. It's a way of life. Some of us lead lives like that and we have a good time.

One more. How do you—OK, let's say you're going to meditate. If you're very new to meditation, you're just starting, I suggest that you have a watch or a clock by you and set a minimum amount of time. Chances are what you're going to be doing is referring to it occasionally. Because after five minutes you're going to say (Rama talks like a cranky person) "I have to sit here longer?" (Return to normal voice.) So you set 15 minutes, let's say, as a minimum. You're going to sit there and no matter what you think—songs are running through your head, you're thinking a million things you never would and you think, "This is never gonna work"—doesn't matter. Sit there. Do the 15 minutes. After that you'll find, after a few weeks, that it becomes very comfortable and suddenly you'll look down at the watch and 20 minutes have gone by or 25. What you want to do is sit as long as it feels good. Once you've reached a minimum time and you've gotten used to that, then just sit as long as it feels good.

Sometimes it's fun to set little hurdles for yourself. It depends. There are different ways to go about this. There's not one right way. Some people like to set hurdles so then they'll try half an hour as a minimum time. Other people would feel uptight if they did that. It wouldn't be a natural flow for them. Maybe it's better then just to see how long you sit. When it stops feeling good, you'll just find yourself stopping.

Sometimes you'll start out, you might meditate on the heart center, or one of these various methods that I'll show you another night, or that you're learned elsewhere, and you meditate for 15 or 20 minutes, it's wonderful. Then suddenly you'll feel your consciousness logging back too much on the physical. The thing to do is then maybe do a different technique for a few minutes. What you're doing when you do that is bringing kundalini through and then you're riding that kundalini for a while.

A time comes when you don't have to use meditation techniques anymore. You just sit down and you're nonexistence itself. So as far as length of time is concerned, just as long as it feels really good—once you've reached the point where you're past the minimum time. Good.

We're going to do one more meditation technique to close it out here. This one will be the most powerful, so please listen carefully. This one's a little complicated. I need your second attention here.

What I would like you to do in a minute is to sit up straight again and for the first couple minutes of meditation I'd like you to focus right around the back of the neck. There's a chakra that a lot of people don't know about. Most people are aware of the basic seven or the ones in the hands or the feet. But there are some other, more hidden energy centers in the subtle physical body. There's one around the back of the neck, it's just kind of around the top of the neck. Put your hand back there just for a second. Just feel that area back there. Feel your neck, then come up just about the to the top of it where you're connecting with the head—never thought of it that way did you? It's good thing, huh? Right around there. OK. That's where you're going to be focusing to start with.

What I'd like you to do is to start focusing your attention right there and then take that energy and feel that it's going to transmit from there in two lines to your hands. I don't want you to move your hands or do anything with your hands. Just put them in a comfortable position. You might put them on your lap. Some people hold them like this or just any way you want. But just feel that two lines of energy are going to move out from here to your hands. And when they hit your hands, you'll kind of feel a warming sensation, and then from the hands we're going to bounce that energy right back to the heart center and ground it. We're taking a very occult or a very mystical energy and we're shooting it through, then we're going to bring it into the psychic being. It's done in waves like we did before.

We're going to start with the energy here [back of head] and then just feel it pulsing towards your hands. You can visualize lines of light if you like or not, just feel it going there. It doesn't matter whether it travels in a straight line or through your arms, whatever; it gets there. Just feel the energy going there and it's going right to the very center of the palms and then it's going to bounce back. This is a more advanced technique now, so it's a little stronger. Then it's going to bounce back and go right into the heart center. It's just out and back. Out and back. Just do that in a rhythmic way for a couple of minutes and then stop. Let go. Go with the music. Then open your eyes a little bit and watch me meditate. Just observe without looking too hard. You don't want to focus too sharply. You're not just watching me the body, but you're watching the energy fields here. You're relaxing your eyes, not looking too sharply, gazing. And just watching. You're letting go. Then you might try closing your eyes again, opening them, whatever is comfortable for you.

You're going to start by focusing your attention back here for a few moments and then just feel this energy moving into your hands any way you want to, as long as it gets there. Then you're going to feel it coming back from the hands right into the heart, right into the psychic center. And then it just dissolves. It radiates through your whole being there. What we're doing is taking an occult energy, bringing it into a place—it's like an amplifier, it's amplifying in the chakras and the hands, and then we're neutralizing it and spreading it through the being. Again, the hands can be in any position. It doesn't matter. The energy flows. That would be good.

So please sit up straight and close your eyes for a moment and focus around the back of the neck to start out with. Let us begin.

(Music starts. Rama continues speaking when meditation has ended.)

Could you guys stand up for a minute? Stand up. (Lengthy audience applause.)

Thank you. On guitar, Joaquin Lievano. (Audience applauds.) Bass and synthesizer, Andy West. (Audience applauds.) A lot of synthesizers, Steve Kaplan. (Audience applauds.)

Two blisses, lots of astral beings, lots of energy. Thank you very much. Good night. Hope to see you again. Namaste.

If you meditate deeply several times a day, if that is the center of your practice, then in that meditation you will become light. You will transform and change and you will find that you don't have to inspire yourself to do what's right because you've already become what's right. I respect self-giving and I've tried to lead my life with that as the ideal. But real self-giving is when we take our self, our being, that which is most precious to us—our ego, our bodies, our minds, our values, our past, our present and our futures—and we sit in meditation and we throw that all into eternity with a sense of total offering to that larger, infinite self.

— *Rama Live in L.A.*

When we meditate and we're able to stop all thought, suddenly we're suffused with light. We get a sense of being outside of the body, or beyond the body. Our consciousness expands and we see ourselves as beings of light. And that's certainly true. As we progress in our inundation with light, as we make friends with light, and we come to know it better, we come to know our substance and our essence, then we find that we're not really separate beings of light. That that's a dream that we're having, the dream of multiplicity. Each one of us dreams that we're a separate individual with a history, a future, with a moment, with something to do or nothing to do. Meditation takes us beyond the moment to eternal awareness. Cosmic consciousness. Nirvana. These states of awareness are open to everyone. It's just a question of where we focus our time and energy.

— *Rama Live in L.A.*

Rama Live in L.A.:
[TANTRIC MYSTICISM] AND MEDITATION
1983

Tonight I'd like to talk a little bit about a timeless subject. Meditation. I don't think there's a way we can really define meditation. I think it's easier to say what it's not and perhaps come at a definition that way. Meditation is not being caught in time. Meditation is not being limited to any condition of the mind, body or spirit. Meditation is not being fixated, even on the avoidance of fixation. Meditation is not the awareness of eternity, although in the process of meditation we certainly become aware of eternity. Meditation is not the avoidance of this world and its people, places and things. Meditation is not impractical or unrealistic, nor is it difficult to integrate with any lifestyle or any age, in that it's timeless, although it occurs in time. Meditation is something that is very hard to categorize, which is what makes it useful to us, because we live in a world of categories, of things that are very definable and that's what we're used to, and meditation offers us a doorway to a world or worlds beyond that which we can easily define.

There are ways we can talk about meditation, but in doing so, we should try to keep in mind that they're only ways. The exciting thing about meditation is that we can't pin it down. There's an innate urge in all of us, I think, to try and pin something down, that is to say, to limit it or restrict it in the sense that we want to quantify it and be able to feel, well, these are the parameters of meditation, because I think we feel indigenously more comfortable with something then. We feel it's under control. But that control sometimes usurps the very thing we're seeking, which is awareness.

Meditation, then, is essentially something that's indigenous to the heart, which makes it, I suppose, hard to talk about. But I think that's its very point—it's something that we don't necessarily need to talk about too much other than to get a sense of the practice and the tonality that we're dealing with and then best leave it alone and just do it and see what happens, because too deep an understanding of the subject precludes the study itself. If we get too, too involved with its practicality, we'll get so caught up in the rhetoric of meditation that we'll miss the point, and the point was to go beyond rhetoric. So I think there's an in-between place, and that's what we try and seek. That's always the hardest, to be in the middle; it's easy to run to extremes at either end.

Meditation, for convenience sake, I think, can be divided into three sections—intermediate, advanced and of course beginning meditation. The principles involved in all three aspects of meditation are really not so different regardless of the stage of meditation. The chemistry is really the same in the sense that, I suppose, when we go to school, graduate school is essentially not so much different than first grade or high school or college. Each involves class experience, home study, things like that. While the level and intensity of the material may differ, still the experience is somewhat similar. So I really think that there's not all that much difference, at least in terms of approach.

Now, there are definite schools of meditation. In other words, there are people who say, "Well, there is a definitive way to meditate and this particular way or method is the best, ultimate, supremo, fantastico way." I don't think that's true. I think that there are many, many ways to meditate. Styles of meditation are like languages— Italian, French, German or English. I don't think one language is better than another; each has its own beauty. But the point of the language is not simply the study of the language itself, but to communicate. So with meditation, one shouldn't become so caught up in the fine points of styles that you miss the point, which was to become conscious of God and eternity and to be happy and aware.

Yet there are styles. And I think something can be learned from all of them. In the beginning when you're starting to meditate—the beginning being maybe from the first time to the first four or five years, I suppose it depends on the intensity of a person's practice—simply what we're trying to do is settle down and become aware of that which lies beyond thought. In the very beginning we're just trying to realize that there's some possibility of awareness on other levels.

Now, theoretically, everyone's inner being knows everything. There's a part of us that's aware of all things. But that doesn't necessarily do us a whole lot of good unless we are conscious of that. So meditation, then, is the process of becoming conscious of the part of ourselves that knows everything. Meditation is a bridge between the awareness that we have now and infinite awareness. The problem with the awareness that we have now is it's somewhat limited, in the sense that we're limited by desires, doubts, fears, frustrations, happiness, concepts of the nature of existence and ourselves.

The spectrum that most people exist in in this world, in terms of their awareness from the time of their birth until the time of their death, is not really very exciting. It's very mundane and very unhappy. Certainly human beings are capable of experiencing great joy and happiness. But they're also capable of experiencing quite the opposite. So meditation is the study of fields of attention, fields of awareness— not simply to relax a little bit and overcome stress and tension, but to become conscious of our own immortality, possibly in a religious sense, possibly not, it depends on the individual.

In the beginning what's necessary, of course, is to feel, if you're just starting the process, that there's something worthwhile to be attained because otherwise we won't do it. And this awareness comes to people in a lot of different ways. Very often it comes through meeting someone who meditates and you sense something from them that's appealing. They seem to be having a good time with their life, perhaps, they're more at ease or whatever it may be. There's just a subtle energy sometimes that comes from them. And we feel that and part of us is in consonance with that, we resonate. We're drawn to that, as opposed to most of the people we meet who are just so caught up in their lives that they don't understand their lives or even see their lives before they're gone. People who meditate, depending on their level of awareness and so on, seem to have a better time with their existence.

Some people are drawn to meditation without knowing why. Their inner being just demands it. They reach a certain point where it's not up to them anymore. Their inner being realizes that they've totally fouled up their life so far, and now it's just going to drag them to the local meditation hall and make them sit there. It's kind of like detention. After school, I remember, in high school sometimes you'd get detention because you were out walking around in the halls or doing things you weren't supposed to be doing when you were supposed to be sitting in class being bored. So sometimes you'd get detention and afterwards you'd just have to sit there and contemplate your life. I think for some people that's what meditation is. It works out happily. But they've kind of burned the candle at both ends, if not a little bit in the middle, and their being finally says, "OK, you've had your chance. I tried to tell you, I tried to warn you, now it doesn't matter, I'm taking over." So they find themselves approaching a meditation class or a teacher, reading books on the subject and it doesn't make much sense, it doesn't necessarily fit in with the person they've been thus far, which is exactly the point. It's time to become a new person because this one has exhausted their resources or just reached the point where it's gotten ridiculous to continue.

I don't really think it matters why you start to meditate, the point is that you do. Then suddenly one is barraged with ways, means and methods. When I started to meditate about 15 years ago, there wasn't a whole lot of information about meditation in the West. You could walk into the local bookstore and maybe there were four, five or six books on the subject and that was about it. Today to walk into a New Age bookstore, there are hundreds and hundreds of books, and I wouldn't know where to start. It was easier back then. All there was— there was Alan Watts, there was Paramahansa Yogananda, and that was about it. And Suzuki. That was it.

So we meditate to become conscious, and in the beginning it's simply a question of realizing that if we meditate we'll change, our awareness will change, and we'll become happier and just more aware of the moments of our lives—and isn't that the purpose of life itself, to be aware? To be awareness, eventually. So we then are faced with how to meditate.

Tonight I'm not going to really go into how to meditate per se, in terms of explanation of techniques, I've already done that on tapes and books and places like that. I think we can use your time in a more valuable way, in a more experiential way. Simply, when a person is learning to meditate, essentially what they're trying to do in the beginning is to settle down and for fifteen minutes or half an hour or forty-five minutes, to sit and try and still their mind. This is usually done through a focus, initially, of some type. The idea being that if you just sit there, thoughts will cascade through your mind and you won't have much success. So for the beginning student, it's best to have a focus, and the focus allows them to at least, even if they can't stop thought in the beginning, to direct thought and then once one has mastered directing thought, it's easier to stop thought and move into other levels of attention.

Initially the student in some traditions is given a mantra, a particular word of power to focus on; while the thoughts are cascading through your mind during meditation, you should be absorbed in the repetition of a mantra. In other styles of meditation they use yantras, which are visual mantras, I suppose you might say. They're specific designs that have a great deal of power in them, as do the mantras, which are words of power. These are designs of power that tap into other levels of attention. They remind us of things in other worlds. So we set the little yantra up in front of us on a meditation table, on a little table, and we sit there and we focus on it. And instead of being fully absorbed in our thoughts, we focus on the yantra or we repeat the mantra or sometimes a combination of both. You might repeat a mantra for a while, then focus on a yantra. Then a time should come when you do neither.

After a while in your practice, in an individual meditation session, you might start by chanting a mantra maybe a dozen times, then focus on a yantra for ten minutes or so, or fifteen minutes, then close the eyes and do neither, because to continue to focus on the mantra or the yantra throughout the period of meditation will hold us down to a very specific format. We won't go beyond it. While it's an important way to start a meditation and to develop our ability to meditate, ultimately at least half of the meditation, and one day all of it, will be spent in silence trying to stop thought or go beyond thought.

Now, there are schools of thought, if I can underline that word, that suggest that the way to meditate is not to tamper with your thinking processes, but just to allow your thoughts to go hither and yon, wherever they will, and that what you should do is simply be detached from your thoughts. I think this is a fine way to start meditating, but advanced meditation definitely involves the cessation of all thought. No thought, no image, no picture in the mind whatsoever. I personally have found that people have more success with a focal point.

The other method is a little more sophisticated and doesn't work that well for most people—just letting your thoughts run all over the place. What I suggest normally is that a person should focus on a yantra. I think mantras are more difficult to hold onto. People who do a lot of mantra repetition, I find, don't meditate very well. Because what happens is, as they're meditating and they're repeating the mantra over and over and over, after a while the mantra doesn't mean anything. That is to say, they just get lost in their thoughts and the mantra is going on somewhere in the background, you see. You've got it going and it's going in your mind or you're saying it out loud, but at the same time it's sort of like walking and chewing bubblegum at the same time. You can be repeating the mantra and at the same time completely absorbed in all the different thoughts that are passing through you, and this, in my estimation, is not a higher level of meditation. Whereas I find that when you involve the visual senses, when you're focusing on a yantra, it's easier to curtail thought.

I think mantras have an important place in meditation, but the idea has become somewhat prevalent in the West, and in the East to some extent, that the simple repetition of a mantra will eventually cause enlightenment to take place, and that's usually not the case. The mantra is a very preliminary exercise for the student to begin to just grasp a sense of focus. Mantras also do have their advanced side. When they're used by persons who have reached very high levels of attention, they can open up doorways to other worlds. But for most people the repetition of those mantras would be useless in that you have to have a requisite amount of personal power to make them work.

So essentially, I prefer the yantra method. I've just seen after teaching meditation for quite a while, that people do better with it. I think it's a good idea to start a meditation session by repeating a mantra, perhaps "Aum," which is the most powerful of all mantras, or you may have been given a personal mantra or something like that. Then, after repeating the mantra perhaps a dozen times, nice and slowly, to start your meditation session, with the eyes closed, focus on a yantra.

There are a number of different yantras, and each one has its own subtle qualities. It creates a slightly different type of meditation. Then perhaps for ten or fifteen minutes, focus on the yantra, usually starting at the dot in the center of the yantra quite intensely for a minute or two and then looking at the whole yantra without focusing, more just a gentle gaze. You'll notice that the yantra, this visual design, will begin to appear to move. The lines will move and stuff like that. Do not become too absorbed in that, but just observe it and to try and ignore thought. That's introductory meditation—stage one—not to stop thought, necessarily, but simply to ignore it. And even though the radio is going on in the next room, not to be upset by it but rather to be focusing on the yantra, which divides your consciousness in a way. It doesn't necessarily stop the thought but it detaches us from it.

Normally we're so absorbed in our thoughts that every thought that comes through is a reality. That is our world. We have to just start to detach ourselves from thought a little bit and become aware that there are things beyond thought. But then after focusing on the yantra for a while, close your eyes and simply let go.

Now at this point, some people like to focus on a chakra. There are seven primary chakras and lots of other ones. The chakras are locations in the subtle physical body that have corresponding locations in the physical body that are energy centers. When you focus on a chakra, it's very easy to bring subtle physical energies into your consciousness. Some people focus on the crown chakra, the third eye, the throat chakra, the heart chakra, the navel chakra, and the chakra at the spleen or the very base of the spine. There are also chakras in the hands; you've seen me use those quite frequently when I meditate. I project the shakti, the kundalini, through the chakras in the hands to people I meditate with. There are chakras in the toes and all kinds of places, quite a few in the feet, actually.

Whether you focus on a chakra or not, once you've closed your eyes during the second half of your individual meditation session, that's up to you. But even if you're focusing on the chakra, you don't want to do that for the whole period of meditation—there should come a point where you let go. Now we're moving into a deeper stratum of meditation. The rest is just to get us to settle down, to get off the train of thought for a while, and now we want to look around, now that we're on the train. We've been so obsessed on this train ride that we've just seen a limited aspect of life, but now we want to finally get off the train and look around. That's meditation. It's just looking around, being observant...

Beginning meditation is a process of unhooking ourselves from thought, of being motivated to meditate, and naturally it's very exciting in the beginning because we see the tremendous jumps we make in awareness. We find we are happier, our mind is clearer, we're inspired, our creative talents flourish, an awful lot begins to happen in that first year or first four or five years of meditative practice if we stick with it, and particularly, of course, if you meditate with someone who's a powerful meditator and learn from them. Usually the ascension is more rapid.

The second phase of meditation is very different. It's hard to say when this takes place. It depends on the individual, but I would say around four or five years in of serious meditation, particularly with an advanced teacher. We could say that it begins when you can successfully stop thought for long periods of time. At this point you begin to move beyond the awareness of this world. Now, in the beginning, even when you start to meditate you'll begin to feel different sensations and feelings. You may see colored lights of different types; there'll be a lot of phenomena associated with the practice. For some people there's more, for some there's less. The phenomena are not necessarily a measurement of how well you're doing. You always know you're doing well if you sit and meditate every day, a couple of times a day—that's the sign. One learns not to judge one's level of progress or assess it. It's best to leave it alone and just do it, and you'll find you'll progress very nicely.

But when you can successfully stop thought for longer periods of time, you do move into other worlds. This can also happen in the very beginning if a person meditates with someone who's very advanced, on the verge of enlightenment or enlightened. Because when you meditate with an enlightened person, their field of attention is so strong that you get a free ride.

When I was in college years ago, when I was an undergraduate, I used to have a typical undergraduate car, at least typical at the time, this was back in the 1960s, and I had a Volkswagen, a little VW bug. This was before the advent of the Superbeetle, [it was] the old little one. And when I used to ride on the freeway with it, when you hit a hill it was a problem, to be honest. While it was a great little car in the straightaway, it would lose it on the hill. But I learned—I used to commute a long distance sometimes to school—that if you could get behind a very large truck, the truck had a slipstream and you could get behind it and you'd actually be pulled along a little bit by it. Now the trick, of course, was to be careful because the trucks tend to have very good brakes. You had to be a little bit wary; if he put on his brakes fast you would be in another world quickly if you weren't real attentive. So it involved a little risk, and also saved gas—but that wasn't such a problem back in those days.

So when you meditate with someone who meditates extremely well, it's kind of like entering into a slipstream or a jet stream. You move into a level of attention that you might not have been able to attain for years and years and years or lifetimes, which is the value of a teacher. It's possible to meditate with an advanced person and perhaps there'll be no thought for a half an hour, whereas on your own when you try it, you might be able to stop your thought for 20 or 30 seconds. And as you do that, the more you're able to do that, the faster you progress in your meditation. But it's also important to practice on your own and develop your own ability. Sometimes there are people who would only meditate with a teacher and they ride the teacher's energy and they don't really learn how to meditate. They learn how to ride the energy. It's important to have both, if both are available to you.

Intermediate meditation, then, begins when thought stops for longer periods of time and when thought stops, of course, the world goes away. Time goes away and space goes away. Yet there's still a sense of self as we're sitting there, and there's no thought—there's an awareness of self. It's not quite as manifest but there is a sense of being light. Let's say suddenly you dissolve and you become infinite light—there is this sense of being light even though the mind is not thinking it, one feels it, which indicates that one is still there, at least half of one is.

At this point the study changes and also the changes in one's personal life become accelerated. You begin to live in other levels of attention all the time whether you're at work or driving or running on the beach or whatever it is. You begin to be in a more meditative state all the time and you find that it fits rather well with everything that you do. Your work improves; your life improves. Everything gets better simply because you have the ability to be more focused, and at the same time you can stand back from things that used to drain your power and monopolize your attention. In other words, you begin to get more of a handle on life. You also become more sensitive, which is a double-edged sword in this world. But it's well worth it ultimately.

The second stage could last for the rest of one's life. One could never move beyond that—or [not] for many lifetimes. But eventually a time does come—or it could happen in a particular lifetime, perhaps the one that you're in—where you move into the third stage, which is the advanced practice, which is samadhi. Samadhi is a stateless state of awareness. There are different thoughts about how many levels of samadhi there are. Patanjali classifies a certain number; different people have their systems. As far as I'm concerned, there are really only two and the rest are so close together that it doesn't matter. One can differentiate, but I think that they're about the same.

There's salvakalpa and nirvikalpa samadhi. Salvakalpa samadhi would be absorption in eternity to the point where there's no real concept of self but there's still a karmic chain. Nirvikalpa samadhi is synonymous with nirvana, absorption in nirvana—different words to express the same thing in my opinion—and there, this world and all worlds and the concept of worlds and self and non-self and all these things go away completely. That's enlightenment. If a person sets out to practice meditation in this lifetime and they have a little bit of spiritual evolution behind them and they're quite dedicated, it really is not at all an impossible task to enter into salvakalpa samadhi in this particular lifetime, which is complete ecstasy, complete rapture, knowledge of God, of eternity, all the things that there are no words for.

Nirvikalpa samadhi is another matter. That's not something, I don't feel, that's really up to us. That happens at a certain time when our being has gone through countless changes and refinements, selves have come and gone and shuffled through existence. At that point we become—there are words for it, but I don't think they're really succinct—God realized, enlightened, liberated; all that words do is point in a directionless direction.

Those are really the stages of meditation. Naturally there's a lot more to it. There are thousands and thousands of aspects to the meditative practice. There are different pathways that one follows, be it Zen or tantra, karma yoga, jnana yoga, different ways that have been devised to do the same thing essentially for different types of people according to their temperament. Some people are more emotionally inclined, some more intellectually inclined, some are work-oriented, some are mystically oriented and they are interested in the study of power. There are many different ways to do the same thing. There are many different ways that we can climb the mountain .The result is the same, yet each has its own history, stories, language and culture. I don't feel one form is better than another. I myself teach nine different paths because I think that it's necessary, not so much to be a proponent of one, but to find the pathway that works well for each individual that they'll do best at. It's not a competitive situation in my estimation—at least it shouldn't be.

Meditation then comes down essentially to stopping thought, detaching oneself from thought and eventually even going beyond stopping thought and all such relative concepts. The result is freedom. Freedom not just in the sense of a happy or better life, but freedom in the sense that one is aware that you're not the body, you're not the mind, you're not even spirit, that you're eternity itself. You go beyond the process of rebirth, which doesn't mean that one doesn't take incarnation. But let's say that you are just no longer bound by anything except your love of eternity.

So it's a delightful process, definitely not for everyone. There are those who want to revolutionize the world with meditation, and I really don't think that that's necessary. I think the world is already revolutionized. All too much. It's a very quiet study. It's for people who are completely out of their mind, or if they're not, they want to be, and at the same time, in my estimation, it's something that does not have to take you away from your life. Unfortunately we've seen meditation insulted in a sense with the image of ritual. That you have to dress a certain way, act a certain way, follow a certain type of lifestyle, all that sort of thing. Very culty. And that, of course, has nothing to do with the practice whatsoever. Those are just pseudo forms that people added for their own reasons. The practice is a very pure study, and you can do with it as you will.

There are those who feel that meditation is unrealistic or takes them out of the world, and if that was your experience with meditation, you weren't meditating. If you meditate, you'll find it's easier to blend, easier to understand people because you can see in them, you become psychic, it's easier to do just about everything. Your mind becomes sharp and efficient, you become conscious. You lose your emotions eventually, over a period of time, that are destructive—jealousies, fears, angers, hate. Eventually all those things go away, you just never feel them. Your higher emotional tonal range opens up dramatically, your ability to love and give and care. To be concerned with the welfare of others becomes one's major occupation without any sense of self-importance that one is better because one meditates or leads a certain type of life.

Real meditation engenders humility and purity, always. Yet I don't really think it demands any kind of lifestyle. I think the best thing to do is to meditate and see what you do. Certainly, different teachers make different recommendations that will help a person with the practice. But ultimately you're the filter; the recommendations are only good if they make sense to you inside. You should never do what anyone says unless it touches your heart and you know it's true, no matter how charismatic or powerful they may be. What they say may be true, but if it doesn't have application for you, it's not necessarily something you should try to do.

A lot of people have this live or die attitude with meditation. It has to be all or nothing. I don't think it should be. It's a study that you follow for the rest of your life. It's something that you get better at, and it adds meaning and color to being and eventually to non-being and beyond both. But I don't think it has to be this overwrought emotional business that people make it into. I think all they do is sidestep the actual issues, which are leading a disciplined, clear, happy life and becoming aware of others and seeing what you can do for them, in whatever way that you choose.

At the same time it's necessary to respect, I feel, all other ways and other teachings on the subject because even though they may not make a lot of sense to us, they might to someone else, and it may be exactly the thing that that person needs at this stage of their development. Who are we to say?

But ultimately, I think cosmopolitan spirituality is the best, where we go beyond, "My teacher's better than yours," or "My meditation form is better than yours," or whatever it may be, and we see that that's not the purpose of the entire thing. It's not Ford versus Chevy exactly. But it's rather the transition of our limited awareness into eternity. Just to be able to smile sometimes when things aren't going well, and maybe realize when they aren't going well, they are. There's a lot to the study.

When we silence the mind in meditation, when there's no thought, no image, no pictures, no memories, no desires, no sense of a self that is in any way participating in an experiential ongoing life, we reach a plateau of awareness that is beyond creation, transformation and destruction. It's beyond birth and death. That awareness is within all things. It is all things.

— *Insights:* Tibetan Yoga and Secret Doctrines

Insights: Talks on the Nature of Existence
THE NON-DOING OF MEDITATION
1983

I don't think anyone knows why they meditate. As a matter of fact I'm not even sure that we do meditate. All we know is that we don't know. That's all that we can be absolutely certain of. Meditation is not a doing. It just is.

We think of meditation as something that we have to do, something that we have to accomplish—to do, to accomplish, to be. This is emblazoned on our consciousness by our lives. That's why I think essentially people have difficulty with meditation. They try and do it. You can't. It's not something that can be done, nor is it something that can be undone. You can't even say that meditation is or is not.

If there were no world, no time, no space, no condition, if none of us existed, that would be meditation. Pure and simple. To say that we have to meditate implies that we have to accomplish or do something, that by following a planned series of actions we will reach a destination point. We like to think that all we have to do is know how to implement that knowledge and voila! We've done it.

That's not meditation. Meditation has nothing to do with building a building, taking a journey, not even setting ourselves on fire. Meditation always has been, is now and always will be. Meditation is dreamless sleep.

I think it would be a good idea, as you're setting your sails for the land of meditation, to consider wisely, o nobly born, before you venture forth into the bardo of experience, what it is that you're trying to do. Not so much why, because I think the why eludes us all. We may come up with reasons as to why we meditate, why we live, why we die. But ultimately those reasons will not effect what occurs. Those are just panaceas, things that perhaps make us feel better, inspire us. They're neither good nor bad, it depends on their usage.

Think of meditation as a summer night. The crickets are chirping, life is going on, with or without us, within or without us. Life is going on, on the stage of life in front of our eyes and senses. In the house next door that we may not be aware of, life is going on—in countries other than our own, in worlds other than ours, distant galaxies. Life exists in the sub-atomic regions, in the quasars. Life is all there is. That's meditation.

Beyond this plane, this plateau we stand on that we call life, there are infinite planes and plateaus. Beyond the physical, there's a subtle physical, astral worlds extending forever. All of this is intertwined in the web of nirvana, the unspeakable, that which exists without existing, sustains creation without holding it, transmutes creation without involvement or attachment—the mystery, the riddle.

How is it possible that we are all eternal and yet so ignorant, so forgetful of truth, while we are the truth itself? They call that maya—forgetting truth, or perhaps seeing a lesser truth instead of a greater truth.

We sit here on the shore of existence watching the boats go back and forth. Sometimes there's a vast ocean liner out on the horizon. It approaches us, perhaps it comes right to where we are. We watch the people get off. They embrace each other. People meet them. Whole lives pass before our eyes, emotional whirlwinds, the people who work on the boat. Then the boat leaves, the people go away. The ocean is the same.

Where do these images come from and to where do they return? All answers are only found in the superconscious, and the superconscious doesn't really house answers. It takes us to a point where we don't ask questions anymore because that part of us which would ask or which would inquire goes away, is quietly absorbed in eternity.

Meditation is not a journey. It's not an arrival. It's not an action. Meditation is just awareness. You don't have to do anything to meditate. That's what makes it so difficult. Everybody wants to do something. You're so used to doing or to undoing that the thought of non-doing is baffling. And that's what you're asked to do when you meditate. To just sit. That's all—that's all physically. To become aware.

Well, first our awareness is in our thoughts. We're sitting down to meditate and the thoughts are chasing each other around—thoughts of past experiences, thoughts of ourself, of others, of the world around us. Desires, something that we want. Aversion, something we want to get away from. Personal history. Remembrance of the self: I am so and so. I am a person, I have a history, I define myself by that history. I am the sum total of my experiences. This is what the personal self thinks.

Meditation has nothing to do with that, the personal self, that is. Meditation is timeless awareness. You don't have to do anything to make it happen. You don't have to rub two sticks together vigorously to create fire. The fire is already burning inside. To become aware of that which is, you simply have to stop. Stop all the doings that you do, all the actions you perform, all the rituals, the nine to five rituals. Living in front of the make-up mirror—applying a little rouge to one cheek, a little lipstick, working on our eyebrows, combing out our hair, all the doings, the creations. Preparing ourselves to go on stage, to act, to perform.

There is a place for action and there is a place for inaction and there is a place for timelessness—which is everyplace and no place. It's not necessary to become anything to become enlightened. You don't have to build up to some marvelous pinnacle. You don't have to fulfill someone's expectations of what you should do or be. It really doesn't matter what type of work you do. It doesn't really matter where you live or even why—to meditate that is—because everything is meditation.

Meditation is the cessation of thought. No thought, no mind. No mind, no body. No body, no time. No time, no life or death. It's simply letting go. For people who try to hold on to life, who try and push away from death, it's very difficult. The formula approach was quite popular for a while, fostered by certain groups. They decided that the way to introduce meditation to people in the West was to tell them what to do, to give them a schematic drawing. If you do this and this and this, you'll be meditating. Chant the mantra, say the right words, sit for a specific period of time—this doesn't have anything to do with meditation. It's a doing. It may get you used to sitting down; it may focus your attention in a new way. It may prepare you for meditation, but it's certainly not meditation.

Meditation just is. You don't have to do anything. You don't even have to undo anything. Meditation exists with you constantly. The universe is meditation. That awareness is everywhere, just as the air is everywhere.

You don't have to go to the air; you're breathing it already. You may be unaware that you're breathing; your attention is elsewhere. Well, of course, your attention is on things other than the air. But you can easily become aware of the air. So you can easily meditate. Now, when you've been conditioned all of your life to do things, to accomplish things or to avoid things, it's difficult just to breathe. Of course, it's not just breathing, this meditation, because it's endless. Life is endless. Eternity is endless. The universe is endless.

To meditate, then, we need not do anything. We need simply be. But for a mind that is habituated to thought, to action, that's enslaved to ways of seeing, this meditation will not come naturally. No, rather it's necessary in such a case to do remedial work, to uncondition ourselves. Therefore, we learn gazing. We practice focusing our attention on something other than our usual doings. This is another type of doing. But as Sri Ramakrishna always used to say, you take one thorn to remove the other thorn, then you throw both away. So we use one doing to remove another doing, and then we let go of both.

We practice methods and forms. You've all been living one way. You're so fixated in living in one way, whatever the way may be, that we present other ways for you to live. Each way that we present is less demanding than the previous way. You have one self, one personality. In self-discovery we dissolve that self and we go to another personality that's not as structured, that's freer, more evolved. Then we dissolve that self, and we have a thinner self and a thinner self, until finally the self is so thin that it barely exists.

We use doing to undo what's been done. But each doing must be more universal and less finite. Then one can get attached to doing also, even the higher doing. One can get attached to practice. But first, one must practice. After practicing, if you get attached to practice it will be easier to undo that doing because it's more universal.

The self is a perpetual mystery. Why do we think? Why do we feel? Why are we here? Only because we think that we are. Well, who is it that thinks these thoughts? Where do they come from? Why is life the way it is? It isn't. You only think that it is.

There is no one listening. There are no thoughts in meditation. Meditation is white noise. We know that we can listen to individual sounds, but if we blend all the sounds together, all the tones, it's called white noise. No distinct sounds—all of them at once. Meditation is listening to all of existence, not listening as a doing, but in the sense that one arrives at a point of departure that one had left sometime before without knowing that one has arrived. Or one goes forward to a point of return, not realizing that one has gone forward.

The doings of meditation, those formless forms that we use to go beyond our arrival, which is yet to occur in some future existence, are many. Love, discipline, shock, awareness, self-giving, joy and exuberance, dance, pain—anything can be used as a doing to undo what's been done. Each one of us will find, if we don't look too hard, exactly the right way to meditate. If we look too hard, we'll overlook that which is in front of us.

To meditate, you need to feel, and feeling is a lost art. You need to feel the stillness of existence and also the sound of existence. You need to feel that which lies beyond your awareness field, and that which is within it. Essentially one day you'll see that they're not particularly different. But first we have to extend ourselves. Because within the pattern of our experience and our doings we haven't found the air that we breathe.

Meditation is perfect peace. Well, what else could there be without a self but perfect peace? It's only the self, the personality, the sense of individuality that causes turbulence. When you're sitting in deep meditation and there's no thought, no image of the world, no idea, no sense of self—you're not doing something, you're not even experiencing something because there's no self. How can there be upset? How can there be torment? How can there be pain or frustration? To say that you've gone above it all implies that someone has arrived. But all of these things were only a dream—all the doings. These are the ways we prop ourselves up in the universe and support ourselves. We give life a shape and meaning, which it does not necessarily have. We create it with our thoughts, our feelings, our memories, descriptions of the world, frameworks that are meant to help us go through life. But unfortunately they bind us. They limit us. The creation takes over the creator.

Those of you who seek to meditate, you must be aware of a strange duality. That duality is that you have to try very hard; you have to do. There are many things to be done. You have to deal with your lifestyle, your diet, your habits, your thoughts, your feelings, your memories—but only for a while. Only so that you can become still, which is not something that you will do. It just is. It's always been and it will always be.

One day you will arrive at a station on the train of existence that you've always known has been there. You'll find yourself there with no train in sight, with no sense of arrival. You will have always been there because in fact you always have been there. There was no journey. There was only a perpetual arrival, a timeless condition of infinite awareness. To say that you realized the self is absurd. Who realizes what? What is there to realize? These are useful terms, at some point.

So on the one hand, we have a hand, on the other hand there's no hand at all. Until that point at which there is no point, there is a point; to say that there is not is absurd. And to try and implement a point or a way when the way has become wayless is equally absurd. So know that one day you will go beyond duality. You will find that you're at the station.

We say that everyone is self-realized, everyone is enlightened. But we know, obviously, that we're not; we can look at the condition of people in the world. By that we mean that in another theater, the one down the street, not the one we're in tonight, everyone is enlightened. We're all sitting there enlightened. But here, perhaps not. That's existence. Different theaters of the imagination, of life, of death. To become conscious of that universality, to be in the finite awareness of the moment and to experience, and yet at the same time to not be as we know being and doing and structure, is nirvana.

When you meditate, know that one day you will arrive. But you didn't go anyplace to arrive. We can say that you're always there, but not yet, it wouldn't be true. Because you're not there yet. But once you've arrived, you will have always been there. In other words, the self that exists now, that you're living with and sharing your moments with, will not be for all time. Rather, you will find that there's something else. And once that something else is, there has never been anything else. There is no other possible condition. I would suggest to you that at this moment you are the only self that you have ever had, that you've never had a childhood, that there wasn't a five-minute-ago time.

You may say, "Well, I remember."

I'll say, "Well, show it to me. Does it really exist?"

"Well," you say, "here's the scar I got when I was a little kid. It's on my hand here. Now that proves— "

So I'd say, "Well, it proves that you've got a scar on your hand. That's all it proves. It doesn't prove that it came from anywhere."

You say, "But I have photographs. Here, I'll show you. This is me when I was a little girl. This is me when I was graduating from high school."

I'll say, "Interesting pictures, who's that?"

And you'll say, "Well, it's me!"

I'll say, "Who? Well, you don't look like that, you're right in front of me. Obviously, it's someone else. Listen, I don't know what you're trying to pull here, but you're not going to fool me. I know I've got the genuine item in front of me. Interesting person, though. I admit there is a slight facial resemblance, but this is obviously you. You're trying to tell me that you're here and you're someplace else at the same time? It sounds interestingly metaphysical, but I don't believe it for a second. No, you're here now, that's all we know."

Then you might say, "A moment has gone by, and now I'm here, and of course we were both there a moment ago, so there is a past, and what I am now is an outgrowth of that past, you see?"

And I'll say, "What? What past? What moment ago? What are you talking about? This is all there's ever been."

"History books," you'll say, "look at the history books."

I'll say, "Yes, they all exist right now. I see them. Here they are. Wonderful histories. We can read them. As we read them, history will exist—for that moment in our imagination. Where else can it exist?"

You'll say, "Look at this tree. Now, let's cut the tree down. It's got fifty rings. That means it's fifty years old."

I'll say, "Well, it has fifty rings now, of course it has, how could it be any other way? It's always been this way. It couldn't be any other way. Not now."

There is no future and there is no past. There never has been. There never will be, you just think there is. It's not life that moves, it's awareness. Imagine a number of stage sets. They're all set up. You go and run into one. You run into another—adolescence. You run into another—maturity. You run into another—old age. You run behind the curtain—death. Now, you think it's all changing. You probably think the earth is round. How do you know? Have you been on the other side? Once you were on the other side, was there this side? These are ridiculous questions. But they are to bring you to a point, and that's to undo your doing. In other words, the framework you've set up to view time, space, experience, and so on, is just a framework. It's arbitrary. It's like writing a computer program. We're going to create a program, and it'll be an interesting way to process information. But then to suggest that the universe must conform to the patterns of the program, when it is the program that has come forth from the universe, is ridiculous. But that's what everyone does.

Meditation then, is simple awareness. But simple awareness is eternity. It's endless, but it's not in time. Meditation is not in time. It doesn't take place here because in meditation "this" isn't here—the "this" that you are familiar with. The program dissolves. The information floods away, and it's impossible to say what there is or what there isn't. White noise. Completion.

Why do we meditate? Doesn't it seem rather self-destructive to try and take [away] everything we've worked so hard for, this awareness that we've amassed, this knowledge, this sense of self that we've gradually put together over the years as a bulwark against that awful vastness out there, that incomprehensible infinity? Why would we want to do that? It's because the comprehensible, the understandable, the awareness that we have now in this world is only a dream. It may be a nice dream, but it's just one of many. And then there's dreamless sleep—nirvana.

The dream that we live in is very limited. There is not much happiness in it. Travel the world and try to find someone who's always happy; it's very difficult to find one because everything in this world is transitory. Everything changes. A moment ago I said everything always is. Now I say it changes. There's no difference. There's only difference in the mind. Meditation is no difference. Change is one state of being, it's one idea. Permanence is another. But they're both just ideas. They're little equations that we've written on a blackboard, but that's all they are, just little chalk lines.

What is existence itself? Meditate and find out. When you meditate you are free. Meditation is perfect freedom. In the beginning when we start to meditate, we think that meditation means mastering our environment. Putting our life into a certain order, saying the mantram, and everything will be all right. That has nothing to do with it.

But we need to think that in the beginning, and we need to do those things. But eventually you'll find out that all of the battles, the Napoleonic wars of existence, occur within yourself. You don't have to conquer the world, you don't have to change or transform anyone else. The mat is inside yourself. Your opponent is circling you; you're circling each other on the mat of existence. And each one of you is looking for a grip. Who throws whom? What's the difference?

We fight the self with the self. It's ridiculous. I watch spiritual seekers do it all the time. We try and throw ourselves to the mat. It's like this marvelous Monty Python skit I saw, where this fellow comes out to a boxing match and he's going to fight with himself. They introduce him as the challenger and the defending champion. He bows for both. Then the commentator, one of the Monty Python fellows, comes on and he says, "All right, now, Joe throws a right to his face," and the guy hits himself. "A crushing blow to the chest," and he hits himself in the chest, and this goes on, and he fights himself for about ten minutes. Finally he wins and loses. And that's what I watch spiritual seekers do. That's what self-discovery seems to mean to most people. You're going to beat yourself up. You're going to reduce what you're supposed to be and do to a set of rules so you can defy them, or so you can perform them and feel smug. Either way you're beating yourself up. You're missing meditation, which had nothing to do with any of that

Yet I have the nerve to say that all your battles are within and that you have to fight, even though I know that you can't possibly win and you can't possibly lose. It seems pointless and I agree that it is, but I know that until you've done it for a long time you won't be convinced. After you've beaten yourself up a few times and you've won, you'll begin to see things my way. My way is the easy way, is the way of enlightenment. Complete self-sacrifice. There can be nothing less.

You have to give everything to eternity. As Krishna tells us in the *Bhagavad-Gita,* offer everything, whether you win or lose or draw, to God, to eternity; give everything. Don't worry about whether you should be fighting with yourself or not. You don't really have much choice at this point. The point is not whether you're winning or losing, or in the heat of battle or licking your wounds. The point is to realize that you have to give it all away. That's a doing that is a lesser doing than the doing of ownership, of selfhood—it's the doing of self-sacrifice, the sense that there's something higher and purer and immortal, and that you can give your entire being to that which is high, pure and immortal. True, that's an objectification, but it's a lesser doing. It's less harmful to you than the others. It's part of the way out.

Again, there is no way out. Yet one day you will find that you've always been at the station, and you didn't need a train to get there even though you were on a train trying to get there. When you meditate, it's important to remember not to think. I would venture that most of you spend the majority of your meditation in thought. You think about how well you're going to meditate, next time you meditate. You get wonderful ideas and inspirations for projects and plans. You think about extraneous things, but rarely do you stop thought.

I would suggest that the reason you don't stop thought is because you're trying too hard. In other words, you have made the stoppage of thought into a doing. You feel that it's something that you have to accomplish. I will tell you that no one has the power to stop thought. It's like the Colorado River, it just flows. And you're out there on your raft, and sometimes the flow's smooth, and sometimes it's white water, but it just flows on and on and on. That's why they say in Zen, "The bridge is flowing but the river is not."

Don't try and stop thought. Or try, if you want to fight yourself to the mat, like my Monty Python friend. Ride the river, and then at some point watch yourself bring the boat ashore and get off and go for a walk and disappear. Then you'll find yourself someplace else. The self that you find someplace else will be a different self because the same self never returns, not if you meditate, if you stop thought. This self can never be again. The dream fades, but another dream comes, a higher dream, a happier dream, a more evolved self.

In meditation we return to the source. The source is God. God is Godless. God is an idea that we have, another construct, a prop, which doesn't suggest that God doesn't exist—God is existence. But your idea of God and existence are two different things at the moment.

So when you meditate, observe. Observe the emotions that pass through you. Observe the thoughts. Observe when they stop. When the observer goes away, you will have arrived at the station, and you'll see that you have always been there. Then suddenly you'll be on the train again, and you'll say, "Well, my God, how can I be on the train again? I was just sitting in luminous perfection. My thoughts stopped, the world went away, time stopped, self stopped, and here I am again. How did it happen? I thought it would last forever." It was forever.

Be neither attracted nor repulsed to all these images that you see flowing through you and around you. This is the bardo. When you find yourself at the station without the train there—that's nice. When you're not—then you're in the world. You're in time and space again. However, you will notice something, which is that after a while you'll be in both. There'll be an awareness of being and nonbeing simultaneously.

In the beginning, we go up and down. We meditate, we're down in the world; we meditate, we're down in the world. There's a seesaw. But after a while we move to the fulcrum in the middle, and while we're in the world, we're not of it. This is enlightenment, or some stage of it—the sense that I'm walking around, I'm at work, I'm with my friends, but I'm not here at all. I'm in another plane, another world.

Now, all planes and worlds are transitory. None of them last. But there's nothing wrong with that. Sometimes the nicest things don't last. That's why they're nice; we value them. That's what makes beauty, the transitory. Beauty is just value, a value we assign because it doesn't last, because it's different. Segmentation. There's a personal self that appreciates beauty.

Those who scorn and hate the world and hate themselves miss the point. The point was that there wasn't one. There was no place to go to. All there was was this. This was everything; it was perfect. That's how you should feel about meditation. Don't worry about whether anything comes forth from it. Don't be concerned if you don't seem to be making progress. These are just ideas.

Life is a wonderful mystery. You sit and meditate, and it's beautiful. It's beautiful when you're meditating, it's beautiful when you struggle. When you go away, we can't say anything. Then if you find yourself or another self, what's the difference? It's all light. It's all life. And death is not the end. Because you die when you meditate and you see that it's not the end. You go away and you come back. But is it you who comes back?

Who are you? You are eternity. You're God—in shifting patterns of awareness, in shifting fields of attention, and in nirvana, silence—beyond comprehension, beyond knowing. Beauty beyond description. Perfection. It awaits everyone. Silence.

You don't have to be special to realize God. The point is, people who realize God aren't special. They don't think they're special because that sense of being special is what separates you. That's the ego. But you have to fight yourself, for a time. It's a stage in growth, one backdrop you walk behind for a moment. It isn't really even taking place, it's just a dream. But dreams have their reality too, you know. So watch each stage, and don't be concerned. If you succeed, if you're the hero, if you're the villain, if you fail—don't be concerned.

Meditate. Just meditate. Meditate when you're by yourself, when you sit in formal meditation and fight with yourself to still your thoughts. Meditate when they stop by themselves. Meditate when you're in the office, with friends, when you're in love, when you're out of love, when you're in a crowd, when you're alone. By meditate, I mean be conscious of that which is eternal, eternity in the finite and beyond—within your framework and description and that which you experience. Try and reach out and feel that which is beyond your framework. Then you will know the mystery of existence, which is incarnation, being here without being here.

Self-realization is not a state of being, although all states of being are contained within it. Self-realization is like the thin air. Only you have become the thin air. There is no sense of form. There's no sense of being a person. When you close your eyes and meditate, there's no sense that you are meditating. All there is is the thin air. It's like going down to the beach on a windy day, and there's no one there. It's too windy and cold. All the bathers have gone away. We walk down to the beach, we sit out looking at that ocean and we decide to meditate, so we fold our legs, a half-lotus position or a lotus cross-legged position, we sit up straight, we close our eyes. And at first we have a sense that, "I'm sitting here on the beach meditating. I can hear the wind. I can hear the seagulls when they cry as they go by, whirling in the wind. I can hear the sound of the water slapping against the shore not far away. I'm here alone on this beach, in the wind." Then, something happens. The sense of being there on the beach goes away. The wind is still there, but no one is there to listen to it. So instead of hearing it as a separate wind, as separate from anything else, we don't perceive that. We see that it never was separate. There never was a beach. We were never sitting on it. The sea gulls were never or always were flying. Nothing is distinct and separate... There is no movement in Nirvana. There is no sameness, and one does not consider it to be timeless because one is not one. It is you, my friend, who go away. What we discover is that it was not the waves, or the birds, or the wind that were standing out and being separate from existence. It was we who were standing out and being separate from existence.

— *Lakshmi Series:* Liberation and Self-Realization

Lakshmi Series:
INTRODUCTORY AND INTERMEDIATE MEDITATION
1982

Meditation is the art of life. All of life is meditation. Meditation is not simply a practice. It is an experience, an awareness, a way of perceiving and also a way of life. All of life, from the personal point of view, is dependent upon our perception. When we can perceive life as it really is, then no emotional cloud or discordant melody from the world can distract us from our own original, perfect being. If we trace life back to its source, we find perfection.

Life itself, in essence, is light and consciousness. Beyond this world and other worlds, beyond time and space and dimension, beyond what we call duality, is God. God is not a person. God does not have a history. God does not have a future. God is beyond definition. We can say that your perception of this world is God. We can say that this world is God, that perception, this world, and you who are having the perception are all part of God. As a matter of fact, there's nothing that isn't God.

When we think of God, normally we have an apprehension of a celestial being. We think of a big person who lives in heaven. God is not particularly personal. God is existence. Try to redefine the word through your experiences in meditation. Let us just say that there is an all powerful force or energy that creates all, sustains all and draws all back into it again. This is God. It is beyond intelligence, beyond analysis.

Now, in meditation what we do is something original. We experience God. That is to say, we experience that essence of existence from which we have come forth, which sustains us and to which we will eventually return. From the point of view of meditation, there is nothing that is not God. So when we meditate, we are participating in a spiritual experience. We are seeing that life is not perhaps as we thought, but a little bit different—vastly different.

The results of meditation vary. It depends upon many, many different things. Have you meditated in your past lives? How hard are you trying to meditate? How long have you been meditating in this life, or are you just starting? How old are you? In what condition is your psyche? What kind of influences do you have around you? What are the people like that you associate with—your family, friends, acquaintances, people you work with or study with? All of these people have fields of energy and through your association with them, you touch those energy fields and they enter into you, as does your energy field touch and affect everyone in your life.

All of these things affect us. Our past affects us, our present affects us, even our future can affect us. We live in a relative world of time and space. We're born and we die. The space in-between we call life. The space on the other side of life we call death. We've developed a very complex filing system for existence. We see things in terms of good or bad. We feel happiness, joy, pain, loss, guilt, remorse. And very few people are happy in this world. Most are miserable. Even in their so-called happiness, they're unhappy because compared to what real happiness can be, the transitory happiness that most human beings experience is ephemeral; it does not last and it's so short of complete ecstasy, of God consciousness, of true being, that it's almost pitiful.

You as a human being are capable of so much more than you realize. You are capable of being consciously eternal. You are not a body or a mind or a group of perceptions. You're not a history or a future, or even a present. If you can look beyond the physical and the mental, you'll see that that essence which we call God, that perfect reality that is within all things and sustains and nurtures all things and transforms all things, that essence is you.

At the moment you're suffering from what we call maya. Maya is illusion. Maya is a Sanskrit word that suggests that we have forgotten. We're suffering from temporary amnesia. We've forgotten the purpose of life, how to live life. We've forgotten what we are. You could be the son or the daughter of a very, very rich person, a great king, but if you were wandering in a strange land and you had amnesia, you might think yourself an impoverished beggar. If, one day, you were able to remember that you were the daughter or son of a king and if you were able to return to your land, your poverty would fall away. You would be reinstated to your rightful place. So in life, most of us have forgotten. We've forgotten what our rightful place is. Our rightful place is to merge our awareness with the perfect being of existence. Anything short of that is frustration.

We live in a world of wars and war's alarms, of famines, of oppression. While there are many wonderful people in this world, you'll notice one curious fact about the—they all suffer, they all die, and sometimes those who are the nicest seem to suffer the most. There is an end to suffering. There is a way beyond limitation. The way is meditation. When you meditate, you take charge of your life. You bring your conscious awareness to a new high point, where the vista, the view, is beyond any horizon. To do this you're going to have to go through a lot of changes. We're discussing, in other words, the fact that you are going to become perfect. Perfect awareness. There's a definite way to do this. There is a training program that you will go through, and it's delightful. It's absolutely beautiful.

When you meditate, you feel joy, harmony, peace, stillness, ecstasy, laughter, certainty, courage, strength, awareness and immortality. In the beginning you will feel these things vaguely, a distant knocking at your castle door. But then, as time goes on, they will no longer be vague but strong and certain. In the beginning you will only feel these emotions during meditation. But as time goes on you will feel these emotions and have these perceptions constantly.

We're going to alter the structure of our beings together. We are going to not only modify but also totally change what we are. This is the possibility and inevitability that meditation offers us. The practice of meditation is an ancient practice. It's been practiced in many lands, for many lifetimes. You may have practiced it before. But I feel it is best in the beginning to not worry too much about the past or the future, or even the present—to approach the study for the first time. You should always feel, each time you sit down to meditate, no matter how many times you've meditated before, that this is your first meditation. You have no idea what will happen or what won't happen. Only by meditating will you find out...

The wind of existence is blowing all around you. All you have to do is listen to hear it. The truths of eternity are ready to be revealed to you, truths that will free you from unhappiness, that will bring joy and beauty into your life, and completion. But you have to listen to them. The truths of eternity speak very, very softly and can only be heard when your mind becomes calm and quiet and still. Meditation is a practice of detaching and then stopping ourselves from thinking; our thoughts are interruptions in the flow of awareness. Think of a lake without any ripples. Now a lot of rocks are thrown into it, and there are waves and ripples everywhere. So consciousness, in its highest aspect, awareness, is perfect and formless. But thought and perception create lots of waves and waveforms in awareness itself.

What you will be doing in meditation is learning to stop thought. This is done in a number of stages. The first stage is simply to ignore thought, to become conscious as you're sitting there meditating that there is something beyond thought. To feel yourself as being separate, in other words, to sit and think and perceive that you are not your thoughts, that you are rather the person who is listening to the thoughts.

Your thoughts are like birds. Birds come into the sky and we see them. Then they fly by and they're gone. But the sky, which is the element through which they travel, remains the same. The sky was there before the birds came; it was there while they passed through and while they left.

We want to know what our self is. We are the sky. Our thoughts are the birds that come and go. You can enjoy the birds and their beauty, but it is the sky that endures, that lasts. If the birds squawk and make too much noise, we can't hear the stillness of the sky, the sound of the wind. If the birds are angry and attack us, we have a terrible problem.

So, we're learning for a while to perceive existence in separate phases. One phase is to see that we are not our thoughts. As you sit with your eyes closed in meditation, try and feel what is beyond thought and sense that you're separate from thought.

Then, the second stage, after you've become somewhat accomplished, after meditating for several months, is to begin to eliminate negative thoughts. You've learned to practice detachment—now you can pay no attention to your thoughts, even though they whirl by. But now you want to actually change thought. In meditation, when you have happy thoughts, creative thoughts, thoughts of good things you can do or be or become, let them come. But when you have unhappy thoughts, frustrating thoughts, anger, fears, jealousies, things like that, just don't let those thoughts inside you. The angry birds are flying around your house—you're simply going to close the door and not let those critters in. If a beautiful, happy bird comes, then you can let the bird inside and play with it. But you must practice discrimination.

Discrimination means keeping the negative and unhappy thoughts away and allowing the pretty thoughts to come inside you. Then a day comes when we don't worry about whether the birds are nice or ferocious. We leave the house behind. We go up into the sky ourselves, like the birds. We fly among them and then we fly beyond them, into space and into eternity. We leave them all behind. So eventually in meditation, you'll learn to go beyond thought. You'll leave the body and mind and this world behind. You'll go beyond time, space, and all relative conditions and you'll fly through eternity, perfectly free. You'll merge with God, that basic awareness of existence—total joy, total happiness and total completion.

How the heck do you keep those nasty birds away? Well, consider it this way, as "a" way. There are many. One of the things that you can do is practice meditating on the heart chakra. There are many, many ways to meditate. This is only one of them, but it's one of my favorites and it's quite good for the first few years of your meditative practice.

We have a body, but we also have a subtle body, a body of energy that looks like our physical body, if you could see it. The subtle physical body, which is approximately the same size as our physical body, is made up of energy, of light, a light that vibrates at a very, very high rate so that the human physical eyes can't see it. When you develop your psychic vision after some meditation, you will be able to see the subtle physical of others, or perhaps of yourself. At first you'll see it as an aura, a light that seems to appear around someone. But eventually you can see the whole subtle physical.

Just as your physical body is composed of tissue, organs, bones and different parts, so your subtle physical body has many different parts. There are seven primary centers, junctions, within the subtle physical body. They run from the base of the spine to the crown of the head. These are called the seven chakras. When you meditate and focus your attention on any one of the chakras, it will open a doorway into a specific world, another dimensional plane. Each chakra leads to a different floor in the building.

For the first few years, it's most beneficial to meditate on the heart chakra. The heart chakra, called the anahata chakra in Sanskrit, is located in the center of the chest, dead center. It's not in the exact location of the physical heart but rather more to the center. If you focus your attention on the center of your chest while you're meditating for the first few minutes, you'll feel a warm and tingling sensation. The heart chakra takes you into the plane of beauty, humility, purity and love. As you focus your attention on this area, you'll begin to feel your thoughts slowing down. You'll begin to feel your mind becoming calm and quiet. And even if there are lots of birds flying around, even if you have lots of thoughts, they'll become distant. They won't bother you. You'll hear the birds flying above you, screaming and cawing in the distance; you'll be down at the beach, sitting and meditating, but they won't affect you. You'll go so deep within yourself that you won't even notice them.

While you're meditating, after you've focused on the yantra, focus your attention on the center of the chest and gently begin to meditate. Pay no attention to your thoughts, let the birds come and go. Don't try and stop them, if you're a beginner, but rather just focus your awareness on the center of the chest. Relax, sit up straight and let go. Meditation is letting go. Not letting go to your thoughts—they're in the distance—but letting go to something deep within you, releasing your deeper self, which will actually meditate for you.

Focus your awareness on the heart chakra. As you do, you'll feel your consciousness shifting. You may feel different perceptions of energy in different parts of your body. Pay no attention to them. Let

196

them come and go, like our friends the thought birds. Just keep focusing on the center of the chest, not too hard, not too aggressively, but gently.

As you begin to meditate, as you sit there and the thoughts become quieter, you'll begin to become conscious. Don't think about it, those are just more birds you're inviting in to scree and caw and create more problems for you. If you do start to think about your experiences while meditating, don't become upset. Again, just ignore thought. Sit there very passively but happily, feeling. Meditation is feeling. You're trying to feel what lies beyond the doorway of existence. You may not be able to see it or touch it yet, but with your heart, with your love, you can feel it.

As you sit there and meditate on the heart center, feel love, feel joy. You can actually create these emotions in many, many different ways. Just meditating on the heart center, focusing your attention in the area of the center of the chest will help this process. But now you have to help yourself to your higher emotions. Consciously begin to feel love. Start by feeling love for a friend, or an experience, anything that you like—love for God, love for yourself—and let that love circulate. Let that emotion pass through you. Focus on it for a while. Then you'll find your thoughts will become quieter. You can let go of that emotion. You can even stop focusing on the center of the chest once the meditation begins to go.

You're in the river. If you're in the current of the river, you don't have to do a thing. The current of the river will take you where you want to go. But if you're on the banks of the river, there's no movement, no motion. Focusing on the heart center, feeling love, thinking beautiful thoughts gets you into the river. Then, as you meditate, you'll find that consciousness itself will move you beyond time and space and condition into a larger, vaster, more beautiful state of awareness. Once you enter into that state of awareness, you'll start to know things. Knowledge will come to you of this life and that which is beyond this life. This knowledge comes from God. You're accessing eternity. You're plugging yourself into that source which is all light and all beauty and all perfection.

But as you meander down the river of consciousness, at times you'll get stuck on the bank. You'll find that you're thinking a lot of thoughts, the birds are becoming annoying again; they're screeing and cawing and you've forgotten that you should be meditating. You're so busy thinking about what you're going to do tomorrow or what you did yesterday, or you'll be worrying that you don't have enough money to pay your bills or that someone doesn't love you or just something's not right, that you'll become upset and you'll stop meditating. Everyone does this again and again. Don't be disturbed by this. But thinking about the things of this world is not going to help you. The world is always in a state of transition, and thinking about it isn't going to solve any problems. Instead, forgetting about everything for a while and looking at something that is perfect will help you deal with the world better.

You need to regain your perspective on life. You're down in the valley and the valley is filled with smog. You can't see too well. But if you go up on top of a very high mountain, you have a point of view, you have a vision, you can see. Then when you go back into the valley, you can remember that vision and it will help you. So when we meditate, we're going beyond the smog to the top of the mountain, to a point of clarity. Clarity is stillness. You need to stop all those thoughts. All the birds must become silent eventually. As you meditate more and more deeply, this will happen automatically, by itself.

After you've meditated for 15 or 20 minutes or half an hour, an hour, whatever the time limit you've set for yourself, at the end of the meditation, chant Aum again. Repeat the mantra seven times, or as many times as you like. Chanting a mantra at the beginning of your meditation helps you to clear the mind and takes you deep within the self. Chanting the mantra at the end of meditation helps you seal the meditation. It helps you bring the awareness of the meditation down into your daily life.

After meditation, it's important to offer the meditation to eternity. It's a good idea to bow and offer your meditation to God, to that stillness and perfection that is existence, and just feel that you're giving your meditation away. Then sit quietly, for just a minute or two. Very often you won't be aware of how good a meditation you did and how much benefit you've received from it until several minutes after the meditation. While you're meditating it seems that you're working away and not much is happening sometimes. You don't realize how high you've gone until afterwards. But there's a period of time right after your meditation session in which you have to be a little bit careful. If you start to think a lot of thoughts and become very active, you can prevent some of the meditative awareness that you have worked so hard to receive from coming into your mind.

So for a few minutes, sit quietly. Or if you need to do something, do so, but remain meditative. If it's the morning and you've just finished your morning meditation, then take a couple of minutes to just walk around the house, do a few dishes, organize things, but keep the mind quiet. Stay in a happy state. You might like to read a meditation book or a spiritual book of some type. Something written by myself or Ramakrishna, something about Buddha, something about Christ, about Yogananda, about any spiritual teacher or written by them—something that will elevate you. If you give yourself a few minutes, you'll find that you'll absorb the meditation. Then suddenly the mind becomes clear. The world is shiny and luminous; you're seeing correctly.

It's a good idea to avoid eating for an hour or two before you meditate. If you try and meditate on a full stomach, you'll find that it's difficult to meditate because you're just too heavy. You feel your body too much. Try to wear clean, comfortable clothing, and always be physically clean before you meditate. Try to take a shower or a bath. If you can't, if it's an evening meditation and you don't have time, at least wash your hands and face. You need to bring a sense of purity and cleanliness to your meditative practice.

There are some other things you can do during meditation to help facilitate the practice. There are many methods or ways of meditating. Now we're moving more from basic meditation, which I've just described, to more of an intermediate meditation level.

In intermediate meditation you have a number of choices. At this point you should be used to meditating twice a day. In the morning, before you start your day, this is your most important meditation. The morning meditation clears the mind. While you may be a little bit sleepy after you've just gotten up, the mind is not yet filled with impressions. After you've started your day and you've been out in the world, it's harder to meditate. When you first wake up, all the birds are quiet and they've been sleeping. They're not too active yet and they may make a few sounds. But once they've been up for a while, they're chirping away and active, and it's harder to quiet them down. So in the beginning of the day, meditate.

It doesn't really matter what time you get up, but whenever you do get up, set aside enough time before you have to leave the house to have a good meditation, and then remain for a few minutes and just enjoy the feelings afterwards. Doing this will clear your mind and put you into a very sharp and aware state of consciousness so that you'll do a good job and have a good day. Then, around the end of the day when you come home, you'll be tired and you will have picked up a lot of different energies from the world. It's a good time to relax for a while, and before dinner have another meditation.

Sunset is a good time. At sunset a doorway between the worlds opens up. It's a very powerful and easy time to meditate. You may meditate again for another half an hour. Clear the day away and return to a very beautiful and clear state of awareness. As you meditate day after day, twice a day or three times, if you like, you'll find that the awareness of meditation will begin to creep into your daily life. You'll be sitting at the office or talking with a friend, exercising, going to the movies or having some type of experience, but you'll notice that you're high, your mind is clear, you're at peace with yourself. You're feeling joy for no apparent reason, simply because joy is and you are.

But now it's time, now that you've gotten this practice a little bit together, to start to work on refining your meditative level. To do this you need to intensify the practice. Try some of the following methods. When you're meditating, after you've started to meditate and you've meditated on the yantra or a candle flame, instead of meditating on the heart center, now instead, simply try feeling gratitude. Sit and feel grateful to existence or to eternity or to life because you are, because your life is good, because you're meditating and if you're meditating, that means that your life is going to continue to become more beautiful, you'll become happier and clearer and more aware. Feel grateful for the people you love, for the beauty of the day or evening. If you can't feel grateful, if you're discouraged or depressed, then think of the fact that things could be a lot worse than they are, and you should be grateful that things are not worse because believe me, no matter how bad things may seem, they can always get a lot worse.

Just start gratitude. Create it. Gratitude is a bird that soars very, very high, and you can get on its back and fly with it, way above the clouds. Gratitude is a good method.

Try will power. When your thoughts come and you're trying to stop them, simply say "No." Learn the mantra, "No." N-O. Every time a thought comes in your mind, say "No." Just repeat the thought, "No." This is the method endorsed, in a sense, by Sri Ramakrishna, the great spiritual teacher from many years ago. He said that when you have a thorn stuck in your foot, you can take another thorn to help you get the first one out, and then throw both away.

In this case, as you sit there and you're trying to make your thoughts quiet, you're using one thought to negate another. Every time a thought comes, whether it's beautiful or not so beautiful, just think "No." Don't let it happen, push it away. Then once you've done that, push the thought of no thought away.

The inner cry is a very good way to meditate. As you're sitting there in meditation, just cry inwardly to God, to that source, to your spiritual teacher if you have one, to a particular god or goddess, a celestial being in a higher plane that you're drawn to. As you sit and meditate, reach with your whole being. Cry like a child, not with tears or unhappiness, but just reach. So, for example, if you were meditating with your whole being on Lakshmi, the goddess of light and beauty, you might repeat her name. You might, with your whole being, just say, "Lakshmi, Lakshmi, Lakshmi" silently inside yourself. If you do this with great intensity just for a few minutes, it will bring your heart out, and the power of your love will attract a higher reality to you.

Try the inner cry. Cry to God, cry to your spiritual teacher, if you have one. Cry to a favorite god or goddess or whatever you consider noble and divine. If you do that just for a couple of minutes with your whole being, just like a child who so badly wants a cookie is going to say, "Oh, Mom, pleeeease can I have a cookie? Pleeease?" The child wants that cookie more than anything else. If you feel that you want eternity and light more than anything else in your meditation—just for a few minutes, you don't have to go on and on—you'll break through the barrier of the mind. You'll go beyond it. Then just sit quietly and feel, and you'll see that light will enter your consciousness and fill your meditation.

These, then, are a few ways that you can progress a little further. Practice them at different times—the inner cry, when you reach with your whole being to eternity; willpower, when you're just saying, "No," when you reject thought; focusing, of course, on the heart chakra and feeling love and gratitude; detachment, simply ignoring thought and having nothing to do with it, not thinking of the thought or no thought.

Try to be creative in your meditation. Don't get hung up or stuck. Try meditating outside on a nice day. Meditate with your friends if you like. But try and have at least your morning meditation to yourself. Don't meditate with anyone else. Because when you meditate with others, there will be lots of different energies around, and you're trying to center in on the stillness of existence. You have enough birds flying through your own mental sky creating a disturbance without picking up those of others.

There are many different mantras that you can use when you meditate. I have several favorites. I like Aum, of course, which is the most powerful of all mantras, but I also like Lakshmi's mantra. Lakshmi is a celestial being who lives in a higher plane of existence, another world. Her mantra is "Sring." S-R-I-N-G. When you chant it, it brings beauty and light into your consciousness. Someday you might try starting your meditation with Sring instead of Aum. Chant Sring as follows— (Rama demonstrates chanting Sring.) Try chanting Sring for five minutes and see what happens. You'll find that your whole consciousness will fill with light.

Another time you might try Kali's mantra. Kali, of course, is another celestial being. She offers very fast spiritual progress through intensity. Her mantra is "Kring." K-R-I-N-G. When you chant Kring, chant it very intensely and sharply. (Rama demonstrates chanting Kring.) When you chant Kring, you'll feel power entering your being.

Only chant Kring, though, when you're in a high meditation. While you can chant Aum and Sring and most other mantras at the beginning of your meditation, or any time you like, Kring will only really work when you're already in a meditative state. So you would chant Kring towards the end of your meditation a few times very intensely and then sit and meditate for a few more minutes.

These are a few different mantras that you can use. Experiment. See how they feel.

An advanced way to meditate, of course, is to focus on your teacher. If you have a spiritual teacher and you focus on them during meditation, then you access the light that flows through them. For example, I am a liberated teacher. After many lifetimes of meditation, I've reached a point where I can no longer be separated from meditation. I'm always in the state of meditation, or you could say I am meditation itself.

A person who meditates with me, even though they may be thousands of miles away, focuses their attention on me. If they think of me, if they chant my name a few times or just in some way focus on me, then they'll connect inwardly, psychically, with me. Well, "me" is light, to be honest with you. That's about all there is inside me anymore. When you focus on me that light will be drawn into you. You're not taking anything away from me. It's not my light to begin with, in a sense; it's the light of God and the light of eternity. So take all you want. This is how real spiritual teaching takes place.

You can focus on myself or on any spiritual teacher. Spiritual teachers who have left the body, who are no longer on earth can help you too. I'm on earth now, but I won't always be here. When I leave the body someday, I can help people just as effectively if they focus upon me.

You can focus on Jesus or Buddha or Krishna, Ramakrishna, Lao Tsu, Yukteswar, Yogananda, Vivekenanda, any of the great spiritual teachers who have lived, or on a living teacher, and draw light from them, energy from them. This is a more advanced way. You see, what we really have to teach you in meditation can't be expressed in words. This is a tape to help you get started. But to be honest, deeper meditation can only be learned from a teacher.

When I sit with my students and meditate with them, I channel the kundalini, the energy, directly into them. I bring them to plane after plane of consciousness. What they would do in 100 years of meditation, I can do in an hour with them. This is how meditation is learned in its advanced stages. But regardless of whether you're working with a teacher or not, everyone must meditate each day on their own and do their daily meditations.

As you do your daily meditations, your life will change. A new power and energy will enter your life. Most people change between age zero and four. Then around age four or five the personality begins to become structured and our growth slows down. The older we get, the less we change. When we meditate we become perpetually young. We make the personality structure more pliant.

Each time you meditate you hold the possibility of completely changing your life in one meditation. If you meditate with your whole heart and your whole soul, with your whole being, you will become light itself. You will not only see and feel God, existence, eternity, Nirvana, samadhi, but you will become quite happy, very humble and pure, and yet you'll deal with the world very effectively. Your mind will become razor sharp. Your memory and retention will be superb. New talents and abilities will develop. Your artistic nature will begin to unfold. In other words, you'll start to grow again. You'll become younger each day yet wiser. You'll develop a good sense of humor so that you can laugh at yourself, which you need to do in this world. You'll be able to look at both the beauties and the horrors of life and accept them with an equal mind. You'll love more and be kinder to those around you.

Meditation is existence. When we meditate, all we're simply doing is letting go and allowing ourselves to dissolve back into that which we really are. Our amnesia is fading away and we're consciously becoming the source again. We're merging with life and light. When you meditate deeply, you'll see beyond life and death. You'll see that you can't die and you can't be reborn. You are existence itself.

Learn to meditate, practice and don't get frustrated. It will take you years to learn to meditate perfectly but every time you try, you're growing. It's not as if you have to learn to meditate perfectly to make progress. Even your first, most basic attempt will bring you something. In the beginning your experiences may be sporadic. Nothing will seem to be happening. It is! But you must be patient.

Try to find a teacher of meditation and meditate at least once a week in a group with people who meditate a little better than you do. It's good to meditate in a group every week. It will inspire you to keep meditating and if you have a teacher, even if the teacher isn't really advanced but even just a little more advanced than you, then you'll grow and develop and learn. Also, meditation is sharing. You learn to share your experiences with others. As you develop more and more, you'll learn a new language that other people who meditate speak.

It's important not to move while you meditate. Sometimes when you're sitting there meditating you may find yourself swaying. As the prana current and the kundalini and different energies begin to move through you, you'll feel yourself moving and rocking. Keep the body still at all times, otherwise that energy will be lost as it expresses itself through the physical. Whereas if you keep very, very still you'll find that that energy will just take you higher in meditation.

Never expect anything from a particular meditation. Don't try and meditate a certain way. Once you've gotten started, once you've chanted the mantra a few times and practiced concentration on the yantra or a candle flame and meditated maybe for a few minutes on your heart center, or tried gratitude or willpower, all these different methods just to get you into the stream, then just let go and let the meditation take you wherever it would like to. Be free in your awareness and free in your love. Relax and let it happen. Remember you have lots of help. God is meditating in you and through you. The beneficent forces of existence are glad to help you. You can focus on me or any spiritual teacher. We're glad to help you. You've got lots of help. All you need.

Try to read books about meditation, but not so many that they get confusing. You know, there are so many different viewpoints and ways to meditate that you can begin to wonder which is best. There is no best way. It's just what works for you at the time. Ultimately you won't use any techniques. One day you'll stop using the yantras and the mantras. You'll just be able to sit and instantly stop thought. As soon as you do, the curtain of reality parts and you are lost in the immortal rapture of existence. You will see perfection in everything. You will see that there is no time, there is no space. All there is is light. Death is no threat. Life is no threat. All there is is perpetual joy, perpetual existence, perpetual oneness with the source. You'll see this not only in your meditation but also in your work, your service to others, your lifestyle, your play and everything that you do.

Don't try to be someone. Be yourself. This is what meditation should teach you. Oh, you'll learn the great truths of eternity and infinity. You'll learn to be perfect. You'll overcome your jealousies and your depressions and your fears. But don't try and force it. These things will happen gradually, on their own.

Just meditate each day in the morning and the evening and maybe for a few minutes at noon—that's a nice time. Whenever you like. Be free and be open, and trust. Trust that life is guiding you and showing you every step that is necessary to learn to be perfect. Have faith in yourself. You'll come through OK. Have faith in existence. Try to find a spiritual teacher who can teach you the more advanced things. Practice what I've told you every day and your life will be beautiful. You will see beauty in all things. You'll learn to accept the transitory nature of existence of the body and the mind happily because you'll see eternity in everything—both in this world, in the other worlds and beyond the worlds, in the void and nirvana. Meditate with feeling and with love and then take your realizations from meditation and give them to others.

Don't preach about meditation, but as you change and grow, as you love more, as you become kinder and more sensitive, help people. Help the world in any way that you want to. Do something with all that good energy and you'll find, as I have found, that the more light you give and spread, the more you share, the more you will evolve, the closer to God you will be, until one day you'll be like I am, you can't tell yourself from God. There is no difference anymore. You become existence. You've merged with the source. You've gone back. Yet you'll still be a person with eternity expressing itself through you as a person, or in its absolute form, you will be dissolved into the ecstasy of nirvana. You'll go back and forth as long as you're in this world and then some day, of course, you'll go beyond this and all other worlds.

So good luck, do well. You will.

Meditation clears the way and makes the way possible. Selfless giving is the practice that burns away the layers of the onion. Meditation makes selfless giving possible. Purity and humility keep meditation and selfless giving clear. Love radiates through the entire practice because we do all of it only for love.

— *Lakshmi Series:* Tantric Mysticism

Lakshmi Series:
ADVANCED MEDITATION
1982

There is no end and there is no beginning. There is only eternity. Eternity can be warm, assuming the shapes we love, the petals of the beautiful flowers of existence. Eternity can be cold and ruthless— the solar systems and worlds which begin and end, the winter of our death and then the spring of our rebirth. As human beings, we try to understand, in the brief span that we're given here in this world, why we're here, what we should do while we're here and where we'll go from here. And, of course, we wonder how much time we have.

At first glance, we appear to be people. The world appears to be physical and solid. There appear to be universes, stars, planets, our planet, seasons, different species of animals, plants, protozoa, bacteria— the visible universe. There are many universes, countless universes, and many of them are invisible. As you know, we call these the astral planes, but they are as real as this world is and they're filled with beings and forms that have life spans, as do the beings and forms in this world. They too wonder about the nature of existence, where they've come from and where they're going to and how much time they have.

Meditation is wondering. It is both wondering and wonder at the same time. When we meditate we quiet the mind and open ourselves to our limitless possibilities. As a human being you are capable of a higher level of perception than you may now be cognizant of. You are not really who you think you are. There are many selves inside you, not just one. In introductory and intermediate meditation we seek to know ourselves. We get a sense of the countless selves within ourself, the different forms that they take. We become acquainted with them. We find that some selves agree with us, some don't. Those that don't seem positive or helpful we push aside. Those that seem progressive we enjoy.

Meditation means the cessation of thought. For years we practice meditation, like any art, and we get better at it each day. In the beginning it's just enough for us to sit down and focus our attention for twenty minutes or twenty-five minutes, to chant a mantra for a minute or two to start, practice a couple of gazing exercises, concentrate, and to try and still the mind as best we can—and if we can't stop our thoughts, to ignore our thoughts and just let go and feel. Feel beyond our thoughts.

Our thoughts will swim around and talk to us while we're sitting there, make fun of us, ignore us. We'll think about everything that one can think about. But if you pay no attention, if you don't look in the direction of your thoughts, you meditate. Your consciousness expands. You are no longer focusing on the thoughts, but now you're increasing the spectrum of your focus. As you meditate, as a singular meditation evolves, you'll find the nature of your thoughts will change.

At the beginning of a meditation session your thoughts will be relatively earthbound; you'll think about yourself, your world, problems, difficulties and anxieties. Then as the meditation evolves, your attention, as it passes into higher realms of consciousness, will cause a resulting change in your thought patterns. Your thoughts will become more pleasant, more creative. You'll think about positive things you can do, good feelings will start to flood your being, feelings of hope, joy. You'll have visual experiences—you may see flashing lights, hear bells, feel energy changes inside your body, have a sense of being weightless, as if you're floating, and feel altogether pleasant.

Sometimes you won't feel pleasant during a meditation session. Sometimes it just seems like it's an uphill run. But then when you get to the top, the view is rather beautiful and breathtaking. So you should learn not to judge your meditation. Just meditate, do your best, set a minimum period of time and meditate. When that period of time is past, stop meditating. If you're inspired to keep going, keep going by all means, but don't meditate less than a specific time. If you're a beginner, it's good to meditate for twenty minutes or a half an hour twice a day. If you're more advanced, 45 minutes to an hour, two or three times a day.

It's really not necessary to formally meditate longer than that. Naturally if you're going to a meditation session with your teacher, as my students do with me, we may meet for three or four hours. During that period of time, some will meditate, doing the defined meditation session when I formally meditate. Others will meditate the entire time that I'm there. Others will meditate even before I arrive. It depends on their level of attention.

So we have longer meditations, we have spontaneous meditations. After you've been meditating for a while, you'll just be sitting in a room, your living room, talking to a friend at a restaurant, working, and suddenly you'll feel yourself enter into a meditative state. You'll find that it will always come at the right time; it will never interfere with your work or with anything that you have to do on the physical plane. Sometimes these meditations occur because our soul is reaching to the infinite, even though our mind is not conscious of it. Sometimes they come because a being, a spiritual teacher, or something or someone else is reaching out to us and filling us with something, giving us an inner present.

For most people this is meditation. Getting up in the morning and as soon as you get up or whenever you get up, meditating and never leaving the house until you've meditated. Your mind is most receptive at this time, even though it may seem more difficult to meditate because you're a little sleepy. Still, the mind is quiet, you haven't been thinking, so you'll find it easy to meditate. Meditate then for half an hour or an hour. Then, don't think about your meditation. Go out into the world, do your best all day, try to think higher thoughts, try to be kind and compassionate, but don't let people take advantage of you. Then at noon, try and meditate again for a few minutes.

I always meditate every day at noon, the time when the kundalini is the strongest. If you have to work at noon, at least try and think about eternity, think about your ideals, what you're trying to do with your life. Feel the pulse beat of the universe. It's very strong then. Try to meditate at sunset or in the early evening. It's very easy to meditate at sunset; there's a feeling of peace and there's a transcendental awareness from about 4:00 in the afternoon on. It's a very high energy time, from about 4:00 until about 8:00 or 9:00. Try to meditate then, before you start your evening. If you've been out in the world or working, that meditation will clear off all the energy you've picked up during the day, the unhealthy energy, and it will balance you and progress you.

Some people like to meditate for a few minutes before they go to bed. You won't really gain quite as much from this meditation because you'll be sleepy, you won't absorb as much. But you can gain something.

One who practices basic or intermediate meditation is learning to still their thoughts; trying to get on a regular schedule with meditation, which may take a while; getting used to meditating a couple of times a day and never missing; learning what the different basic experiences are like; and of course, dealing with the resulting changes that occur in your life from your forays into the infinite.

As you meditate and you move from the introductory phase to the intermediate phase, your life will begin to tighten up, you'll change again and again. You'll become smoother, more collected and crazier, in a positive sense. You'll begin to be yourself. There'll be an ease to your being, a deeper joy to your life. You'll see your own eternality. You'll remember a little bit more of who and what you are. And you may never go beyond this point in this life, if you just can meditate regularly.

Try to meditate with a group, hopefully with an advanced teacher, once a week or so if your lifestyle permits that or by yourself. Just reach to God, and you'll feel God and you'll feel eternity. Light will come into your being and you'll have a remarkably beautiful life. The world won't necessarily change but your understanding of it will, and therefore the world will change. A tree won't appear to be a tree anymore, a person a person, an experience an experience, because you'll see level upon level within it and beyond it. Your attention will no longer be confined to the physical body and the physical world.

If you never go further than that, then you've advanced to a very nice, safe place. And when death comes, it won't frighten you. And when life comes, it won't frighten you or excite you. You'll care more for those around you and you'll be able to do more for them, because as your own awareness advances, everyone who comes into your field of energy is positively influenced. This is as far as most people get.

Then, of course, there's graduate school. Graduate school is advanced meditation. Advanced meditation assumes certain things. It assumes that one has meditated for many years, five, ten, fifteen years, and learned to meditate well. You can meditate for an hour, stop your thoughts completely at some point in the meditation, even if it takes you half an hour or forty minutes, and enter into a timeless state of existence. You've worked out the basics in your life. You become a very nice person.

You can't really go into advanced states of meditation if you're holding a lot of baggage in your hands. You're too heavy. So over the period of years that you've been meditating and studying and practicing, you've let go of your attachments. You can live in the world and have friends and family and possessions if you like. But you don't take them all too seriously because you know that death removes everything. And you feel that death is every moment, as life is every moment. You enjoy, but you don't fixate. If it all goes away tomorrow, that's OK, you trust God implicitly. The universe will always do what's right for you. You have this feeling.

Emotional storms may pass through your being, upsets; the sea of life is not always smooth. But these things don't affect the deeper you. You have a link, you've established contact with your deeper self. You no longer envy others. If someone gets the larger piece of cake, you're happy for them. They'll get fat and you'll stay thin. You feel a comradeship, a kinship with life, a deep love of nature and existence. Like the whales that we see here off the California coast this time of year in February and March, it's just enough sometimes to play. As I'm speaking to you now, I'm looking out a window and there's a whale playing in the surf about 150 yards out beyond the beach. Every once in a while it surfaces and it just plays in the waves and goes back under.

So the self plays among the waves of existence. It surfaces, it comes up for a while, and then it disappears again. We are that self, playing in the waves of existence as my friend the whale is—I've just spotted it again, breaking through. So in deeper meditation, then, we're no longer concerned so much with putting our life into order. We live in a spotlessly clean house, our papers are in order, there's no extra accumulation in our closets. In other words, you lead a totally tight life. Your relationships are as good as they can be, you don't feel the need to possess anyone or be possessed by them. You've learned to love, to share, to be fair and to be humble. Your only real concern in life is either being absorbed in eternity or working for the welfare of others. And there's still time to have plenty of fun. You're very busy, reflective and the thousand voices of existence speak through you. This is the preparation.

Anyone who really practices advanced meditation has spent quite a bit of time, of course, doing karma yoga. You have to work for others. Usually such a person will live in a spiritual community where they have the opportunity to give to others, as the personal family doesn't mean as much to us. The personal family is a fixation. Not for you, perhaps, but for people who are advanced meditators. You can enjoy your family and your friends and your career, and that's fine. There's nothing wrong with that.

A person who practices advanced meditation has gone a step further. It's like joining an order of spiritual aspirants. The family, career, money, the things that most people strive for don't mean that much to you. You may have them, you may not. But usually such people don't have families anymore. They're usually not married, some are. They usually don't have children, some do. But the chances are, if they've become an advanced meditator, they will not marry or have children because it demands too much time. This isn't selfish, it's just that God is directing them in another way. If they become an advanced meditator after they've had children or married, they may choose to leave their family, feeling that it was a nice stage that they went through and now eternity's pulling them in another direction. They know that God will take care of their family as God would if they died—which they have, because in advanced meditation we die and another self is born.

Or, they may choose to stay with their families and see that it is the dharma for them to be with their children, with the person that they married, and that they can practice selfless giving right there. It's a wonderful opportunity to raise their children without trying to make them into anything special. They're not trying to make them into spiritual aspirants, but just let them be and give them what they need to love and be kind.

But, you see, when you enter into the world of advanced meditation, you no longer fixate on an individual. It is not your husband or your wife or your child or your parent that matters anymore. I realize this may be hard for either you to accept or for the child or the parent or the husband or wife to accept, but if they truly love you, they'll understand.

I was raised in the Roman Catholic Church, and it was understood that if you became a priest or a nun, your family would understand that. You'd chosen another way of life. You weren't expected to marry or have children. You wouldn't see your family too much because you'd given your life over to God. That was understood. Well, people who practice advanced meditation have done that. It wasn't a hard choice to make. No one forced them into it. As they progressed spiritually, those things just didn't matter. It's easy.

Now, you shouldn't be afraid that if you meditate, you will suddenly feel that way. Meditation will give you a clear mind and a solid purpose and a wonderful life. As I said before, most people won't go beyond that. It's only by your personal choice, something in you will elect to go to a higher level of power and knowledge, and then you'll choose a different way of life and it will be fun for you. You won't miss anything. You don't even have to force yourself to give anything up.

Such a person can live in the world on their own, which is unusual, or they join a spiritual community. Spiritual communities come in two packages basically. One package is the ashram where everyone lives in the same building or on the same grounds, like a monastery or convent. You get up in the morning, early in the morning, usually, and you meditate, and then you may work in the community, helping to sustain it, or outside of it. You go to work all day and you come back in the evening, and there may be a group meditation or private meditations. You get together with your friends and spend time. It's a big family; it's like a kibbutz. The single-family unit is nonexistent because you just feel that it's selfish for you to devote your life to one person. You don't just love the one—you do love the one but you love the many also. Your politics have changed. You've become a larger being. If everyone felt this way there would be no wars, no hatred, because you don't have to rush to defend anything because you love everything.

The other type of community, of course, is like the one we have here at Lakshmi, and that's where we have a spiritual community but everyone lives where they want to. Many of the people in the center live in the same area. I recommend certain areas to live because of their power, and most of us live near each other and we see each other at the supermarket, or whatever. People get together and go to the movies or on hikes or meditate together, but everyone maintains their own independent domicile. Some students live alone. Some share places with each other. And in that way, not only now but as they grow older, there's no loneliness. There's no loneliness because when you meditate well, you feel eternity. How could you ever be lonely? You just feel God's love for you and that sustains you. It's totally clear; it's part of every aspect of your being.

Of course, whenever you want to do something at night you just call up one of your friends and get together, or a group of them have dinner together, whatever. There's so much love between people, there's just not a sense of absence. That's what a spiritual community is for. You join it, it feels right, it's a group of advanced souls who have had many, many lifetimes, many incarnations, in which they practice spirituality, who now work together and play together and enjoy their lives in a very different, but very fulfilling way.

Meditation is a way of being, and it assumes so many shapes and forms. But there is a spirit that guides us, if we will listen. It speaks softly. In order to hear it we must still our thoughts and meditate.

Advanced meditation is the entrance into the superconscious. When you can successfully stop your thoughts for a period of time, you've started to move into advanced meditation. In advanced meditation we not only pass through other planes of consciousness or awareness but we become them.

There are primarily two levels of what we call samadhi. Samadhi is a Sanskrit word for the advanced states of meditation. There's salvakalpa and nirvikalpa samadhi. Some people say that there are a few other levels of samadhi, which are beneath salvakalpa samadhi. But from my point of view, it's sufficient to say that there are two.

Salvakalpa samadhi is a rare experience for most people who meditate. It not only means stopping all thought, but the awareness of this world vanishes totally. Unless you've had many high births, unless you've practiced self-discovery for many lifetimes, it's unlikely you'll experience salvakalpa samadhi in this lifetime, unless you have tremendous intensity, unless you just burn and ache for God, for eternity, for absorption, or unless you study with someone who is enlightened.

If you study with a fully enlightened teacher, a liberated one, then that person is samadhi. They are just a being of light and when you meditate with them, particularly in person, they have the power to give samadhi. That is to say, when they meditate with you, if you meditate well, they can actually bring you into some of the lower levels of samadhi at will. But they will only do that, of course, if you've developed yourself sufficiently so you can retain that light.

You have to be somewhat formable. You can't be too rigid anymore. If you've done your homework and meditated for a number of years, then they can transmit samadhi to you. You can experience it on your own, but you have to meditate very, very intensely with complete willpower and purpose for long periods of time. That's why most people go to a teacher.

I am a multilevel teacher. I teach introductory, intermediate and advanced meditation. And of course, I run a spiritual community called Lakshmi, named after the Indian goddess of beauty, purity and prosperity, which opens its arms to people who are beginners, people who are on the intermediate level and advanced seekers.

My specialty is advanced seekers. I've had many, many lifetimes as a teacher, but what I really have to offer are the fine points that a person needs in advanced meditation. While I enjoy teaching people on the basic and intermediate levels to work them up to those levels, my real talent, again, is for the advanced students. You could say I'm like a ninth-degree black belt in martial arts. While I can still teach a beginner's class or an intermediate class, my real skill is not even teaching the first-degree black belt, let alone the lower belts, but those who are in the fifth, sixth, seventh and eighth range. But I'm happy to do either, personally.

The way advanced meditation is taught, the way I teach it, the way all enlightened people teach it, is through transference. We transfer light and power to someone else. We teach someone how to hold that light, how to eliminate their attachments, the holes in their beings through which they lose light. We teach how to become selfless, pure and humble and just generally how to have a heck of a lot more fun with their lives. But the way we do it is all inwardly. We use the powers that we have developed in previous lifetimes, or in this lifetime, to bring a person through a series of altered states of consciousness, different planes of existence, very quickly, to expand their being, to dissolve their selves. It's a very, very complex, sophisticated process, which I really can't describe to you in words. It's something that you may have experienced if you've ever worked with someone who is enlightened. If you've sat with them and meditated with them, you have a sense of what I'm speaking of. Otherwise, these will just sound like words. You can do your best to imagine it, but it's nothing like it.

Advanced meditation is taught, then, in most cases, by a self-realized teacher, one who is liberated, enlightened—not through words but through transmission. That transmission does not have to take place physically, that is to say, the student doesn't have to be sitting across from you. But it's easier if they are because the vibration of the teacher is strongest in the physical proximity of the teacher. Once the student has spent some time with the teacher and learned the frequency, you might say, the student can be thousands of miles away and tune in and gain quite a bit. But it's still a good idea, whenever possible, to be in the physical presence of the enlightened teacher because it's not physical. You can hear the ocean from quite a ways away, but if you're standing right in front of it, it's easier. Then of course you can just jump in, like my friend the gray whale, who seems to have vanished from sight, which is not a bad thing for all of us to do—you can just be absorbed.

Advanced meditation has an awful lot to do with nothing. You become friends with nothing. First you experience salvakalpa samadhi. Salvakalpa samadhi means that there's no thought, no form. As you're meditating there's no idea of this world, time goes away, and as you sit there meditating, there's no sense that you're sitting there meditating. You become consciousness itself. But there's still a slight sense of self. There's still a vague feeling, "I'm eternity, I'm God, I'm all of existence." You become that. Your awareness has merged with the transcendental awareness and it is the sense, without having to think about it, without you as a perceiver or a person thinking about it, that you are the transcendental awareness. This is salvakalpa samadhi.

If you experience salvakalpa samadhi even for a few minutes, you'll never be the same because to enter into salvakalpa samadhi, the human self, the old self, has to die in a sense, or be reborn. You're composed of an aggregate of different forms and energies, and those energies are held into focus or line by your past life development, what we call the samskaras. These are lines within your being. When you enter into samadhi, these lines dissolve gradually so you become less formed. You're freed each time you enter into samadhi.

For years and years you enter into samadhi every day in order to attain liberation. For years and years you enter into samadhi every day and each time you enter into samadhi for five minutes or five hours, whatever it may be, it's as if your inner being, your substance, has melted down in the core of eternity. And eternity fashions a new self, which you find yourself with when you come out of samadhi. But you never quite come out. Each time you come out a little less, you might say, or your real self comes out a little more. There are different ways to talk about it. None of them will be exactly what it's like, except to say it's an experience of such absolute beauty, radiance and completion, such life, such depth, such joy, such indifference and such love, that nothing else is really like it or worthwhile in comparison, yet it gives shape, color and meaning to everything. In other words, there's nothing you should be afraid of. It's not going to take away your humanity. It will give it to you. But you will become more cosmopolitan, more conscious, more infinite.

Nirvikalpa samadhi, of course, is the pearl in the oyster. Nirvikalpa samadhi—there's nothing we can say about it. I use the term "nirvana" interchangeably with it, meaning that you've gone off the board, you've gone off the map, there's no way to describe it. You've attained liberation, you no longer are bound by the cycle of existence. You can't be born and you can't die anymore. You just are, and yet you're not at the same time. There are all these paradoxical ways of discussing it, suggesting that it's beyond discussion, though it happens to some of us. It happened to me and to not me. You just become eternity.

When you're absorbed in nirvana, there's not even a sense of self as eternity. There's no way to describe it. Then you're liberated. Liberated while living, what they call a jivan mukta. And when death comes you won't be reborn, unless, of course, you're reborn, in which case you won't be reborn as other people are. You'll be reborn as a liberated being. While a number of years will go by after you've been reborn—if that's what happens, if you choose to be reborn to come back to help others—a number of years will pass and you may look like everyone else. But then one day you'll be drawn to the light, you'll meditate, you'll study for many years and then your liberation will return without you having to try a whole lot, in a way. It comes back. You dissolve again. It was never really gone; it was just dormant. It was sleeping for a while. But then your old personality comes back, all the selves from before and then liberation, of course, that which is beyond.

There's not really a whole lot you could say about liberation. The closest experience you can have of it is to come meditate with someone who is liberated. Many people claim to be liberated. Oh God, if we were to believe everybody who said they were liberated and self-realized, I mean, it's an endless list. According to "moi," as Ms. Piggy would say, there are currently on this earth 12 beings who are self-realized. Eleven are men, one is a woman. Most of them are in the Far East, most of them you've never heard of and probably never will. They work with a very small group of advanced students. A couple don't even have students. They have friends, I suppose, but they just meditate a lot.

Liberated souls are a rare commodity in this world. They're no better—it's just you, a little later, in the next act or in the next play. But if you yourself seek to learn advanced meditation, that's really how it's done. You devote your life to such a person, you have to, but they will never ask it. A real liberated teacher never asks for a commitment from a student. They realize that that's absurd. How can you ask for a commitment? That's looking at it the wrong way. There's no commitment—a person wants to be there and they want to learn everything they can.

When I was a graduate student and I was studying English literature, working on my Ph.D., on my Master's, there was nothing else I wanted to do in the sense that I wanted to find the best teachers and learn all I could with them, study everything that was possible, learn the art. It was fun. I suppose you could call it commitment. I never thought of it as being commitment, it was just what felt right.

So when you find a teacher, you devote your time and energy to what they believe in. If they think you should all go to the movies, you all go to the movies together because obviously you feel they see something beneficial about going to the movies that night, maybe just to have a good time. Or if you should meditate for five hours, you all meditate together. You surrender not to them but to the infinite, which operates through them.

Now, here, of course, as you know, I'm always a stickler on this point, this is where the abuse of power manifests with the phony spiritual teachers and phony gurus who tell you how to run your life and what to wear and what to eat and all that sort of stuff, what to do with your money. They abuse. People who don't realize that, of course, listen to them and ruin their lives. They [phony gurus] make themselves objects of adoration and worship. Real spiritual teachers aren't interested in adoration and worship. They like respect only because they realize that that respect will actually help the student. When you respect something you do better with it or for it. If you respect your teacher, you do better. You feel, "Gosh, this is someone very knowledgeable, I have to give them my best. There's a lot to learn from them." If you don't respect them, you're not going to give them the time of day.

Respect is good only because it will help you. But a real liberated teacher or liberated person, what can you do for them? They've got everything; they are everything. They don't need to be worshipped, they don't need to be adored. It's nice if you love them and you should because they love you. They're lovable. They're children playing in a very, very unusual world filled with vortexes of dancing darkness and light.

A sense of eternity, that's what you need, a sense of timelessness beyond time and within time. So if a spiritual teacher says something that doesn't make sense to you, you should always listen to yourself and not to the teacher. A little common sense would end all cults. Of course, one person's cult is another person's spiritual organization. There are many sides to it all, I suppose, I don't know.

Advanced meditation. I'd love to find some people to teach advanced meditation to, I've been looking for many years. I travel all over the world, lecture and meditate, and I'll continue to do so. I'd love to find some people eager and enthusiastic about the higher aspects of the rebirth process, who have already put in the time and the energy to reach that point where they're ready for the advanced study. But there aren't many in this world. There are a few around. Once in a while I run into another one. But it's a very limited league at this time in this world. So the next best thing to do is to work with those who are not quite there yet to bring them up to that level.

What I'm suggesting then, is that advanced meditation requires a level of complete dedication to existence. Complete dedication is not forced, it's easy. You don't think of it as dedication. The sign of a spiritual person, an advanced spiritual person, is that they don't think they're an advanced spiritual person until after liberation, and after liberation, you can say whatever you want because you don't really care, because it doesn't matter, because you're no longer a person. But on the way up, there's a way to do it. In other words, you've got to shine, you've got to work.

I remember in college, I had a Doctor Klein. He was a biology professor I studied with—he was a marine biologist, he was great. He used to tell us what it took to become a successful research scientist and how, for someone who became a successful research scientist—you know, there were so few positions available, there was a sequence they had to follow. At a certain age they would start. They'd do really well in college and really well in graduate school, they'd get a post doctorate. If they married, they'd hardly ever be home with their family, and even when they came on at a university, if they got a job at a university, they'd have to shine because there'd be four or five other people and only one or two would be able to stay, so they'd just have to work intensely all the time. You have to pay your dues; you have to be an apprentice, putting in 15, 16, 17, 18 hours a day. You have to do the same thing if you become a physician. If you become a physician, my God—medical school, internship, years of residency. Anything that you want to bring to perfection—if you want to be a ballet dancer, if you want to be a first violinist with the Chicago Symphony or the London Symphony, you give it your whole life, it's all that matters.

Now you don't have to do that. There are lots of people who are happy—they listen to music, they play a little music, they study and go to college. There are lots of people who have a wonderful time in life just going to college and learning. College is a wonderful place. A handful goes to graduate school, five or ten percent. And of those, how many go all the way? Do you see what I'm saying? It's a small number. You shouldn't worry about being in a small number because if you're supposed to be in a small number it will be fun, it will happen by itself. You'll just be inspired. If you're not, then that's not the track life wants to take you on at the moment.

The people at the top are not happier, they just have more responsibilities. Yet there is a way beyond this life and beyond death, and that is the path of liberation, and in order to be liberated, you have to enter into the world of advanced meditation. One path leads back to this world, to rebirth; one path leads beyond. Your soul stands at a crossroads, trying to make a decision. Flipping a coin. A nice image for the soul, I think.

I'm just trying to say that advanced meditation is not just a little bit of meditation; it's not just sitting and meditating. That's not advanced meditation. True, you have to sit there and be able to still all your thoughts and move into the superconscious awareness. But the reason you can do that is because you not only practice meditation for many years in both the good times and the bad times, when it was easy and difficult, but because of the type of life you lead, which doesn't mean it's a strict life. It doesn't mean that you necessarily have to be this or have to be that. You don't necessarily have to be celibate or necessarily have to not be married. There are variables.

It's not what you do, it's the intensity of your feeling that determines how far you go in the spiritual life. If you were that dedicated and that committed to sports, to medicine, to music, to business, to whatever it may be, if you take that same total level of dedication that anyone had to get to the top in any field, and apply it to self-discovery, the same thing happens. Except that when you get to the top in anything else, it washes away, it's transitory. You've devoted your whole life to working and endeavoring, and then you'll die and you'll lose it all, whereas here you'll never lose it. It loses you. The only thing that stays with you forever is your awareness.

To some of us it makes sense. We don't even know why. We're drawn towards the light like moths to the flame, and into the flame we go and burn up and then suddenly we become someone and something else, all the time. But you have to excel. You have to be exceptional, you have to be impeccable. You have to care about nothing but light, all the time. Then, of course, you put that caring into action, not in a sloppy way but in a perfect way, in order to enter into the world of advanced meditation. It's a very strict school.

The other schools, introductory and intermediate meditation, are easy schools. But advanced meditation is like graduate or professional school; it's much more demanding. In one year of graduate school, you might learn what you learned in five years as an undergraduate. But if you've done a good job as an undergraduate and if it's what you want to do, it's fun. You're ready for that level of professionalism.

But don't even think about advanced meditation until you've meditated for many, many years, burned your bridges behind you and the bridges in front of you and you can feel that your life is very stable. You've got your physical life together; your economic life together, in most cases; your emotional life is tight; you no longer feel the need to have someone in your life, rather your interest is in serving people. And you don't just think these thoughts because they sound correct, this is how you genuinely feel. When you wake up in the morning, all you think about is, "What can I do for my spiritual teacher, or our spiritual journey that we're on, our community, or for others?" Or whatever the thought is, for God, it's the same thought, just taking different forms.

It's not an obsession, although you're definitely obsessed. It's just the way you feel. It's not right, it's not wrong; it just is how you feel. You feel that way all day long. You feel that way all night long. You don't care about anything else the same way. You're the same as the research scientist who has just given up his life to do that, the doctor or the artist, for whom nothing matters more than their art. You don't have much of a personal life, is what I'm suggesting. If you want a personal life, it's definitely not the world of advanced meditation.

Advanced meditation is if you want a personless life, one filled with people and with love and with beauty but without that fixation. It's if you're brave enough to stand alone, even when you're surrounded by others. It's if you have the courage to live your convictions, even when things aren't going your way, even when you make a fool out of yourself. Even if you fail a thousand times, you get up a thousand and one times and each time try to be more creative, and at the same time you accept your destiny and accept what God gives you.

People who are advanced meditators don't worry about liberation and self-realization anymore. They're not trying to become liberated. They instead are interested in the welfare of others and aiding others in their liberation. They know that when it's time for them to be liberated it will happen. They're not even desirous of liberation anymore, that's just another attachment. There is no liberation. There is no bondage. These are just ideas in the mind. They're children, children of light. They're ageless, timeless and wonderful. We call them saints, sages, fools, different names. They glow, those who practice advanced meditation, they glow.

Then, of course, there are the old hardcore teacher types like me who just sit around and tell jokes, realizing that what's the difference anyway, it's all timeless, and looking for someone who wants to play a good, fast tennis game sometime. If there's no one around to play a good, fast tennis game, then you teach them how to hold the racket and how to get the ball over the net, as patiently as eternity, and just wait. And if no one ever comes, that's nice too because what's the difference? You're the finite and the infinite, you're the beyond and the near, everything and nothing.

So advanced meditation is life. It's the pure acceptance of life in its totality. It's climbing up to the highest point and beyond and observing the view. It's being alone with yourself and facing the immensity of eternity, and even at its most awesome, even when it's most frightening and terrifying, embracing that which terrifies you and frightens you and loving it because it's God, you're God.

It's not being afraid to stand alone and do what's right, through life or through death, and realizing that you never had anything to do with it anyway—not because you were good or wonderful, it was just the way it worked out, the way the cards were dealt. There is no sense of self, but a great love for all, and total trust. You must have total and impeccable trust in eternity. Whether you have it or not, eternity's in charge so you might as well trust, you'll feel better.

Advanced meditation. Never leave the body without it.

Nirvana is waiting! Don't keep it waiting too long!

— Rama

Meditation: The Bridge Is Flowing But The River Is Not

Meditation: The Bridge Is Flowing
But The River Is Not

Rama - Dr. Frederick P. Lenz
The Frederick P. Lenz Foundation for American Buddhism

For
Lakshmi

PART ONE

THE WAY OF
MEDITATION

Meditation is the natural state of existence.
Whatever you see is meditation.

If you did not perceive the universe as being
Separate from yourself – then you would not
Need to meditate.

Meditation is the awareness of timelessness,
Both in and out of time.

There are few, if any, instructions
That are useful for meditation.
Formulas tend to catch us up in the
Trap of formulation.

Meditation is beyond Formulation,
Becoming and being:
Yet it exists always in all places
At all times.

Meditation is not a practice,
Nor is it a 'way' of being:
It is being:
Being natural,
Being humble,
And being pure.

Is there anything else of value?

When you practice meditation, you
Come upon the ease of your own being.
It is easy to meditate unless, of course,
You think otherwise.
Nothing is or is not so unless you
Think otherwise;
Until you stop thinking, that is.

Meditation is not thinking:
Not thinking about
Things, people, places or ideas,
Not remembering, not planning,
Not dreaming, not scheming,
Not craving and not avoiding,
Not thinking about not thinking.
This is meditation, pure and simple.

The only thing that stands between you
And the infinite ecstasy of existence are thoughts.
When you stop your thoughts,
You stop the world.
When the world stops, time stops.
When time stops, matter stops.
When matter stops, self-consciousness stops.
When self-consciousness stops, there is nothing.
Nothing left to stop, start, begin or end.
The person who did all of these things
Has gone away,
Vanished without a trace in the
Ecstasy of existence.

-2-

There are two types of meditation:
Simple and Profound.

Simple meditation involves stilling the mind
Quieting your thoughts and senses
Until you have reached a point of perfect balance
Between timelessness and time,
Between becoming and being,
Between mortality and immortality.

Simple meditation is self-conscious meditation.
Sitting in an up-right position with eyes
Opened or closed you gradually detach yourself
From the storm of your thoughts.

Begin by focusing on a cosmic pattern or yantra,
Repeating a sacred word or mantra,
Observing the patterns of your breath,
Ignoring your breathing and focusing on love,
Listening to the silence of Eternity,
Thinking of God, an enlightened person,
Or a deity,
Focusing on the subtle energies,
Visualizing the junctions of prana – the chakras;
There are so many different methods.

The ocean of your mind is agitated,
The waves of thought prevent you from seeing
Beyond the surface of existence.
By focusing your attention, you gradually quiet
The waves of thoughts within your mind.
When the waves stop, your mind becomes still
And you can see into the depths of Eternity.

4

-3-

Desire obscures the soul.
The soul is Eternity.
It is the source of all — it is all.

Thoughts are manifested desires.
When they enter your mind they
Fragment your awareness.

You are awareness — undifferentiated awareness:
Smooth, shining and perfect.
This is Nirvana.
Smooth, shining and perfect.
You are Nirvana.

Desire obscures the soul.
Desire is neither good nor bad,
Although there are both good and bad desires.

Desire obscures the soul.
Desire has brought all of this into being:
Being in time,
Being in pain,
Being in love,
And death;
Desire brings death.

There is no life and there is no death.
Life and death are moving shadows
Cast upon the ground
By clouds that sweep across the sky.

The soul shines.
Its light is being.

Desire gives shape and form to life and being.
Where there is no desire there is no death.

HOW TO MEDITATE

Desire divides the cosmos,
It separates you from yourself.
Desire creates time, the pairs of opposites:
Attraction and repulsion.

You cannot overcome desire.
It is like the wind.
You are but a leaf in that wind.
Can a leaf stop the wind?
Can you stop your desires?

If the leaf were no longer a leaf,
And it lived in a world without wind,
What then?

Hard to imagine?
Even harder to describe;
Particularly to leaves that have only
Known the wind.
Is the wind talking to itself?
Or is this just another dream in a succession of
Waking dreams?

You will only know
In a windless world
Where you are someone other
Than yourself.

Meditation is the wind.
It blows out the flames of our desires.
Beautiful the flames, the flames of our desires.
More beautiful still the leaves that burn in those
Flames.

The leaf smoke rises into the skies
It drifts closer to heaven.
Nirvana has nothing to do with any of this.
It is neither here nor there.

-4-

You must look beyond the surface,
You must probe more deeply still in your
Search for Truth.
The surface is filled with Worries, Problems,
Excuses and Death.
Beyond the surface is Eternal Life.

Consciousness comes about through awareness.
Awareness is the dream of consciousness.
In Nirvana there is pure being.
There is no individual awareness of form.
You have returned home and
Everything is complete.
There is no craving or disappointment.

We call Nirvana God.
God is ceaseless and timeless existence.
God is the source of everything and
Everything is God.
This is the dream of God.

The creation comes forth from God.
God is divisionless Ecstasy.
As a branch puts forth leaves and shoots,
God puts forth the countless manifestations
We call Life.
God gives Her creations a resting place
We call Death.

God fills the worlds with beings,
Experiences and dreams,
All of which are not quite what they seem.

From time to time She cleans house,
She sweeps away all of the worlds.
We call these seasonal housecleanings

The cycles of existence.

God recycles some of Her creations:
Characters from one cycle are
Transposed into another,
Some characters are short-lived,
For them there is no second play,
Their reviews were less than the
Best.

Then there are new characters
Who have just come into being.
They are new cycle souls.
They have no karma to work out.
It is opening night
And the stage has just been set.
The lights come up and the overture begins.

You are not what you seem to be.
You are one of God's endless dreams
In search of wakefulness.
Meditation is wakefulness.

When the alarm clock goes off
And you awaken from all dreams
You will see that
You are God.

Things are different for God;
For Her there is no time, no worlds,
No housekeeping and no existence
As you have come to know it.
For Her there is only perfect awareness,
An awareness of the unity of all things,
A timeless awareness beyond
Suffering, Transmigration,
Change and Death.
She dreams Herself into
Samsaric forms and beings,
Allowing Herself to be both within and beyond Her own dream.

From within Her dream, she can faintly
Remember what is beyond Her dream.

She creates dreams for Her dreams.
In dreaming. Her dreams are free to explore
Her countless worlds and experiences.
They awaken to the dream of life.

There is a way out.
Out beyond the threshold of all dreaming.
She dreams the way out.
She dreams a way for Her own awareness
To be free:
Free from dreaming forever:
This is the dream of Nirvana.

Into Nirvana you go.
It's like skiing
In perfect powder.
Faster and faster into darkness,
Without knowing why,
Without caring,
Faster and faster until there is only the
Whiteness of snow.

When you meditate, you will
Become this awareness.
Your awareness and God's awareness
Will be one.

There is simple meditation:
Nothingness and everythingness,
The color and the form,
Death and the Void,
The End and the Beginning,
A Beginningless end with an Endless beginning:
Pretty clever if you ask me.

-5-

Existence is the awareness of awareness.
Without the awareness of awareness
There is Nirvana:
That which is beyond description.

From existence, existence comes forth.
Into existence, existence returns.
This appears to be so to one who seems to exist,
In a world that is a dream of Nirvana.

When you visit Nirvana, there is neither
Existence
Nor nonexistence.
Your baggage never arrives
Because there is no one there to claim it.

-6-

Profound meditation cannot be described,
There are no instructions.
All that can be said is that when you are ready,
Something or someone will show you.

To find Nirvana on your own is difficult.
The path has disappeared in our hike
Through the woods.
We cannot find it.
There is no trail to show us where to go.

When the trail gives out, we need to find
Someone who knows the way.
This is the guide.
Our search for the trail is a search for the guide.
The guide is the trail.
Follow the guide and you will reach Liberation.

-7-

The Guide was once yourself;
In another time, in another world,
In a different dream.
He struggled, loved, wept and lived as you.
Then he changed.
The dreams he was dreaming of
Separativity and desire went away.
This did not happen all at once.
It occurred over a circuit of
Many, many lifetimes.
Countless incarnations in
Different planes of being:
Endless experiences in the Eye of God.
All forgotten now.
No Self.
No Separation between anything:
Only existence:
Shining, perfect and perennial.
No zip code.

Self Realization is a strange term.
You don't actually realize your 'self.'
If anything, you go away.
The caterpillar enters the
Cocoon of meditation:
A butterfly emerges.
Metamorphosis.

You are no longer what you were.
You cannot say what you are.
Sometimes you are, but most of the time
You are not. —

HOW TO MEDITATE

If I may digress for a moment:

> *Pleasure and pain are outgrowths of desire.*
> *If there is no desire, then there is no pain.*
> *Pain is frustrated desire.*

> *All suffering comes from desire.*
> *It is impossible to stop your desires.*

> *That is why we meditate.*
> *We cannot stop our desires.*

Many people in spiritual practice
Become very frustrated.
They are told to overcome their desires.
How can you overcome your desires?
Can you stop the wind from blowing?

You cannot stop desire.
But you can stop yourself.
You can reshuffle your being
Endlessly in the white light of Eternity.

If there is pain and you are not there
To feel it
Will the pain still hurt?

This is profound meditation.
You will no longer be there.
The butterfly has flown to a safe place:
Out of sight, out of mind.

Timelessness:
> *Avoid it as long as you an.*
> *When you find that you*
> *Can no longer avoid it,*
> *It will come to you and you will*
> *Become it.*
> *It is your destiny.*

-8-

Don't blame others.
This is the mistake that most people make.
If you have a problem —
If you are not happy —
If you are in any kind of pain —
If you see injustice in the world —
Don't blame others. It will not change anything.
You will not improve by blaming others
For your problems —
Even if they are the cause of your problems.
All you will succeed in doing is to
Further bind yourself to
Pain and frustration.

If you want to overcome pain and frustration
I will show you a simple way.
Meditate.
It is the way out of hell.
Hell only exists because of desire.
You can end it.

Hell is everything.
Heaven is nothing.

Meditate.
Still your thoughts.
Don't blame others or yourself.
Nothing will come from it.

Meditate.
When you meditate you will become a
Clear and shining Instrument of Immortality.

There is no way out of the maze.
The entrance has been sealed.
You will walk through endless lifetimes,

Endless and countless
Dreams of the Self —
Never knowing why.

Listen to me.
I know why.
You have dreamed me to remind you.

Meditate.
Be absorbed in Eternal Consciousness.
Then there will only be Light;
The Light that existed before this world
And that will exist long, long after this
World has passed away.

Meditate and be absorbed in this Light.

Each time you meditate, the Light of Eternity
Refines your being.
One transfusion after another until the
Patient is no longer there.
A complete cure.

Exposure to the primal Light of Existence
Restructures you;
The deck of life is shuffled and you are
Dealt a new hand.

Don't blame others.
Don't' blame yourself.
Instead, meditate on the Absolute.

Learn to still your thoughts and
Be absorbed.

Don't run away from the world.
The world is God.
Don't run towards the world.

God is the Void.
Don't be afraid of the
Complexities of this life,
Nor the stark simplicity of death.

Accept whatever life gives you with a
Friendly attitude.
This can only be done when you meditate.
Without meditation these are only
Abstractions.
Meditation is the glue that binds all of this
Together.
It is the solvent that dissolves you in
Eternal Light.

When there is nothing but Light —
Blinding Light stronger than
Ten million suns —
Then you will understand.
Until then, meditate.
The way will be shown to you.

Meditation: The Bridge Is Flowing But The River Is Not

PART TWO

---

1. THE ART OF MEDITATION

In meditation we turn our attention inward and watch the transformations of eternity taking place within us.

Meditation allows us to be everything at once. In this world, we try to succeed at many different things. We occupy ourselves with friends and relatives, with careers, with hobbies and interests, with our hopes, dreams, plans and loves.

Meditation is nothing like this at all. Meditation takes us beyond the world of daily living and acquaints us with the immortal worlds of silence and consciousness.

To meditate with humility, consider existence. It is infinite. You are finite. You are a finite portion of the infinite existence. Let this be your meditation.

Meditation means complete awareness. This awareness is not finite. It is infinite. To be aware of yourself is finite. To be aware of the universe is also finite. But to become awareness itself is infinite. Meditation is the ability to move beyond the subjective to the limitless and fathomless ecstasy we call existence.

Meditation is letting go. Meditation is the way to eternal knowledge of God. When you have become advanced in your meditation you will come to realize that God is not a big person who lives in a celestial palace in the sky. Nor is God an aimless idea in the minds of those who seek to explain away the mysteries of existence. God is all. At the same time, God is beyond all. There is nothing that is not God. To limit God to a particular conception is to prevent yourself from seeing the totality of God.

Meditation is like taking a bath. When we bathe, we wash away all of the impurities that have become attached to our bodies. Meditation is a constant washing of the psyche. It cleanses us of our impure thoughts, attachments, desires and frustrations.

Meditation is the way out. It is the only escape from the continual change of cause and effect. Without meditation, you are tied to y our body and desires. With meditation, you fly into the unfettered skies of the infinite.

Meditation is the ultimate act of refinement. You must bring your best aspirations to each meditation session. If you are fortunate enough to have an Illumined teacher to guide you, the process will be easier. However, the voices of eternity is present to guide each of us, if we only will take the time to listen.

How to meditate? The question constantly arises. First, ignore your thoughts. Whether they are good or bad thoughts. Whether they are good or bad thoughts, be neither attracted nor repulsed by them. Watch them pass through your mind as you would watch a flight of birds pass through the sky.

Then begin to eliminate your thoughts. When you think thoughts of this world, push them aside with thoughts of the Infinite. Instead of thinking about problems and difficulties, consider your opportunities.

Finally, begin to meditate on the spaces between your thoughts. Expand these spaces into the Infinite. Then — when thoughts come knocking on your inner door — ignore them. Let your awareness roam at ease in the infinite stillness of the Void.

Use your imagination. Be creative. Meditate as you go along. Don't always be a slave to direction.

Try repeating the word "Supreme" with your whole being. Close your eyes and enter into meditation. Then silently repeat the word "Supreme" with all of the sincerity you can command. The Supreme *is* the highest reality. Beyond both form and formlessness, the essence of all existence — your true Self. Reach to your Supreme Self; cry to it. As you do, you will feel yourself lifted into a high and pure consciousness.

The goal of meditation is to go beyond the ego. The ego is the limited self. Within you is a limitless self. The ego experiences doubts, frustrations, sorrows and limitations of all types. But your deeper self is always in a state of constant illumination and joy.

Gratitude is self giving in its purest form. Whenever you feel gratitude growing inside your heart, you are diverting your attention from your ego self and directing it towards something or someone else. Gratitude enables you to transcend the ego and become conscious of your limited self.

Try to forget your past. It is an old story which does not need retelling. Whenever you think of your past you limit your present. You are not what you were. You are what you are. You are immortal consciousness. Immortal consciousness inside a body. Forget and forgive your past. Meditate on immortal consciousness.

When you meditate, you move from the world of ideas to fluid realities.

Meditation is listening. When you begin to meditate, you will only be aware of your thoughts. Ignore your thoughts. If you fight against them, you will only become caught up in them. It is like trying to escape from quicksand. The more you struggle, the faster you sink.

To meditate with gratitude, all you need to do is think of someone you feel gratitude for. You may feel grateful for your friends or loved ones. You may feel grateful to for the beauty of nature. You may feel grateful to God. Whatever the cause, if you can feel grateful just for a few minutes, you will start a chain reaction of gratitude within your heart.

Take that feeling of gratitude and expand it. Immerse yourself in pure feelings of gratitude. Feel grateful for all of existence. Smile and feel that nothing but gratitude exists. Then let go. You need do nothing now but let go and flow with the currents of eternity.

Meditation is liberation. When you meditate, you purge yourself of all conceptions of self. No matter what you think of yourself, no matter how you see yourself, you cannot fathom that which you truly are. Ideas about yourself only interfere with the natural flow of your own awareness.

Willpower. Use willpower to eliminate all thought. Each time a thought enters your mind, silent say, "No!" Continue to do this until you have rejected all thought.

Sri Ramakrishna used the analogy of the thorns to explain this concept to his students. He would say that if you get a thorn stuck in your foot, you can take another thorn to remove it, and then throw both thorns away.

You are using the thoughts of your willpower to reject your aimless, wandering thoughts. Once you have silenced your aimless, wandering thoughts, you can let go of your willpower thoughts and enter into complete silence.

The Inner Cry. The inner cry is the quickest and easiest way to meditate. The inner cry means reaching out for help. If your load is too heavy to carry, you can call out and someone will help you.

When the child cries, the mother comes. When you cry, God the Infinite Mother of all life comes and rescues you. To cry inwardly, you do not need to be unhappy or shed outer tears. You need only reach to the Infinite with your whole heart and soul.

Try meditating with your whole heart. When you meditate with your whole heart, feel that God is standing right in front of you. Then feel that God has entered your heart. Now feel that you have entered into God and that you are everywhere.

Meditate with your eyes closed and feel the space in the center of your forehead about an inch above your eyebrows. This is your third eye. Focus your attention here and you will see the past, present and future. If you focus on this spot with total intensity, you will go beyond this world into a world of static bliss and immortal beauty.

When I meditate, I become the source of all Light. An ocean of infinite Light – shimmering and shining – rounded and perfect.

Meditation makes you happy. If meditation is not making you happy, then you are not meditating. You are doing a great deal of thinking, but you are definitely not meditating.

ॐ

Silence and sound: these are our two meditations. Silence brings us to the white, still heart of Light. Sound encompasses the movements of Time.

ॐ

Sound is silence and silence is sound. Seen together they are a seamless reality. Seen apart they are complementary points in a limitless and formless universe.

ॐ

Sound is the experience of this world. Life appears suddenly — raging and careening down the highways of existence. Then, mysteriously and quickly, it vanishes. Where does it come from and where does it go? This is the mystery of eternity.

ॐ

Meditation is the boat that takes you across the sea of life to the shores of eternity.

ॐ

Think well of yourself. Know that you are the source of all existence. You are an infinite awareness in a finite body. Release yourself with a smile. Lose yourself in the eternal silence and stillness of your heart.

ॐ

I hear the voices of eternity calling me. The river of life flows into the vast ocean of immortal consciousness. I am sailing in the boat of my heart down the river of life into the ocean of immortal consciousness.

Meditate alone. When you meditate with others, you must not only eliminate your own restless thoughts but also the thoughts and vibrations of those around you. In your daily meditations, meditate alone.

At least once a week, it is good to meditate in a group. A group meditation offers you an experience of power. If the meditation is led by a spiritually advanced person, then that power will help you to increase your velocity towards the immortal consciousness of perfection.

Meditation clears your vision and sharpens your mind. Razor-sharp, your mind will cut through the illusion of self to reach Illumination. What will your razor-sharp mind cut then?

I have seen the silver fountains of eternity. At the eternal springs of timelessness I have renewed myself. Now – drenched with the immortal nectar of happiness and bliss – I roam alone in a world of changeless change. I am alone with my own pure delight. I am existence itself.

2. Mantras

The highest type of meditation is done in silence. In silence there are no mantras. Mantras can help you to enter into silence. Mantras are not essential, but they can be very helpful.

There are thousands of mantras. Everyone has favorites. I prefer three – *Aum, Sring* and *Kring.*

Aum is the most powerful of all mantras. It is good to chant "Aum" seven or more times before and after each meditation. Chanting "Aum" puts you in harmony with the vibration of Eternity. "Aum" opens the gateway to the infinite highway of light.

Sring is the mantra of beauty. Traditionally it is connected with Mahalakshmi, the Indian goddess of beauty. Chant "Sring" slowly, elongating each sound. As you do, you will see the consciousness of beauty everywhere.

Kring is the mantra of power. It is used for rapid spiritual transformation. You can chant most mantras whenever you like – while you are meditating, driving your car, or walking down the street.

"Kring" should only be repeated when you are in deep meditation. Towards the end of your meditation session, or when you feel your meditation is deep, chant "Kring" seven times. Repeat it with sharp intensity, *without* elongating the syllables.

Mantras can be chanted out loud or in silence, whichever you prefer. Mantras do not need to be repeated for long periods of time. A few times is usually sufficient. It is more important to repeat a mantra several times with total absorption than to parrot it for hours on end.

3. Meditations on Eternity

That which is real has always existed. That which is not real can never exist. Since existence itself is the source of all life, then existence is all that can truthfully be said to exist.

How to unravel the knot of reality? Slowly and patiently. You cannot run away from it. You cannot run towards it. Yet Truth runs in your footsteps. It is the face in the mirror, the light of the sun, the winter rainstorms, the heat of summer in the city.

Break away from your thoughts. No matter how beautiful they may be, they are limitations. No matter how important they may seem, they are only reflections – phantoms in the night.

Beyond thought is silence. Within silence is stillness. Stillness remains throughout time. Stillness exists beyond change. Find yourself in stillness.

You are a product of a linear sequence of life-times, karmas, thoughts, actions and interactions. This is what the mind states. You are a composite of emotions and pure feelings. This is what the heart says. The soul doesn't speak at all. She passes no judgment and lays down no laws. She accepts her children whether they are moral or immoral. For her there is no question of morality. She simply accepts her children with love.

In each lifetime we lose and find ourselves. Suddenly we appear. Then we are gone. We look closely and catch ourselves in the action of becoming, being and dissolution. This is the Supreme act of awareness. To observe ourselves in the act of becoming-being-and-dissolution.

Infinite space surrounds you. Truth is contained in infinite space. And equal amount of truth is also contained in finite space. Yet Truth is neither finite nor infinite.

Student: "I have had conflicting thoughts on the nature of reality. When I first started to meditate, I thought that reality was this world. Then, after some time, I began to think that what I experienced in meditation was real and the world we live in is unreal. What is the truth of this matter? What is real?"

Teacher: "Everything is real. Everything is truth. But the shape of reality and truth changes from plane to plane. When we are in the world of men, reality is this physical world. When we are in the subtle physical worlds, then the words "real" and "truth" can no longer apply. They no longer apply because we can no longer distinguish ourselves from that which is real and that which is true."

To die is only to continue in your current cycle. To meditate is to go beyond the cycle of birth and death.

To die is easy. To live is difficult. To die takes only a few moments. The world fades and you find yourself in bliss. To live takes many, many lifetimes. To live you must have continual courage. To die you need only let go.

Death leads to rebirth; rebirth leads to death. The chain appears to be endless. Suffering, sorrow, joy, happiness, suffering, sorrow. The chain appears to be endless.

Everything in this world is transitory. All who come here are born, and all who leave here die. Nothing and no one escapes death and rebirth. We live in a world of constant transitions.

Love is pure power. Its power is measureless. The first ten or fifteen years of your meditative practice should be spent learning the ways of love. Love will take you very, very high. One day, however, you will have to go beyond love. While love is certainly the best of all spiritual qualities, it is still only a partiality. Eventually you will go beyond all partialities in your quest for identity.

To reach the infinite we go through the finite. Those who shun the finite, or condemn it, condemn and shun themselves. The finite exists in the infinite and the infinite in the finite. In this finite world, we explore the infinite through the finite.

There is only one time and that is eternal time. On the clock of eternal time there are no hands. There is no movement. All is, and all has always been. But in the relative world this truth cannot be seen.

Time binds you. Time destroys you. Time brings your death. This is one face of God.

Time liberates you. Time creates you. Time gives you your very life. This is another face of God.

Today exists. I can feel it. But tomorrow, who knows? And yesterday — what need have I of yesterday? It has already been. What I need is happiness and completion *now*, not tomorrow, not yesterday. Happiness and completion can only occur when I get out of the trap of time.

The Void is not empty. Emptiness is a quality of this world. The Void is not full. Fullness is a quality of this world. The Void is like a diamond that endlessly reflects itself. Place this diamond inside your mind and seek the golden dust of eternity.

Speculations about the nature of God never cease! Is God infinite or finite? Dies God have form or is God formless? Is there anything beyond God?

God is everywhere and nowhere. God is finite and infinite. God exists and doesn't exist. It all depends on your understanding of God.

Everything is reality. For a child, a toy is reality. For a corporate executive, a business merger is reality. For a lover, her beloved is reality. For a holy person, the unmanifest is reality. But for an Illumined person, there is nothing but reality.

We think of our minds as obstructions to the attainment of enlightenment. We think of our attachments as obstructions to the attainment of enlightenment. We think of ourselves as obstructions to the attainment of enlightenment. But from the point of view of the Enlightened, there are no obstructions to enlightenment. All that exists is enlightenment. How could there be anything else?

Beyond the form is the formless. Beyond the formless, who knows? It is what we call Nirvana – that which cannot be said to either exist or not exist. That which has neither form nor formlessness. Yet out of this changeless reality comes both form and formlessness. Both exist within Nirvana and beyond it. This is our meditation.

The forest will bring you peace until it is cut down. The ocean will bring you peace until it dries up. This world will bring you peace for a short time. Then all the worlds recycle. The cosmic game begins anew. Peace is lost and peace is regained. That is the way of the samsara.

Eternal peace exists beyond change. Everything in this world is bound in a cycle. But "beyond change" does not signify a physical location. "Beyond change" implies a shift in perception rather than location.

Perception is the root of all existence. Someone caught in the web of illusion sees change everywhere they look. An Illumined person sees the changeless wherever they look. A Liberated person sees the Self changing its changeless form. A Self Realized person no longer sees. They have gone beyond the perceptions of change and changelessness. They have become eternity itself.

All things, persons, worlds and realities come forth from, and return to, the transcendental Light.

This fathomless source is our true self. While we cannot necessarily understand the nature of God within our minds, we can experience God – the transcendental Light – in and through meditation.

The eternal all is ever-present. I have seen and know it. This you can say. The eternal all is ever-present. I have seen, known and become it. This you can also say, but it is not true. When you have become the eternal all, you will be in samadhi. There can be no seeing, knowing or becoming then.

When you can enter into samadhi, you will no longer use meditation methods and forms. When the land is flooded, the reservoir becomes superfluous. When you have perfected your meditation, you will dispense with all meditation methods and forms. Until then you must practice these forms again and again. They are the short path to liberation.

The stars meditate constantly. They burn their very substance to give Light to others. This is constant and conscious meditation.

Intention and volition. Intention is good will. To purify and strengthen yourself against the cold winds of adversity. To do what is right in all situations and circumstances no matter what the consequences to yourself may be. This is intention.

Volition is the action of intention. You will do more than promise to be good. You will become goodness itself. You can do nothing but follow the will of the Infinite. You have surrendered the limitations of the ego and accepted the white cloak of forgiveness and perfection. Whom to forgive? Yourself. What to perfect? Your smile.

Life can never end. It is changeless, immortal consciousness. It may vary in intensity and hue, but it can never end.

You are life. You are the conscious awareness of your own immortality. Your mortality is but a small portion of your immortality. While the forms you adopt may vary, you are the endless dreamer of eternity.

The idea that one can escape from reality is a false notion. There is no place to escape from. There is no place to escape to. All that exists is reality.

Dance with life. Don't sit, a wallflower on the bench. You can never be sure of who you really are until you throw yourself into the Infinite. Whomever comes back is who you are.

When in doubt, throw it out.

4. Meditations for Self Improvement

Willpower is within me. I must only exercise my free choice to bring it alive. My free choice is to use my unlimited willpower to free myself and others from bondage. My only choice is to *will* freedom.

When I give of myself, I expand my consciousness infinitely. When I share my inspiration with others, I live love. When I choose to share my life with God, I become a flame of perfect perfection.

Courage enables me to live in the present and shun my past. When I am courageous, I am willing to accept that I am imperfect. When I am courageous, I am willing to give up my life for others. When I am courageous, I have put a permanent and complete end to fear.

Love comes naturally when I think more of others than I think of myself. Love comes spontaneously when I free myself of emotional obligations. Love comes endlessly when I allow my love for the Supreme Source of Existence to be fathomless and endless. Love is complete when I allow its very madness to permeate my mind and intoxicate my soul.

Self doubt is an expression of falsehood. When I doubt myself, I go against the will of my soul. Self doubt is what I used to be. Self assurance is complete acceptance of my immortal destiny.

I don't have time to be jealous of anything or anyone. Death may come sooner than I expect, so I don't have time to be jealous of anything or anyone.

God makes all of existence perfectly. Wherever I am supposed to be, I am. Whomever I am supposed to be with, I am. Whatever I am supposed to be, I am.

I am humility. Nothing more and nothing less. I am one blade of grass in a sea of grass. I am one wave in an endless ocean of waves. I am one glowing star in a galaxy of stars.

The way to Truth is easy. Following that which makes me happy leads me to Truth. Doing that which makes others happy leads me to Truth.

I love myself because I am Truth. My body will come and go. My personality will change. Everything I see with my eyes will cease to exist one day. But the Truth I am is immortal and perfect.

I live in the constant newness of aspiration. Whatever I think, I ignore. Whatever I feel, I don't trust. Yet I listen to my thoughts and follow my feelings.

5. Meditations on Life

The breath of eternal existence is all-where. The moments of complete fulfillment are fleeting. The road to eternity winds through these moments. I am formless – yet remain the same.

This world is a grain of sand on the beach of Eternity. Eternity is a grain of sand on the beach of Infinity. The ocean of Nirvana connects both Eternity and Infinity without connecting them. Know this and you will be free.

The memories of your past lives are unimportant. They only prove what you already know. Forget your past lives and live in the ever-present. It is here that you will gain freedom from bondage – not by looking at pictures of the gone world.

This world is of little account. It is only one brief stage in a succession of endless stages that we play upon. This body is of little account. It is a passing flower in the bouquet of life.

The time we waste never comes again. The opportunities we miss never come again. The loves we lose never come again. Indeed, in this world of constant change we are fortunate that these things never come again.

To know yourself you must be willing to suffer. To know the Void you must be willing to give up suffering.

I know one day my heart will bring me through the gates of Eternity. If I can only remain true to myself, my heart will remain true to me.

The possibilities of Immortality are endless! Here you sit reading these words – a butterfly resting on a flower.

Never before have you had so many reasons to celebrate yourself! You are immortal. You are infinite. You are mortal. You are finite. By celebrating yourself, you commence your education in the eternal schools of consciousness and becoming.

Whenever you make a mistake, remember that you are God. God doesn't make mistakes. God only has experiences.

We are only aware of what we know. Although we may think we know more – we don't. Try to remember this.

Running away from your attachments only brings you closer to them.

I know that you may be confused by much of what I say. But confusion is only a relative state on the way to total enlightenment. Don't be afraid of confusion. When you are confused, you are definitely making spiritual progress.

Humor yourself – laugh at yourself – make a few mistakes – be human. You are.

Trust yourself. Do you really think that after all of the incarnations of practice you've had you are going to blow it now? Trust yourself. You will do exactly what is right. Why should you do anything else?

Plan not to plan.

The circle of life is complete. You now know who and what you are. You are the silence of meditation. You are the stillness of the Void.

Think of what you love most in this world. This is what you will come back to in your next life.

I have tried constantly to point out one eternal truth to seekers of the Infinite. I will continue to do this. Simply be yourself. This is constant and conscious meditation.

I am not important. Today I am here and tomorrow I will be gone. This is my freedom. I am not important.

I can claim no credit for what I am. I am nothing and no one. How can I take credit for someone I am not?

Above the clouds, the sun is always shining. Beyond the moon, the stars are twinkling. Beyond this life, Immortality is silently waiting. Fear not – the best is yet to be.

Try not to be afraid of death. Think of death as an old friend who comes to help you when you are ready to begin a new adventure. Death comes to all. Let your body die when its time has come. Then you can begin your next adventure.

Life and death coincide. Work and rest sleep side by side. Yesterday and today bring themselves into one another. You and your awareness — make all of this come alive.

HOW TO MEDITATE

6. Thoughts for Higher Living

I believe that all systems are good, provided they bring one to an awareness of that which lies beyond good and evil. However, I don't believe in any system. I don't follow any creed. I enjoy systems and use what is useful from them. I respect others who use and believe in the systems. But I find Truth in Truth, not in systems.

You and you alone know how far along the pathway to Truth you have progressed. Your heart tells you at every moment. Go to your heart and embrace it. Love it. Make friends with it. Then go to your soul and bid it farewell. Go beyond your soul, beyond this world, beyond all worlds and the creator of all worlds. Go beyond birth, death, change and changelessness. There alone will you find the Eternal Reality which is your Self. Beyond form, beyond description, brimming with life, form and description. This is completion. This is rest.

It is good to have a teacher of meditation as your guide. A real teacher is able to go beyond the confines of this world and become one with the Self. A real teacher helps you to ascend to the Self. Once you have learned how to go up and down the ladder yourself, you no longer require a human teacher. At that time Samadhi becomes your teacher.

When you meditate, try to go beyond form and thought. Always remember that the very highest meditation is done without thought. You will have thoughts in your meditations for many years. But constantly strive to eliminate all thoughts from your mind. Thoughts are enchanting. As you sit and meditate, the oceans of thoughts will swirl around you. Be neither attracted nor repulsed by your thoughts. If you can simply ignore them, eventually they will go away.

The question of thought is endless. How do they get into the mind? How can you stop thought without employing thought to stop thought? If you strive, isn't that a limiting thought too? There are many questions and distinctions. Zen has some, Yoga has some, Buddhism has some. But the ideas of striving or non-striving are simply ideas. The concepts of going higher, or of non-duality are still ideas. Any way you look at it, you are looking at it with ideas. So you may feel that your ideas are better than someone else's. And well they may be. But in my eyes they are still ideas. Ideas limit and bind you to this world.

You are complete. Completion has taken place in you eons ago. Accept yourself. Enjoy yourself. This time will never be again, so fulfill the moment with your own self-joy.

Miracles are all around you. A Spiritual Teacher sees miracles in his students. A spiritual person sees miracles in everything. But where do these miracles come from? Where do they go to? This is perhaps the greatest of all miracles.

Desires are neither good nor bad. Only thinking makes them so. Friends are neither good nor bad. Only thinking makes them so. Life is neither good nor bad. Only thinking makes it so. Death is neither good nor bad. Only thinking makes it so. Therefore, if you don't think, you will live in a fluid existence that is beyond judgment, beyond salvation, and beyond damnation.

People enjoy pomp and circumstance. They like their Presidents to be Gods. They like their parents and teachers to be Gods. They like their spiritual liberators to be Gods. However, Presidents are Presidents, parents are parents, teachers are teachers, spiritual liberators are spiritual liberators and Gods are Gods. It's a good idea not to get them confused.

Pedestals were invented by a wise man who perceived the need in human consciousness to cast people down. The wise man realized that it would be impossible to cast people down unless you had put them up on something first. So he invented the pedestal, which is now employed on a regular basis. You put people on it so you can cast them down later. Indeed, he was a wise man.

It is not necessary to have a specialized knowledge of occultism or higher spirituality. This knowledge will come to you when it is needed. If it does not come, it is not needed. What is needed, though, is to learn to still your thoughts. If you can do this then there is nothing left for you to do.

Happiness is the fountain of all expression. While heaven may be wonderful, and the cosmic Deities sublime, happiness gives you freedom from unhappiness. Is there more?

Worship life in newness. This is the secret of happy people. Each moment is new. It has never existed before. Look into its depths and allow it to delineate your existence.

Ultimately, it is impossible to will your Self Realization. Self Realization will occur for you when it does. Not one moment sooner and not one moment later. Once you have realized the Self you will see that you were one with the Self all along. There was never a time when you were not Self Realized. There has never been, nor can there ever be, anything but Self Realization.

Don't be upset regarding the circumstances of your life. If they were supposed to be different they would be. When they are supposed to be different they will be. Detach yourself and learn to enjoy poverty if you have poverty, and wealth if you have wealth. Trust the Source. It brings you precisely what you need at each moment.

Experience has shown me that when ideas vanish, the world vanishes. Karma vanishes, man and woman vanish, love vanishes, hate vanishes, life and death vanish, Gods and Goddesses vanish, I vanish, you vanish, nothing and everything vanishes. Experience has taught me this.

I prefer happiness. Happiness is fun. Unhappiness isn't. So you choose which you prefer. Either happiness or unhappiness. Neither will change your destiny. But choosing happiness will make you joyful until then.

7. Some Secrets of Meditation

Meditation should always be practiced with love.

Meditate on Light and you will become Light. Meditate on Peace and you will become Peace. Meditate on Eternity and you will become Eternity. Meditate without trying and you will go beyond all suffering and enter into Nirvana.

If you want to meditate well every day, then never evaluate your meditations.

Try to imagine that you are God. Consider yourself to be as old as eternity, as vast as infinity and as young as immortality.

Let go of your thoughts! They only bind you to a worn out conception of what you are not. You are endless Light. You are perfection in the garment of the body. You are the play of the infinite sun – the glory of the radiant moon. You are not what you seem. You are the morning star.

The world is filled with people who understand. I personally value people who don't understand. People who understand have nothing more to learn. People who don't understand have hope. Do you understand?

Try to remember your name. Not the name that your parents gave you at birth. But your real and eternal name: Truth.

To see the Truth is indeed a difficult thing. To live the Truth is harder still. To offer Truth to others is more than difficult — for they resist; in spite of their sincerity, still they resist.

When you meditate, never be afraid of anything. You may see the worst hell demons you can imagine ready to tear you limb from limb. Or all of the Gods and Goddesses may come by to take you out for lunch. Essentially it doesn't matter. Everything that you see is part of the samsara — it is all a projection of your own Self.

Embrace everything you see and then step outside of yourself. Very quietly, circle around behind what you see and enter into it. Then, leaving yourself inside what you see, zip back into your old self. Now you have it! You are inside yourself seeing yourself outside yourself. But who is watching you?

The best things in life are free. Sunsets and sunrises are free. Air is free. Love is free. Death is free. The best things in life are free.

To meditate with perfection, you need only care. Care for both the Infinite more than you care for yourself — then you will meditate perfectly.

How can you lose in the game of life? There is no winning and there is no losing. These are ideas that some human beings have fostered, but they are not true. They are only empty ideas of persons who no longer exist.

When you meditate, try to forgive yourself. Forgive yourself for all of the wrong things you have done to others in all of your incarnations. Then, forgive yourself for all of the wrong things you have done to yourself in all of your incarnations. Finally, forgive yourself for all of the things you have failed to do in all of your incarnations. Once you have done this you will be free to go out and make more mistakes.

There is nothing but hope. How could anyone dare to even think anything else? Hope is the bridge that binds all of the worlds together. Hope is the dream that lies just beyond sight. When you meditate with hope, there is no end to your meditation. You will be bliss – light – and perfection. This is hope.

Smile.

You have forgotten how to meditate. You knew how to a long, long time ago. You will remember. In the future, I can see that you will remember. Keep meditating. You will remember.

8. The Bridge is Flowing But the River is Not

The bridge is flowing but the river is not — from the river's point of view.

Immortality is the time between here and there.
Simplicity is the sun upon the grass.
Purity is the morning.
Love is knowing.

The intensity of knowing who we are and what we cannot do is almost overwhelming. Try not to fight against yourself and your urge to change. Become a shadow in darkness and a light in the day.

When I see suffering, I don't know what to do. When I hear laughter, I don't know what I'm hearing. When I feel love, I am always alone. It seems to happen only when I'm alone.

I am eternal consciousness. I have nothing to build and nothing to break. I have come into this world from a forgotten place. One day I will return again. I am the perfect freedom of my own God-becoming.

The cause of my life is unknown. The purpose of my life is my life. I have nothing to fear because I have nothing to lose. I am immortal life — how can I lose what I am?

Nothing matters quite a bit. I have made this point repeatedly. Let me try again. When I say that nothing matters, I do not mean anything. I mean everything. Everything matters precisely because nothing matters.

How strange to be human. For a short moment we are conscious of the glories of life — then we become silent again. Perhaps there is more — look more deeply into the matter.

The river of Dharma is endless. Your only duty in this world is to flow along with the river of your Dharma. Don't be afraid of who or what you are. Accept the challenge of time and destiny — be all that you are capable of being.

The Golden Light of the Beyond is incomprehensible. It is ecstasy beyond direction. Join me in this Light — be my brother — be my sister — in the timeless dance of Eternity.

I have longed to be with you. I felt you in meditation so long ago. I waited as long as I could and then, when you didn't come, I had to write these words. So they could be with you when I could not be.

The circle is complete. You are your own God. All conditions of *maya* bow down to you. I invoke you, Oh God of the ages. May you shine forever.

Oh God — may we be as perfect as you like. May we wait for you as you will. May we deviate from Truth as you direct. May we never want unless you want. May we never be unless you are there. May there never be an end and a beginning — may we remember you until we are forgotten.

Try to meditate each day. You will not find it all that difficult. The secret is to be patient. If you can be patient you will learn to enjoy your conscious becoming.

Sing the songs of immortality. Drink from the streams of love. Sleep in the dream worlds of happiness. This is my heart's wish for you.

Be fearless! Never give up your search for Truth and God, no matter how difficult it may seem. At each moment you are beckoned by the smile of Life. Don't fight yourself. Be fearless!

How can you possibly overcome your fears, doubts, worries and other problems? You can't. You simply don't have the capacity. Fortunately, the Infinite can do all of these things for you. How? Because it is lacking in nothing.

When you consider the opportunities you have had to be perfect and free, you should realize something. You have had more than enough. What you need now are not more opportunities. What you really need is to be of service to others.

Grab hold of immortality and you will lose it. Hold on to love and you will hate it. Escape from this world and you will be bound to it. Forgive yourself and you are free.

PART THREE

HOW TO MEDITATE

If you want to meditate, think of God.

You can think of God as a person,
As a Light,
As Beauty,
As Truth,
As Your Friend,
As Your Lover,
As Your Child,
As Your Mother,
As Your Father,
As Yourself,
As The Void,
As Eternity,
As Perfection,
As Nirvana,
As you like it.

Meditate in a clean and quiet place.
Try to take a shower before you meditate.
If you don't have time to take a
Shower or bath,
Then wash your hands and face.
Water has a very pure consciousness.
When you take a shower,
The subtle physical vibrations of
The water neutralizes a great deal of the
Negative energy that your body accumulates.

Try to avoid eating for several hours
Before you meditate.
If you eat too much before a
Meditation session, you will find it
Difficult to meditate.
Instead of meditating on peace, light and bliss,
You will meditate on pasta.

If you are very hungry, then
Drink some fruit juice or
Eat something very light.
If you try to meditate when you are too hungry,
You will sit there and think of food.

Wear loose and clean clothing;
Otherwise you will be uncomfortable.

Set up a meditation schedule:
I suggest that you meditate
Two or three times a day.
Set a minimum amount of time for
Each meditation session.

If you are a beginner,
Meditate for fifteen minutes or more.
If you have been meditating for
Over six months,

Then I suggest that you meditate for
At least 45 minutes.

It is not necessary to meditate for
More than one hour.
Instead of meditating for over an hour,
Increase the intensity of the hour,
Until the hour becomes Eternity.

Needless to say, if you meditate for
More than an hour and the
Meditation is going well,
Don't stop simply because you have gone
Beyond your normal time.

Pick a spot in your bedroom or another room
To meditate in.
Put a small table there.
Place a pretty rug in front of your
Meditation table.
Place candles on the table.
Flowers are nice too.

It is easiest to meditate by candlelight.
During meditation, your eyes become sensitive.
Candlelight is a soothing and natural light.
When possible, burn incense.
Good incense contains aromatic oils that
Soothe your central nervous system.
The fragrance of incense is beautiful.

Meditation is an act of supreme beauty.
When you meditate, you will discover
Your own inner beauty and the
Beauty of Eternity.
Anything that you can do that will
Add to the beauty of your
Meditative experience will be helpful.

Sit on your rug in a cross-legged position.
If you find it more comfortable,
Sit in a chair.
The important thing is to sit up straight.
Don't meditate lying down.
If you lie down, your body will
Relax too much and
Your attention will waver.
You may feel comfortable, but you won't
Meditate well.

Now close your eyes.
Chant the mantra "Aum," or a
Favorite mantra, seven times.
Chanting a mantra to start your
Meditation makes it easier to enter into a
High and pure state of consciousness.

When you chant "Aum," or any mantra,
Do so softly and gently.
Extend the sound.
Focus your awareness on the sound of the
Mantra and become absorbed in it.
After you have changed a mantra seven times,
Or as long as you like,
Open your eyes.
Focus your attention on a candle flame,
On a flower, on a yantra,
Or on anything small and finite.

It is not a good idea to continually
Repeat a mantra during meditation.
Repeating a mantra throughout your
Meditation causes you to fixate on a
Specific level of consciousness.
In meditation you are trying to
Quiet your mind and stop your thoughts.
A mantra is a thought.
Use a mantra to help still your mind initially,
And then move into silent meditation.

Focus your attention on a candle flame
And gaze at it.
Begin by looking at a small part of the
Flame for a minute or two.
Then look at the entire flame.
If you start to get a headache, or
If your eyes bother you, then you are
Trying too hard.
Relax.
Don't be afraid to blink or
Change positions if you need to.

Meditate. Look at the candle flame —
Or whatever object you have chosen to
Gaze upon — with intensity.

After several minutes of gazing,
Close your eyes.
Enter into the world of feelings.
Ignore your thoughts or enjoy them;
But let them go.

Meditate.
Focus your attention on your heart chakra.
Your heart chakra is one of
Seven psychic energy centers in your
Subtle physical body.

Each chakra is a gateway to a different
Level of reality.
The heart chakra is the central chakra:
It is the best chakra to meditate on
For the first five or ten years of your
Meditative practice.
The heart chakra is the chakra of
Love and purity.
Meditating on this chakra each day will
Give you humility, purity and
Spiritual balance.
The other chakras are fine to meditate on
Occasionally. But, for daily meditation,
The heart chakra is the best.

Your heart chakra is located in the
Center of your chest.
If you don't know how to find it then
Here is an easy way:

Hold either your right or left hand out
In front of your chest.
Extend your index finger.
Now say "ME" out loud and,
As you do so, touch your chest.
You will automatically touch your
Heart chakra.

Your heart chakra is not in your
Physical body.
It is in your subtle physical body,
But it connects with your physical
Body in this location.

The first few times you meditate,
Use this method to find your
Heart chakra. After you have
Practiced gazing for several minutes,
Place your finger on the
Spot you have located,
Close your eyes, and simply "feel"
The spot your finger is touching.
Then, after a couple of minutes,
Let your hand down.
Continue to hold your attention on
This spot just as you did when
Your finger was there.

This becomes easier with practice.

NOTE: After two or three sessions of meditating
On your heart chakra, it will no longer be
Necessary for you to physically touch your
Chest with your finger to locate it.
You will sense the spot automatically and can
Start focusing on it as soon as you have
Finished gazing.

Focus your attention on your heart chakra.
Ignore your thoughts.
As you focus more intensely, you may feel
As if you are floating.

Sensations of peace, joy, and love
Will enter into you.
They will be very subtle at first.
Then they will grow stronger.

Don't expect to be able to stop your
Thoughts for sustained periods of time until
You have meditated for many years.
You don't have to stop all thought to have a

Good meditation.
Simply pay no attention to your thoughts and
You will unhook yourself from them.

Let go of your thoughts.
Let the current of meditation take you
Where it will.

As you meditate, you will observe your
Thoughts changing.
At the beginning of your meditation session,
Your thoughts will be very worldly.
You may be thinking, planning, or worrying.

As the meditation progresses,
Your thoughts will become more pure.
You will think of constructive things that
You can do for yourself and others.

As your meditation progresses even further,
You will notice the phenomena of meditation.
You may see dazzling lights,
Feel energy coursing through different
Parts of your body,
Feel as if you are floating,
Hear sounds, or
Smell fragrances.

Be neither attracted nor repulsed.
You are watching a movie.
If the visions are beautiful or horrible,
Don't get caught up in them.
Enjoy your popcorn.

Enjoy the experience.
Don't expect anything.
Whenever you expect something
From a meditation, you set yourself up for
Immediate frustration.

Don't program your meditation.
Sit and enjoy it.

Then, when you have grown accustomed to
Sitting and meditating,
Try to stop your thoughts.
That's the bottom line in
Meditative practice.

At the end of your meditation session,
Chant "Aum" seven times.
Chanting a mantra at the end of your
Meditation session will help you to
Retain the Light.
Bow and offer your meditation to
Eternity, as you would offer a
Flower to your lover.

If you have a Spiritual Teacher,
Then think of your Teacher at the
Beginning of your meditation.
Your Teacher is your mantra.

Repeat your Teacher's name
Several times.
Think of a nice moment you
Had together —
When you meditated together,
When you talked — Something intimate.

When you think of an Enlightened Teacher,
You contact them inwardly.

An Enlightened Teacher is Light.
When you focus on them,
That Light psychically enters into you.
The Teacher will teach you how to meditate
From within.

You can meditate directly on God,
On a spiritual Teacher who is no longer
In the body,
Or on a Cosmic God or Goddess.

Do whatever works best for you.
Be creative. As you progress,
You will meditate in
New and different ways.

Never analyze your meditation experiences.
Meditate and move on.

Meditate each day as soon as you
Wake up.
This is important.
It may be easier to meditate
Later in the day;
Do so.
But also meditate each day
When you wake up.

Your mind is calm when you wake up.
You may be a little tired,
But a shower will perk you up.

HOW TO MEDITATE

Meditate.
You will enter into stillness and peace.
Then your entire day will be wonderful.

Meditation.
It's like your American Express Card:
Never leave home without it.

Meditate each day at noon,
Just for a few minutes.
The kundalini is strongest at noon.

Meditate at sunset or at night.
It's easiest to meditate at night.
Night is Eternal.

It is good to meditate at any time.
You will find that some times are
Better than others.
Do what works for you.

Be creative in your meditation.
On a nice day, it's fun to meditate outside.
Meditate with friends.
Meditate alone.

Never get discouraged.
Each meditation will change your life.
Sit and meditate with your whole
Heart and mind.
Cry to God.
You will change.

Enjoy the process.
Your meditation is only limited
By your powers of concentration
And your ability to surrender to Eternity.
Anything else you need to know,

Meditation: The Bridge Is Flowing But The River Is Not

You will learn as you go along.
Trust the Force.
It is with you.

Biography

Rama - Dr. Frederick P. Lenz

Rama - Dr. Frederick P. Lenz was born on February 9, 1950, in San Diego, California. When he was three years old, his family moved to Stamford, Connecticut. His father worked as a marketing executive and later served as Mayor of Stamford. His mother was a housewife and an advanced student of astrology. His mother told Dr. Lenz that she knew for many months before he was born that he was an exceptional being.

"When I was very young, three, four, five, I used to go into samadhi, a very high state of meditation," Dr. Lenz recalled. "I would be outside in the backyard of my parents' home, and I'd look up at the sky and go away, dissolve, go beyond this world. Naturally, growing up, I never realized that I was essentially different from other children. Of course, I noticed that I was, but I didn't realize that other people didn't see life the way I did."

Dr. Lenz attended schools in the Stamford area. While he described himself as a rebel in high school, he excelled at the University of Connecticut, where he majored in English and minored in Philosophy. While in college, he was inducted as a member of Phi Beta Kappa and graduated Magna Cum Laude. After winning a highly competitive State of New York Graduate Council Fellowship, he received his M.A. and Ph.D. in English Literature from the State University of New York at Stony Brook. His doctoral dissertation on the poet Theodore Roethke was directed by the Pulitzer Prize-winning poet, Louis Simpson, Ph.D.

During the years he pursued his academic education, Dr. Lenz also became deeply involved in meditation and the study of self-discovery. "I started to meditate formally at about 18 and began to go into samadhi right away," he recollected. "I can remember sitting on a mountaintop in Southern California. I had been meditating for maybe six months, just on my own. I'd read a book or two about it. The books reminded me of something, and I would sit out there around twilight and focus on my third eye, and everything would become still. Rings of light would appear, and I'd go through them. Then suddenly, I would be beyond time and space, beyond life and death. I would dissolve for what, an hour, a lifetime, eternity? There are no words. And I was changed by this experience."

At age 19, Dr. Lenz started formal studies with various meditation teachers. During this period, he wrote two best-selling books based on his own research—*Lifetimes, True Accounts of Reincarnation* (1979); and *Total Relaxation: The Complete Program for Overcoming Worry, Stress, Tension and Fatigue* (1980). While promoting these books, he appeared on numerous national television and radio programs. He taught meditation and yoga at universities around the United States and the world—representing the teachers he studied with.

As time passed, Dr. Lenz decided it was time to teach on his own. In early 1981, he formed his own school of American Buddhism. Making himself available, sometimes over 200 nights a year, to those interested in living "an uncommonly fine life," he embarked on teaching Buddhist principles and meditation, ultimately to over 100,000 people.

The Early Years of Teaching, 1981 - 1988

As a student, teacher and representative of enlightenment, Dr. Lenz described himself as "innately tantric." The Sanskrit term "tantra" means using everything in one's life to grow. It is a sophisticated path where one does not shun experience. Dr. Lenz's body of teaching reflects his classic tantric approach. From his earliest teaching years, he did not restrict himself to imparting a single framework of knowledge. Rather, he presented the best of many teaching traditions and constantly incorporated current American experiences—books, films, field trips, shopping malls—into his American Buddhist coursework.

In 1981, when he founded his first school, named Lakshmi after the Indian goddess of harmony and prosperity, the overlying theme was Vedantic philosophy—the classic paths of Indian yoga: love and devotion, wisdom, action and selfless giving. At the same time, he introduced his students to Tibetan teachings and those of the American mystic, Carlos Castaneda.

In 1982, he adopted a teaching name from the Indian epic, *The Ramayana.* "Rama is the name of an enlightened warrior who lived thousands of years ago in India," he explained. "I really don't know whether I picked the name or it was given to me. One day I was meditating on a cliff overlooking the ocean in Southern California and I was absorbed in a state of high meditation. As I came out of the meditation and became aware of the sense world, the world around me, I knew that I had a new name. And the name was 'Rama.'"

Throughout 1982, he offered numerous public meditation workshops to ever-larger audiences. Although he had started his teaching career with 15 students, by 1983 close to one thousand people were enrolled in his teaching seminars. In late 1983, Dr. Lenz scaled back the number of students he worked with directly to less than half but continued to hold frequent, popular public workshops.

Dr. Lenz was a strong believer in advertising. His approach to reaching people and giving them the opportunity to meditate with an enlightened teacher included taking out full-page ads featuring striking photos and text that challenged and awakened minds. Drawn by his mastery of meditation and his unusual ads, often close to one thousand people attended his public lectures.

In 1985, while continuing to teach in Los Angeles and San Francisco, Dr. Lenz journeyed with a number of his students to Boston. Recurrent themes in his talks with his students and to the public were meditation, career success, spiritual balance, the Tibetan rebirth process, psychic development and the enlightenment of women.

By 1986, as Dr. Lenz planned a series of public talks in the San Francisco area, he felt that his eclectic approach to self-discovery most closely resembled Zen Buddhism. Accompanied by one of his students, he traveled to Japan and met with Zen masters in Kyoto. As he described it, "When I go visit my brother monks in Japan and sit down with other Zen masters, and I walk into the monasteries, and I meet the abbot, drink tea with him and have discussion or silence, they look at my long hair, and they have their shaved heads, and they look at my crazy clothes and my strange expression—but they feel the power that emanates from my dedication to the practice. So they are comfortable... They don't quite know what to do, yet they find they have to accept me because I'm one with the practice."

Dr. Lenz stated that he himself was the ultimate koan. When he walked onstage in San Francisco wearing black leather clothes, sporting sunglasses, drinking Diet Coke, with a wide ring of curly hair around his head, many minds snapped—how could a person who looked like that be an enlightened teacher? Throughout his teaching years, those who could not penetrate this koan did not continue to study with him. Those who remained found this koan challenging, intriguing and uplifting.

In early 1988, Dr. Lenz began to shift his seminar program to the East Coast. While he continued to teach on both coasts, by late 1989, he considered himself a New York-based teacher.

The Later Teaching Years, 1989 - 1998

With the move to New York came an increased emphasis on career success and absorption in career (particularly computer science) as a form of meditation and mindfulness, while at the same time leading a full, balanced life. By 1990, Dr. Lenz began to emphasize Tantric Zen Buddhism—an approach inclusive of Vajrayana Buddhism and Tibetan yoga—as the pathway to enlightenment most suited for Western living.

Dr. Lenz described the 1990s as a time of tremendous freedom. "Just be truthful," he advised. "Determine where you are and where you wish to be, and then use all of your self-effort to make that happen. It's an exciting time. It's a time of battle—battle and journeys and teaching and learning. But it's an open time. Who could ask for more?"

In early 1992, Dr. Lenz perceived that one of the best ways for his students to grow was to begin teaching on their own, with the option of inviting their students to sit in on one or more of his lectures. Many of the new students subsequently chose to enroll in Dr. Lenz's seminar program. The new group stepped rapidly into the fast-paced environment of Dr. Lenz's American Buddhist program, balancing meditation with career, travel and adventure. Adapting his teachings for this new and younger group, Dr. Lenz demonstrated how to balance hard work with play—scuba diving with his students in islands all over the Caribbean, the Fiji Islands and Hawaii; journeying with his students to Europe, the California deserts and the American Southwest; holding rave dance parties in some of the most elegant settings in Manhattan, including the foyer of the World Financial Center and the Guggenheim Museum. Everyone danced.

During this period, Dr. Lenz also wrote two books about Buddhist teachings—the bestseller *Surfing the Himalayas* (1995, St. Martin's Press) and a popular sequel, *Snowboarding to Nirvana* (1997, St. Martin's Press).

Dr. Lenz believed that electronic music suffused with the energy of enlightenment could greatly assist the aspiring student. From 1987 - 1994, working with the band Zazen, he co-wrote and produced 14 musical albums including "Canyons of Light," "Enlightenment," "Cayman Blue" and "Samadhi." These albums featured music geared towards advancing the practice of meditation. Intently listening to Zazen meditation music, focusing on every note, was the equivalent of a "listening meditation."

Dr. Lenz was also a software designer. In conjunction with those working in his companies, he created a wide range of helpful products. He emphasized the importance of career success for his students, stating, "I define career success as using your work to advance yourself spiritually." He emphasized computer science, "because if you study computer science, you will find that it will develop your mind. It makes your mind very strong. And it's literally like doing Buddhist exercises all day long." Dr. Lenz was active in the introduction of educational, client/server, networking, medical, banking, trading systems, encryption, internet and intranet software and technologies.

Dr. Lenz achieved excellence in a variety of challenging sports. "Sports and athletics are zazen," he said. "They're meditation—moving meditation. As you are running down that field or shooting that basket, putting that golf ball, taking down your opponent in martial arts or just competing with yourself, there are moments of timelessness and ecstasy and challenge and emptiness." Dr. Lenz himself was an avid runner, a PADI-certified Divemaster and technical scuba diver, a world-class snowboarder and a black belt in martial arts.

As a philanthropist, Dr. Lenz was a major contributor to National Public Radio in Connecticut and a donor and supporter of the American Civil Liberties Union, the National Cancer Institute, the AIDS Fund, Amnesty International, the National Museum of Women and the Arts in Washington, D.C., Shotokan Karate, The Cousteau Society and the Audubon Society.

In spite of all his achievements, Dr. Lenz was self-effacing. He said that enlightenment was not "special" but simply "different." A listing of his many achievements belies the fact that his greatest achievement was in consciousness. He attained the highest states of awareness in the midst of numerous obstacles and never wavered in his commitment to teach and help others. He accomplished all tasks with integrity, enthusiasm and an incredible sense of humor.

Rama - Dr. Frederick P. Lenz passed away on April 12, 1998 in Long Island, New York, giving his students another powerful koan to decipher. He willed the majority of his estate to the Frederick P. Lenz Foundation for American Buddhism for the purpose of supporting Buddhism in America, "in the context as I have taught it."